Dancing in the Rain

By the Same Author

The Sound Of A Miracle
A Child's Triumph over Autism

Dancing in the Rain

*Stories of Exceptional Progress
by Parents of Children with Special Needs*

Edited by
Annabel Stehli

The Georgiana Organization, Inc.
Westport, CT

Dancing in the Rain
Stories of Exceptional Progress by Parents of Children with Special Needs
Copyright © 1995 by Annabel Stehli

ISBN: 0-9644838-0-7
Library of Congress Catalog Card Number: 95-75177
Cover design © by Martha Vaughan
Book design by Martha Johns Lambert,
        The Write Type, Riverside, CT 06878
Printed in the United States of America
97 96 95   6 5 4 3 2

Contents

Introduction

by
Annabel Stehli

Dancing in the Rain is a collection of case histories written by parents about the progress of their children with attention deficit disorder (ADD), dyslexia, hyperlexia, central auditory processing disorder, pervasive developmental delay (PDD), and autism. The title is taken from my previous book, *The Sound of a Miracle*, (Doubleday, hardcover, 1991; Avon, paperback, 1992) and refers to a passage where Georgie, my learning disabled, autistic daughter, after having her dysfunctional hearing corrected by auditory integration training, asked to go out to play in the rain. "The rain doesn't sound like a machine gun anymore," she said.

Auditory integration training (AIT), a new intervention developed in France, addresses the hearing distortions, hyperacute hearing, and sensory processing anomalies which cause discomfort and confusion in learning disabled and developmentally delayed children. Discussed in detail in *Hearing Equals Behavior*, by Guy Bérard, M.D. (Keats Publishing, New Canaan, CT, 1993), auditory training seeks to retrain the auditory system by correcting hearing distortions. During the twenty half-hour training sessions, participants listen with headphones to a musical program modified and filtered through an electronic device called an "AudioKinetron" (or similar equipment).

According to the Autism Society of America, autism is a neurological disorder of communication and behavior affecting one child in every seven hundred and fifty. This definition applies to learning disabled and developmentally delayed children to a lesser degree, with a common thread being sensory processing dysfunction. Characteristics include assets such as phenomenal memory and sense of balance, genius, and unusual gifts and talents in the areas of art, music, and math (e.g., Einstein). Delays are usually present in the development of physical, social and language skills. Responses to sensations are often unusual, as well as ways of relating to people, objects, and events. AIT has proved to be often effective in remediating the hearing distortions which are present in attention deficit disorder, hyperlexia, central auditory processing disorder, hyperactivity, and dyslexia. Ten percent of the students and 80 percent of the convicts in this country are learning disabled, according to neuropsychologist Julia Grenier. In some areas such as the Aldine district in Houston, the special ed population is 20 percent, a high figure which perhaps could be associated with pollution. (In my Parents' Network the number of children with special needs often appears to relate to the degree of pollution to which they and their parents have been exposed. Anitbiotics are an additional factor.)

Double–blind clinical trial results for AIT have been promising. As reported in the May 1994 issue of the *American Journal of Speech–Language Pathology,* "significant behavioral improvement was observed on both the Aberrant Behavior Checklist and the Fisher's Auditory Problems Checklist for subjects in the experimental group. These changes include decreases in irritability/agitation, stereotypic (repetitive) behavior, hyperactivity, and excessive speech, as well as increases in attention to auditory stimuli, memory for routine things, and comprehension."

Although many professionals in the fields of special education, medicine, psychology, audiology, speech pathology, and occupational therapy have been receptive to auditory training, there has been enormous skepticism, and initially, my daughter's recovery was regarded as a fluke. As I made the rounds of talk shows and conferences, I was astounded at the degree of negativity I encountered. I began proudly to claim my amateur status in the face of professionals who were invested in their occupations, methods, and viewpoints (livelihoods and egos) to an unethical degree, and were threatened by anything they hadn't learned in graduate school. Guy Bérard, M.D., who developed AIT in France, was about as popular as Edison at a candlemakers' convention.

One of the most galling experiences occurred at a conference in Greenville, South Carolina, given at a pediatric center. The pediatrician hosting us (myself and AIT practitioner Deborah Woodward) closed the conference by saying that auditory training worked only because the poor kid had his mother's undivided attention for ten days for the first time in his life. Since the doctor had had the last word, I couldn't speak up about the double–blind clinical trial where the control group and the experimental group both got Mom's undivided attention for ten days, and the control group did not show the improvement of the experimental group, even with all that wonderful mother–love.

Little by little, prejudices were broken down as other children, like the children described in this book, began to make progress similar to my daughter's. My husband, Peter, invited Dr. Bérard to teach seminars on AIT. Later, Dr. Julia Grenier, mentioned earlier, and Jackie Rockwell, a speech pathologist and audiologist, conducted training workshops. Attending the seminars were professionals working with the special needs population, primarily speech pathologists, audiologists, and psychologists.

Leading professionals in the learning disabled community such as Dr. Donna Geffner began to show interest in AIT. In an article in the January 10, 1994, issue of *Advance*, a journal for speech–language pathologists and audiologists, Dr. Geffner reported, "Our preliminary findings. . .reveal significant improvement in speech discrimination in noise and increased tolerance levels to loud sounds. Improvements in other auditory behaviors were noted, such as increased auditory memory span, improved auditory closure and auditory motor skills." Dr. Paul Hardy, a neuropsychiatrist on the faculty of the New England School of Medicine at Tufts, and pediatric neurologist Margaret Bauman, with psychologist Stephen Edelson and audiologist Jane Rudy, conducted a double–blind study on AIT, and speech pathologist Joseph McLaughlin at the University of Connecticut at Storrs is currently studying its potential as an educational intervention.

In terms of etiology, parents in the Network generally report that when autism was present from birth (in 10% of the cases), there was an anoxia factor (loss of oxygen) during the delivery. The other 90% of the children in the Network have late-onset autism, PDD, or language delay, developing after a normal first year. According to Dr. Margaret Bauman, the sensory processing area of the brain is involved, with sensory overload and apraxia (the inability of the mind to order the body) a common thread.

With its complicated coordination of muscles, delayed speech is common, and misperceived auditory input no doubt contributes. If cup is heard as cuh and spaghetti as poggi, as in the case of my daughter, it was difficult to learn to talk because her auditory system was malfunctioning.

How would I have dealt with my daughter Georgie's problems had I known what I know today? Certainly my approach would have been very different. First of all, as I did with subsequent children, I would have breastfed on demand for years in order to avoid allergies and ear infections. It would have been difficult, because Georgie fell asleep so easily and needed to feed so often that it was impossible not to become exhausted. I would have persevered, however, knowing what I know today about the immune system and bonding. I would have made far greater attempts at interaction, and would have enlisted others in the same effort, ideally following a blend of the Lovaas and Option Institute methods described in some of the stories in this book. I would have looked for a pediatrician trained in conventional, preventive, nutritional, and alternative medicine. Georgie would have had auditory integration training at the age of two or younger, and visual retraining as well. Because of her phenomenal sense of balance but poor sense of rhythm, I would have kept her away from modern dance and stuck to gymnastics, skiing, and skating. They are also quiet. I would have hoped to find a nurturing early intervention program (like Giant Steps in Montreal) which is geared to mainstreaming and which starts at age three. With all we would have done had we known, and had it been available, Georgie probably would have gone to school without a label.

As it was, I had read to her, sung and talked to her, validated, respected and enjoyed her, but it was not enough. When she was two, she had learned to tie her shoes; use pencils, pens, and Magic Markers; build fantastic card houses; and line up Leggos in perfect rows. She had learned to feed and dress herself, and help me cook, but she had needed so much more than that. Structured, full–time intervention wasn't begun until she was four, and it was extremely helpful, but late.

One of the crucial factors in Georgie's recovery was the fact that for the two years following auditory training, we lived in Switzerland, where my husband had been transferred. Georgie learned French, played in a neighborhood with French–speaking children, went to school in French, and was given a fresh start where no one knew the extent of her history. In her school, auditory training was known to be effective, and she had been expected to do well. We expected her to do well at home, as well. How important those expectations were cannot be over emphasized.

After our return from Switzerland in 1979, with Georgie well, I received occasional calls from interested parents. After my book came out in the *Reader's Digest* in a condensed version, the telephone rang solidly. Until Georgie's story was told, autistic, developmentally delayed, and learning disabled children were not generally thought of as having sensory processing anomalies, although Dr. Carl Delacato's book, *The Ultimate Stranger, the Autistic Child* (Doubleday, 1975) had made a case for it. Painful hearing had not been measured, and audiologists generally did not think that audiograms could change. But parents knew that their children had peculiar reactions to certain noises, and they could see similarities between them and Georgie, and they called me up to talk about it in a state of great excitement, hope, and relief. Their children, who had been diagnosed with everything from mild dyslexia to severe autism, often could hear sounds others couldn't hear, such as noise from fluorescent lights, or falling snow, or an airplane long before it was audible to anyone with normal hearing. (After receiving auditory integration training, one six–year–old said, "The motorcycles are gone from my head, and I can still hear people blink but I can tune it out.") Typically, the children were language delayed and isolated from their peers, had high tension levels, and often were given little chance of a normal life or regular education. Cloaked in patronizing kindness, negative labeling (classifications given in order to receive necessary funds) had unwittingly contributed to the creation of an educational underclass. Most alarming was the consistency with which severe and prolonged ear infections treated with antibiotics were reported.

Everybody who called me wanted to know where they could get auditory training, and I had to tell them it wasn't available yet in this country. Dr. Bérard had retired, and others carrying on his work were in Europe. Finally, a homeopathic physician/psychologist was discovered in Canada who could accommodate them, and people began streaming to Dr. Gerard Binet in Montreal. As children improved, the demand for AIT grew.

I felt that a network of parents was needed, and when parents asked me what they could do in return for the time I gave them, I asked them to be there for the next person. I linked people who either lived near each other, or who I intuitively thought would simply get along, or whose children were same age and/or functioned at the same level. I kept a record of the people in the Network in a notebook, and eventually in a database, but out of respect for privacy, it was never published. Perhaps because the crucible of having children with special needs is such a character building experience, I didn't worry about the fact that I was dealing with strangers. They didn't seem like strangers to me.

When professionals began to express an interest in learning how to administer AIT, my husband and I formed The Georgiana Organization in Westport, Connecticut. The mission of the Organization was to establish AIT in this country by offering training, certification, equipment, information, and network support. Soon there were hundreds of people in practice, including a speech pathologist/audiologist in South Africa and a developmental pediatrician in Hong Kong. We have answered, by telephone and letter, thousands of inquiries in the last three years, often spending an hour on the telephone with parents.

Given the spectacular success of Georgie and others like her, we tried to shift the focus to the assets of autism and learning disabilities. When Georgie and I appeared on the *Sally Jessy Raphael* show in May 1992, Georgie was asked if she could draw a map of Africa, with all the countries labeled and the boundaries accurately drawn, to demonstrate the "bionic" memory function of the autistic and learning "disabled," memory function which has contributed to their success in law school, computer training, and language study, to name a few areas. (Interestingly, this kind of memory function is often described in special education vernacular as a "splinter skill," i.e. useless, as in Rain Man's memorization of the phone book.)

In May of 1993, in Stamford, Connecticut, we held our first conference, calling it "Celebration of Breakthroughs." We invited speakers who were authorities in the fields of auditory training (Dr. Bérard), visual retraining (Dr. Melvin Kaplan), tactile desensitizing (Dr. Temple Grandin), nutrition and allergies (Dr. William Crook), facilitated communication (Dr. William Ashe), and vitamins (Dr. Bernard Rimland). Professionals and parents attended from all over the country, and we were thrilled at the turnout, the atmosphere, and the feedback. We are still receiving requests for tapes of the lectures.

In the last few years, thousands of children and adults have made significant progress as a result of auditory training. Some have had spectacular breakthroughs; others have made gradual changes. When Dr. Rimland, Director of the Autism Research Institute, flew in recently from San Diego to give a lecture in Fairfield, Connecticut, near my home, he said that because of Georgie and others like her, the prognosis for autism has changed, that there now exists the potential for recovery. This is certainly true for children with learning disabilities as well. As a bonus, if a child with a developmental delay or a learning disability makes it out of the abyss of special ed into the relative joy of mainstream education, he gets to keep his prodigious memory as an asset to run with for the rest of his life. ■

Dancing in the Rain

Chapter 1

Jason

by Jean Jasinski

Autism is like a volcano. Many families feel they were dragged kicking and screaming up the side of the mountain by their professionals and thrown into the abyss where they are left desperately grasping for hand holds and waiting for the next eruption. Our family followed a slightly different itinerary. We, not doctors or educators, initiated our cautious climb up the mountain. We dropped to our bellies, and poked our heads into the black hole, and we looked around for other travelers. Then WE dragged our professionals up the side of the mountain, kicking and screaming, and forced them to look into that black hole and say the word *autism* and our son's name in the same sentence.

It seemed more than a little strange to "the professionals" that we were seeking that diagnosis for our son Jason. Although many of their hearts were in the right place, their knowledge of the spectrum of the disorder was woefully weak, and what they did know about autism evoked dread and fear, making Jason's diagnosis difficult to obtain.

We suspected that something was not right with Jason's development from the time he was about two years old. In retrospect, our early concerns focused too much on some aspects of Jason's development, i.e. his physical development, and not enough on his social and language development. When I was ten weeks pregnant with Jason, our first child, Kayla, just days past her first birthday, was diagnosed with osteogenesis imperfecta, a rare genetic brittle bone disorder. At that time, there were no tests to detect whether Jason was also affected before or after his birth. Since Kayla appeared normal at birth and for a year afterwards, we could not be sure that Jason did not have brittle bones until he had mastered the dangerous feats of learning to crawl, stand, walk, and run without breaking any bones. We watched him for any sign of muscle weakness or delay in motor skills, but they never appeared. It wasn't until we could relax about his physical development that we noticed his social and communication skills were not only delayed, but impaired as well. Jason's expressive language was poor. He used the fewest words possible when requesting things, yet he would often repeat entire sections of the dialogue from a Disney video. Rather than babble, Jason hummed monotonically. We never heard that inner voice of children, quietly talking to themselves at play, cataloging what they are doing/ thinking. Jason's articulation rendered his speech incomprehensible to almost everyone. Most of Jason's conversations were either echolalic regurgitations of his favorite TV shows or movies, or obtuse references to past events that he assumed everyone else understood or experienced as he did. Having shared most of his experiences, his nanny and I served as Jason's primary language interpreters until he was three–and–a–half years old.

Jason's language was quite literal. He called himself a "horse–boy" rather than a cowboy because he rode a horse, not a cow. Not knowing the word for a high chair, he pointed out the "baby sitters." In the fall, he called the greenbelt behind our home the "yellowbelt." When singing a song that included the line, "This is my address," Jason sang, "This is my a–T–shirt," because he knew that wearing adult T–shirts to bed was like wearing "a dress" but they were really T–shirts. If Jason was asked if he was feeling "sick, too," he replied "Yes, I am three–sick." Jason says that his balding father has "five heads" which must be bigger than a forehead.

One of Jason's pretend babies was named Eka (pronounced ee' kuh'), and it took us several months to figure out that Eka was derived from Eureka's Castle on television. Eka is what is modified by possessive adjectives, "My Eka, Your Eka, His Eka."

Jason was very astute at learning appropriate dialogue for specific situations from his older sister. For instance, if he was standing in line, he would say "I was first" but he didn't reinforce those words with any actions like moving to the front of the line or pushing other children out of his way. Or if one of us poured two cups of juice, he would echo "Me first" but would display no disappointment or resentment if he was not given his juice first.

His vocabulary of nouns and adjectives grew, but Jason could not identify functions of objects nor could he describe actions very well. If you held up a car and asked him to identify it and to describe it, he would. But if you asked him what a car was used for, he drew a blank. If you showed him a picture, he could point out all the objects in the picture but was unable to state what was happening in the picture. He'd tell you the page number, he'd tell you how many people were in the picture, but not what they were doing.

Jason's play skills were limited. His favorite playthings were toys that came from TV shows or videos, and his play consisted mostly of repeating the dialogue and reenacting situations from the shows. He fooled one psychologist with this behavior; she ruled out autism as a possible diagnosis because Jason had arranged the Fisher Price Little People in the doll house like a family and acted out appropriate scenes. What she did not realize was that Fisher Price made Little People videos—that Jason was simply echoing the video. Jason preferred perseverative kinds of play, such as walking the pull–toys around the loop of our kitchen, living room, and dining room for hours until we made him stop. He loved to jump off the bed or the back of the couch, over and over. He showed no interest in playing with other children unless it was a simple chasing game.

Jason's sensory system was clearly different. From the time he was a baby, he would crawl into my closet and rub silky blouses or dresses on his face when he was upset. At first we worried that he would grow up to become a cross–dresser. If the priest patted Jason on the head at church, Jason would loudly protest, "Ow–ey, you hurt–a my hair." During Jason's first haircut at the age of seventeen months, he screamed so hard that he broke blood vessels in his neck. Jason found light touch irritating. He slept under four bed pillows. He toe–walked, handflapped, and smelled everything: a bandaid, a cup, the outside of a car door, toys, clothes, etc. He often asked to smell my arm and he sorted objects by smell. Living in Colorado, we are often exposed to the smells of different kinds of manure. Depending on the direction of the wind, Jason would often step outside and proclaim, "Smells like horse poop" or "smells like cow/sheep/dog/(insert favorite animal) poop." Indeed the smells would be different on different days, but we never have conducted a double–blind study to see if his labeling was accurate.

Every spring we would have a tough couple of weeks as Jason adjusted to the sound of flying insects. He would go outside and if he heard an insect, he would become hysterical, cover his ears, and run inside. He would also become hysterical over the noise of the whole–house attic fan. Jason stared at things in different ways. He held toys up to the corners of his eyes and squinted at them. He seemed impervious to pain. Because he didn't cry, we could scrub his skinned knee with a soapy washcloth.

Transitions were nightmares. If Jason didn't resemble his father so closely, we might have been accused of kidnapping as we whisked a screaming, out–of–control child out of public places. Although Jason's tantrums didn't start until he was three years old, they were ferocious. Jason was extremely rigid in his routines. If he went outside, he wore a coat. If he wore a coat, it had to be zipped and the hood had to be tied. If we stopped at the supermarket to purchase one item, we had to use a shopping cart, otherwise Jason would follow us through the market screaming, "I need a cart. I need a cart."

Jason had a phenomenal memory. He could correctly identify sixty videos by the names we had written on masking tape on the spines. He could recall any place where we had purchased a toy or junk food. If anything were misplaced, Jason could locate it. Jason's incidental memory, when combined with his insistence on routine, often led to tantrums because he expected sameness and routine down to the tiniest detail, details so obscure and minute that we had either never noticed or had long since forgotten.

Noncompliance was Jason's normal mode of operation. If presented two choices for a drink, he would reject both or insist on a third choice not offered, have a twenty–minute tantrum, and return from time–out and ask for one of the original selections. If you said it was bath time, Jason would walk up the stairs to the bathroom, loudly complaining, "I hate baths. Baths are yuck," as he stripped off his clothes to prepare for his bath. Saying no or opposing us was so ingrained, it was like a reflex reaction.

We figured out many tricks that made living with Jason more tolerable. We learned to call his name before we spoke to him. We learned that advance preparation with elaborate detail could assist with transitions and new situations. For instance, on the way to the doctor's office, we would tell Jason over and over: "The doctor is going to have to look in your ears, and you'll have to say 'aah' so he can look down your throat. Then he'll have to listen to your chest and back with the stethoscope. And if you behave. . ." Such detailed preparation could also hurt if we omitted some minor detail or if the events occurred out of the sequence we had predicted. We also figured out that Jason could not understand if/then but did understand sequencing. We quit saying things like "If you eat your dinner, then you can have a cookie" and replaced it with a rule: "First dinner, then cookie." Jason understood rules, and even if he didn't like the consequences, he calmly accepted them. He did not understand that he could influence the outcome, i.e. if he ate his dinner, he could have a cookie. They were two separate events in his mind that just happened.

Despite our figuring out tricks for dealing with Jason, we had also subconsciously rearranged our lives to avoid the "near–occasion–of–tantrum." We didn't eat in any restaurant that didn't serve pizza or chicken nuggets and couldn't have the food in our hands in five minutes. We learned never to deviate from the spoken plan of the day, and we learned not to speak of an event unless we were sure it would occur.

We used the year between Jason's second and third birthday to watch his development, to compare it to his sister's and other children's, and to talk to everyone (teachers, doctors, therapists who were treating Kayla) about our suspicions. When Jason was three years old, we were ready for "formal evaluations." We spent the next six months visiting (too many) professionals and acquiring different diagnoses like shopping for blue jeans: trying them on for size and rejecting most of them because they just did not fit well everywhere.

Ironically, the person who helped us the most was not a recognized expert per se, but nonetheless a "real" expert, another parent. Working for a large computer firm, we have access to several worldwide electronic bulletin boards. By luck or divine intervention, one woman responded to my posting about Jason and some strange behaviors we were observing. Her son's behavior resembled Jason's, and he too had acquired many labels, but they had eventually settled on pervasive developmental disorder/not otherwise specified (PDD/NOS). This woman and I spent (and still spend) many hours corresponding electronically about our sons. She shared details about autism and its diagnosis, and SHE planted the seed that perhaps autism/PDD might be a more appropriate diagnosis for Jason. She credits us with being her first "electronic" diagnosis. In the midst of all this hypothesizing, *Rain Man* aired on network television. My husband called me into the room, and after five minutes, we looked at each other and said, "That's Jason." Cold dread seized our hearts, and we girded our loins for the climb up the side of the volcano. On a trip to Princeton, New Jersey, as it turned out, Jason was finally diagnosed as having mild–to–moderate autism in August 1992 at the Eden Institute, a wonderful school in Princeton, when he was almost four years old.

Although the diagnosis of autism connotes many negative images, it relieved us greatly. Having a NAME that accurately described all of Jason's developmental delays, we were able to quit searching. We could shuck all the conflicting pieces of data those well–meaning but poorly–informed professionals had laid at our feet, and we could align ourselves with a COMMUNITY, a community that would help us understand Jason and offer us ideas about how to help him. Realizing that the diagnostic label of autism encompasses a whole spectrum of ability and that some treatments/therapies work for some people some of the time, we had at least some knowledge of where to look for help. We had a starting point, a frame of reference.

We also realized just how much confidence in our abilities as parents we had sacrificed during the process of having Jason evaluated. We began to learn to trust our ability as parents who knew Jason best and to advocate for Jason once more. And we began to try therapies to improve Jason's ability to make sense of our chaotic world.

The first therapy we utilized was Sensory Integration Therapy. Our local school district placed Jason in a therapeutic play group which fortunately consisted of one other boy and Jason. The group, staffed by an occupational therapist and a speech therapist, met for two hours per week. Since the other boy had a language delay and Jason was classified as having occupational therapy needs, he basically received one–on–one therapy for sensory integration. This program lasted three months until the school year ended. At the time, we did not credit the program for much improvement in Jason, but that was due to our naiveté in observation skills. Within three weeks of the program's termination, behaviors returned that we hadn't realized had disappeared! Jason starting jumping off the back of the couch again. His humming was back. The perseverative pull–toy marathons began again. He then started private occupational therapy for sensory integration in the summer of 1992, and it was a couple of months before Jason returned to the same level of functioning that he had attained when the school year ended. He still receives private occupational therapy today.

The next weapon we dragged from the arsenal was speech therapy. We started speech therapy at a local university teaching clinic where graduate students in training offered therapy for reduced rates (about half the current rate for private therapy). We and the teaching supervisor could observe Jason's therapy sessions through a one–way mirror. His behavior quickly drained the trainee's battery of coping skills. The summer of therapy was not successful for Jason, although the therapists probably learned a great deal from him. As his fourth birthday approached, the school district could no longer dismiss his articulation errors as age–appropriate. I had always contended that part of Jason's social delays were due to his peers' inability to understand him, but the school district speech therapist disagreed. Armed with the "official" diagnosis of autism (BIG stick), I held fast in insisting that Jason receive speech therapy. Since his non–compliance was still an issue at this point, he received individual speech therapy so that food reinforcers could be used. We also began private speech therapy with an experienced therapist at the same time. Within two months many of Jason's letter substitutions were gone ("t" for k/hard c and "d" for j/soft g). His ability to make himself understood by adults and peers improved markedly. He continues in speech therapy today to improve his articulation and language pragmatics like eye–contact, turn–taking, maintaining conversation threads, etc.

Because we lived two thousand miles away from the team at Eden Institute whom we trusted, we were unable to attend any of the training sessions or support groups they offered. We were given a twenty–minute summary of behavior modification techniques to use with Jason to improve compliance (don't give any instruction that we could not enforce within thirty seconds, physically enforce any request that is ignored while ignoring any tantrum, and praise all attempts at compliance. The two–finger death–grip on the neck works well too). We were also told that we needed to change our parenting style to authoritarian because giving Jason choices was failing miserably in the face of his noncompliance. This style of parenting had worked very well for Kayla, whose verbal and reasoning skills were above age level, as is true for most children with brittle bone disorder. Regardless of style, the most important thing was to be consistent. Within a month of our leaning on Jason, his noncompliance decreased greatly. If we get sloppy about any of these practices, Jason lets us know by his behavior!

Knowing there was more to formal behavior modification than the basic tenets we were practicing, we searched for local experts who could help us. The school district contracts with a behavioral psychologist whose own parents served as foster parents to several autistic children while he was growing up. We invested several hours in meeting with this psychologist. He observed Jason in the classroom many times and he spoke with all of Jason's private therapists. When it really came down to getting help for things like potty training, the school district drew the line saying it was not their concern; they were only concerned with classroom behaviors. Since Jason would only soil his diapers in comfortable settings, they never had to change a diaper at school. Furthermore we could not contract with the psychologist to work with us privately since it might pose a conflict of interest! It was extremely difficult to consider investing that amount of time and energy with another psychologist and to increase the size of the team which was already dealing with Jason. Meanwhile, Jason potty-trained himself (bladder) days before his fourth birthday, and we ended up calling Eden Institute (Leslie Weitzner) for advice about bowel control. We later visited with a child psychologist in Colorado for the express purpose of learning more behavior modification techniques. Since we were not experiencing major difficulty with Jason's behavior at the time, we spent three hours and three hundred dollars updating the psychologist's knowledge of autism.

By this time, we'd followed the traditional paths conventional medicine recommends for remediating autism: behavior modification, speech therapy, and occupational therapy. Although it was easier for us to live with Jason, the gap between Jason's skills and those of his typical peers was widening. We knew that Jason would not be ready for kindergarten if he continued to progress at the same rate. It was time to start thinking about some of those "eyeball–rolling" therapies, treatments that make conventional practitioners roll their eyeballs when mentioned.

We first learned of auditory integration therapy when *20/20* aired a segment about the Stehlis' success and commitment to promoting Bérard AIT. The whole idea seemed bizarre, but we were ready to cross that line between conventional and eyeball therapy if it might help and couldn't hurt our son. At the time of Jason's diagnosis, Colorado hosted no AIT practitioners. Since we were going to be on the East Coast to visit Eden, we decided to arrange an AIT screening for Jason. Obtaining the audiogram was difficult, but not impossible. At some frequencies, Jason began to grind his teeth, one of his methods for dealing with stress. At other frequencies, he appeared to quit listening. He responded a couple of times but then wouldn't respond again to a sound at the same intensity level. His audiogram showed Jason hearing all frequencies normally between 0 and 5 dB with no peaks or spikes. In order to test sounds at lower than 0 dB, the audiologist needed to switch equipment, and the break in momentum was enough to convince Jason that he was "done" despite our intentions to the contrary. We could not continue. The audiogram was very hard on him. It fatigued and stressed him greatly.

The results did not indicate strongly that Jason would be a good candidate for AIT, but his behavior hinted that hearing might be stressful for Jason. Based on possibly incomplete data, we were not convinced that AIT would be worth the time and money it would take to travel from Colorado to Connecticut for two weeks. We decided to wait until there was a practitioner in Colorado, and we even offered to help recruit practitioners. We stayed in touch with the Georgiana Foundation/Organization and five months later (Jan. 1993), there were two AIT practitioners in Colorado. We visited one of them and attempted another audiogram with Jason. Despite the positive behavioral changes made since Eden, Jason was totally noncompliant. He began to grind his teeth again, behavior we had not seen since his last audiogram. Jason observed that one frequency "sounds like my kitchen" and that he could hear one sound in his thigh. We could not obtain an audiogram this time and would instead have to rely on the previous incomplete audiogram from five months ago. Because we couldn't be sure that Jason did not need filters, we decided to wait until we had more data on the efficacy of AIT without filters.

Then the Georgiana Organization announced their first "Celebration of Breakthroughs" conference to be held in Stamford, CT, in May 1993. The conference brochure read like a "Who's Who in Autism," a medley of big–name speakers: Dr. Temple Grandin, Dr. Guy Bérard, Dr. Steve Edelson, Dr. Bernie Rimland, and a panel of adults and parents of children who had already received auditory training. I reread the brochure several times because I could not believe my good luck in finding such an assembly of speakers at one conference, all speaking consecutively so I would not have to choose between concurrent sessions! I was sold. The mother from New Jersey who first diagnosed Jason also attended, as well as another friend of hers from the computer network from Minnesota.

One of the (lesser–known to the world of autism) speakers at the conference was Dr. Melvin Kaplan, a behavioral optometrist from Tarrytown, NY, whom I had first heard about from Annabel Stehli. Dr. Kaplan's work had been reviewed by a couple of other newsletters for families with autism to which I subscribe. There were a few minor things about Jason's eyes that concerned us. One of his eyes tends to drift in when he is tired. Jason had been examined by a pediatric ophthalmologist twice who said he would not treat it (with glasses) unless he could see the eye drift during the examination. Jason was later examined by an optometrist in our home town in Colorado who recommended vision therapy for Jason based solely on Jason's performance on the standard eye examination. He did not mention Jason's autism or sensory integration problems but instead focused all his attention on the mechanics of Jason's eye movement. Jason would likely wear bifocal lenses during this year of vision therapy and would probably end up farsighted for the rest of his life if we chose this mode of vision training. In relation to all of Jason's other problems, his occasional eye drift seemed trivial. If we were going to commit that much money and time for treatment, it was going to be for something that might help all of Jason's problems in a broader sense. (Our insurance coverage either excluded most therapies or placed annual limitations like $500 on treatments. Only persistent and protracted battling obtained any reimbursement at all, and we never knew from year to year who would win the fights that year.)

Since we have family in Connecticut and New York, we decided to have Jason examined by Dr. Kaplan the day before the Breakthroughs Conference. Dr. Kaplan's office is located in Tarrytown, New York, in the kind of musty old building found in many small New England towns. Immediately I began to question my sanity for spending this kind of money for a one–hour examination. Little did I know that this appointment would be the start of Jason's amazing summer of progress, the start of our trip DOWN the mountain.

Dr. Kaplan's examination started with a functional evaluation, an assessment of how Jason performed tasks in his daily life. Jason sat down in front of a television and VCR to watch a Barney video while Dr. Kaplan observed Jason's body and eye movement. Guided by his remarkable instinct, Dr. Kaplan started putting different pairs of glasses on Jason and noting Jason's reaction. Some glasses made Jason's eyes dart back and forth. Some glasses stressed Jason (his finger would go up his nose, he would close his eyes, or he would pull the glasses off.) But one pair of glasses visibly relaxed Jason. His shoulders dropped. His constant finger fidgeting stopped. He sat quietly and watched Barney, a stillness that I had never seen before.

Dr. Kaplan then progressed to other assessments like catching a ball or balancing on a piece of wood. True to form, Jason resisted every change and every activity, but Dr. Kaplan persisted, putting different pairs of glasses on Jason to see how his performance changed. Jason began to prefer one pair, requesting that pair and verbally objecting to the others. Jason's performance of these mundane tasks was greatly enhanced by the glasses. Instead of trapping the ball to his chest, he would extend his arms to catch a ball when he was wearing the right glasses. He was unable to walk between two chairs and sit down without using his hands. Jason would walk to the chair, place his hands on the back of the chair, put his knee on the seat of the chair, sit down, and pivot. With the right pair of glasses, Jason was able to just walk up to the chair and sit down! Dr. Kaplan started asking questions about Jason. Did he trip often? What caused tantrums? Did he say, "I can't do it" often? He performed the standard eye examination and found no visual acuity problems.

Dr. Kaplan explained that while Jason's focusing system worked normally, he had problems orienting his body in space and organizing what he saw. The glasses he used were organizing glasses, yoke prism lenses. The lenses could be oriented in different directions depending on one's visual perceptual problems. He prescribed these lenses for Jason and recommended the names of some optometrists in Denver who subscribed to some of the same theories and who would follow up with Jason's care. Dr. Kaplan was confident that Jason would improve dramatically by wearing the glasses. He predicted that within six weeks, we would see a great reduction in Jason's tantrums and noncompliance, and an increase in his self–confidence. He promised to show even more dramatic results at the conference the next day.

Dr. Kaplan delivered. He delivered on every promise. He showed a video tape of a little boy whose autism was more involved than Jason's. This little boy stood there looking forward but completely unaware, and did not move, blink, or flinch away from the ball as it approached his face and shoulders. He then showed the same boy wearing prism lenses (approximately ten to twenty minutes later) reaching out to catch the ball. The results were so dramatic, they raised gooseflesh on my arm. The audience collectively gasped, and multiple people raced to the phones to schedule appointments with Dr. Kaplan.

Outside of the one day spent at the Eden Institute the year before, this conference was my first opportunity to meet other people who knew and understood autism from a personal and professional level. The adults with autism spoke about how they perceived sensory input, how certain colors hurt their eyes or how their hearing was so sensitive they could hear both sides of a phone conversation. Their insights fascinated me and would have fascinated me even if I hadn't been the parent of an autistic son. How much different the world would seem if I saw/felt/heard/smelled/tasted the world as they did! Perhaps Jason was paralyzed by his inability to process such an overload of input.

After learning more about auditory training during the rest of the conference, I decided that it would probably benefit Jason. The parents and adults reported decreased tension levels during and after auditory training. Anything to help unwind our tightly sprung child was worth consideration. During this trip, Jason spent the days of the conference with my family, and my brother–in–law, a former kindergarten teacher, asked how we dealt with Jason's intense anger and commented on how little he spoke during the day while I was gone. Between the tension–reduction I had already seen during Dr. Kaplan's examination, and the probability that AIT might relax Jason, we felt real hope for the first time.

Armed with the insight that hyper– and hypoactive sensory processing could interfere with normal development, we returned to Colorado, waited for Dr. Kaplan's glasses to arrive in the mail, and scheduled auditory training for mid–July. Two married audiologists who live across the street know Jason because our kids play together. I brought Dr. Bérard's book over to ask what they thought of his AIT method. They were politely skeptical but they listened to my enthusiastic ramblings about the conference and were particularly interested in the sensory processing insights. Again, as luck or divine intervention would have it, my neighbor, Joan Burleigh, is one of the foremost experts/researchers in the country in the area of central auditory processing disorders (CAPD). She conducts her research which is funded by the Royal Arch Masons, at The Center for Central Auditory Research at Colorado State University in Ft. Collins, Colorado. Joan loaned me a textbook she co–authored and offered to evaluate Jason at her lab. We scheduled the examination for the end of May.

Joan explained that the ears (like the eyes) are responsible for receiving input, but these sense organs make no decision about the input they receive; the brain does that. Therefore it was possible for Jason to have seemingly normal hearing (i.e. a normal pure–tone audiogram) but to be unable to process the speech he heard and to be unable to differentiate and discriminate between sounds that were important and sounds he should ignore. Jason has always been highly auditorily distractable. He could be watching television or playing with a toy, and if a car door slammed three doors away, Jason would stop and ask, "What was that?" Yet he often acted as if he hadn't heard us calling his name. Unlike the Bérard screening which assesses candidates for AIT based on a pure–tone audiogram, CAPD evaluations use both pure–tone audiograms and other functional testing like evaluating a person's ability to comprehend speech in the presence of background noise or other speech— situations that closely mimic everyday life.

Forewarned that pure–tone audiograms had been stressful for Jason, Joan started her evaluation with a "quick" audiogram. She had copies of Jason's previous audiograms and she decided to confirm that his hearing was within normal limits rather than obtain the nth degree of precision on the pure–tone section of the testing. Jason became agitated during this phase of the testing, but he responded consistently. Perhaps he cooperated because he knew "Mommy Joanie" or perhaps it was the bribe of a Polly Pocket necklace. At the end of the pure–tone audiogram, Jason needed a rest before beginning the functional portion of the examination.

The functional test was conducted using headphones and involved Jason pointing to pictures that matched the words he heard or repeating other words he heard. During the first portion of the test, Jason cooperated very well. He pointed to pictures quickly and confidently. Then all of a sudden, he started to act up. He batted at the whole page or pointed to two pictures in succession. He started to scratch the headphones and talk to me instead of paying attention, behaviors that unfortunately I had witnessed often. I was disappointed that we would be unable to continue with testing.

Joan, however, came into the soundproof booth with a smile on her face and said that Jason's poor behavior began when she stopped testing his right ear and forced him to use his left ear. We gave Jason another break, and she proved it to me. She started out testing his right ear (Jason cooperated), switched to his left ear (poor behavior) and switched back to his right ear (Jason came right back to task). Jason wasn't telling us he was tired with his poor behavior, he was telling us that he couldn't make sense of what he was hearing. The fact that his behavior change was so drastic and so tied to which ear was being tested showed that Jason did have a central auditory processing disorder. On one test, he scored 90% with his right ear, and 10% with his left ear. Basically Jason's left ear and right ear did not work together for interpreting speech. His left ear garbled his understanding of speech. It might possibly improve on its own as Jason matured.

The area of Jason's brain involved in his central auditory processing disorder was likely the cerebral cortex on his left side. Tests that could measure his low brainstem function are normal for children six years and older and were not performed.

Historically no treatments for CAPD have proven effective. Instead Joan concentrates on compensatory measures. In Jason's case, that involves inserting an ear mold in his left ear when he is in noisy situations or when he needs to pay attention to the speaker (circle time at school) in order to eliminate the confusion caused by his left ear. Jason should also be seated so that his right ear is given preference with regard to the speaker but away from noise sources like windows or doors. We purchased sound–attenuating earmuffs for Jason to wear for desk work or in extremely loud situations. We could consider use of a personal FM auditory trainer like the EZ Listener device, a cordless microphone worn by the teacher and a cordless receiver placed in Jason's right ear. Jason would not tolerate the earplug, not surprising for a child with sensory integration dysfunction. Joan made a pair of custom ear molds like the ones worn by children with P.E. tubes for swimming. Jason started wearing his left ear mold during speech therapy. We started addressing his right ear and immediately noticed a difference in his responsiveness. Answers to questions became more meaningful. No longer did we get answers like "Disneyland" to questions like "What did you have for lunch today?" Maybe now Jason could make sense of the question. It was my habit to hold Jason's left hand in my right hand in parking lots which meant I was addressing his "bad" ear. By changing hands in the parking lot, Jason was able to carry on longer conversations. We then noticed that when Jason was lying down watching television, he wouldn't hear our calling him if his left ear was up. But if he were lying down so that his left ear was down, he would answer to his name on the first call.

The night of Jason's CAPD evaluation, Dr. Kaplan's glasses arrived in the mail. We were really excited; it seemed as if all the pieces were finally falling into place. Jason put on his glasses, and we noticed immediate changes. For the first hour, he walked around just looking at things. His appetite increased. He started to seem less mechanical in his movements. All of a sudden, he picked up a handful of french fries and ate them at once instead of selecting one and chomping it to bits. My notes indicate that within two weeks of wearing the glasses, Jason had asked to play Nintendo, having silently watched his sister play for a year. He started to invent dialogue when playing with his toys. He started to play with toys that he had previously only carried around and sorted. He responded to my telling him "I love you" with "I love you, too." Before, his response to my telling him that I loved him was silence. His private speech and occupational therapists reported the two best sessions ever. They said he was "sweet" to the adults. He started voicing his feelings, telling us he was afraid to ride a big train whereas before he would only refuse to ride it, which didn't make sense for a child whose obsession was trains! His social learning capacity seemed to increase. We were able to fade cues. He accepted direction better. He also allowed us to use the whole–house (attic) fan again without hysteria.

These improvements continued and held steady. The gains were too numerous to be attributable to simple growth and maturity. A month after Jason started wearing his glasses, we went to Children's Hospital in Denver to obtain the full Bérard auditory screening exam. (Joan Burleigh did not test all the frequencies recommended for Bérard AIT nor did she try to see just how quiet a sound level Jason could hear.) We prepared Jason ahead of time and we settled on the reward/bribe.

Jason expressed his nervousness before the audiogram by becoming verbally and physically hyperactive. It had been only a month since his last audiogram which had clearly agitated him. Based on our past three attempts at audiograms, we suspected that this audiogram would not be easy. Jason surprised us all! He behaved and cooperated so well that the pediatric audiologist asked what his diagnosis was. She seemed surprised when I said autism. She looked at me as if I were a bored yuppie mother, inventing trouble where there was none. Thank you, Dr. Kaplan!

Once again Jason's audiogram was essentially "normal" (no differences between the right and left ears and no peaks). By now we were smart enough to know that passing hearing and vision screenings did not mean everything was normal. Since Dr. Steve Edelson's studies have shown that AIT without using filters was effective, we were confident about proceeding with AIT as planned and hopeful that AIT would bring about as many positive changes as the glasses.

The next three weeks before AIT brought more changes. Jason quit sucking his thumb without any prompting. He started descending the stairs one foot per stair tread, a skill that was emerging when he started wearing the glasses. He stopped reversing she / he pronouns, a habit we had been trying to break for a year. He seemed to quit smelling objects. He tolerated group settings better. He started appending people's names to greetings, "Oh, hello, Dr. XXXX." In fact, on our first visit to our family doctor after he started wearing glasses, Jason was so social and interacted so well that our doctor spent ten minutes telling me how amazed he was at the recent changes in him. He'd also read the literature from Dr. Kaplan and Dr. Bérard and commented on how simple yet sensible their premise that perceptual differences could impact behavior seemed. Now he'd seen firsthand the changes in Jason due to the glasses.

In mid–July, Jason began auditory training with Dr. Pat Rydell in Denver. No filters were used. I was nervous before the first sessions because we had violated one of the tenets of auditory training for persons with autism: we had not visited Dr. Rydell's office nor had we met him before the first AIT session. I had spoken with Pat on the phone several times but that would be of no help to Jason should he object to this new therapy with a new person in a new setting.

If we had had a video camera present, we could have filmed a commercial about how easy AIT could be! Jason walked in, met Pat, put on the headphones, and sat there listening to the music just as Dr. Bérard recommends. No food reinforcers, no deep pressure, and no distractions were needed. During the break between sessions, we visited Dr. Marcy Rose, the Denver optometrist trained and recommended by Dr. Kaplan. During this exam, Jason cooperated very nicely (as opposed to his behavior during Dr. Kaplan's exam two months earlier). Dr. Rose suggested that Jason receive vision therapy in her office and a home program of vision therapy exercises which commenced after auditory training was completed.

Jason tolerated the second AIT session without any distress. His behavior outside the listening sessions began to change. On the seventy–mile ride home, he complained about the wind noise giving him a headache. He fell asleep in the car but startled when I coughed. He began to suck his thumb again and to squeak like a mouse. He squeaked all day, about ten times an hour. That evening, my husband reported more grunting and sound vocalizations than ever before; Jason was using few if any words. (In order to minimize the out of pocket cost of AIT, I would take Jason to AIT and then work swing shift so that I didn't have to burn vacation time. This meant our leaving the house at 6 A.M., doing AIT, returning at 2:30 with Jason going to daycare, and my going to work until 11:00 P.M. with my husband single parenting his way through the evening. I would not recommend this plan to anyone needing much sleep.)

When I woke Jason up for our second day of AIT, the first thing he did was squeak. During the entire first week of auditory training, vocalizations (squeaking, barking, meowing, humming, or grunting) dominated Jason's "free" time, time when he was not purposefully engaged in eating, sleeping, or playing. We kept reassuring ourselves that any change is good.

Not all the changes were negative. Before AIT, while not awake himself, Jason would awaken us by bumping his head into the wall or talking in his sleep. During the first week of AIT, Jason began to sleep more quietly. By the end of the first week, numerous gains in Jason's social language appeared. He backed down from a disagreement for the first time in his life. Normally conflicts never resolve and certainly not by his acquiescing. He began to show signs of more complex reasoning. While waiting for our car to be repaired, Jason wanted a second treat out of the vending machine. His attempts to get a second treat were more creative than ever before. He tried asking me by talking to himself out loud. He tried convincing me I wanted a treat. He commented that while Doritos made his fingers dirty, a candy bar would make them clean. Before AIT, the progression would resemble a broken record—Jason asking for another treat reiterating the same words. "Well" became one of Jason's favorite words as he learned to negotiate, "W-e-l-l-l-l-l, how about cupcakes for dinner and chicken for dessert." He began to use more complex grammar, "I HAVE BEEN playing over here." He literally woke up talking every day instead of needing to be alone for fifteen minutes. He expressed pride in being able to climb a rope at a kids' fitness center, calling from the top, "I DID it! I DID it!" The length of Jason's ability to play with and his interest in playing with the neighborhood children increased.

The second week's sessions of auditory training went as smoothly as the first week. There was one day when Jason tried to hit me because we would not permit him to sing at peak vocal power during AIT. The vocalizations, humming in particular, continued throughout the week. Some days were better than others. We completed AIT hopeful that the positive gains would continue and that the inappropriate vocalizations would taper off.

The day after auditory training finished, we all planned to relax before the traditional August visits from both sets of grandparents. However life has a way of disrupting one's plans; our daughter Kayla fell and broke her leg. Since the fracture was near the growth plate, the doctor couldn't be sure if the shadow on the X-ray film was a fracture or a pattern in the growth plate. So the doctor pushed on the spot to see if it caused pain. Kayla yowled (screamed really), and Jason avenged his sister by attacking the doctor with his pillow cocked over his head.

During August, we witnessed many other "firsts" for Jason. Jason responded to his sister's telling him he was driving her nuts by saying, "Well, you're driving me nuts right back!" While the grandparents were visiting, Jason hopped onto his bike and rode it. Before AIT and the glasses, Jason would either pedal or steer but could not do both at the same time. He could perform both tasks simultaneously only if I were touching his shoulder (facilitated bike riding??). He also figured out that family titles like Grandma and uncle implied relationships and were not just names.

During the appointment when Kayla's cast was removed, Jason enacted a twenty-minute-long pretend play session in which he carried plates and cups from the waiting room to the cast room, preparing lunch for us. He answered questions from me, the doctor, and the nurse about what we were eating, and he asked us for our preferences. When the cast was off, he returned all the playware back to the waiting room without complaint. The vocalizations tapered off. Jason's tolerance for some sounds like the hair dryer and hand dryers in bathrooms increased. Rather than have a tantrum, Jason would ask us to cover his ears when he needed to use a hand dryer in a public restroom. A retest of Jason's CAPD in August showed that auditory training had effected only slight changes but we plan to test Jason again three months after AIT.

It has been two months since we finished auditory training, and four months since Jason acquired his prism lenses. We continue to see such amazing growth and changes today that even the skeptics in our circle credit these "eyeball" therapies for Jason's remarkable progress. Jason rebounds from shutdown periods much more quickly and he shuts down less often. He perseverates less. He accepts direction better. He tolerates other children invading his space. He asks for help with tasks like zipping his backpack rather than having a tantrum. All his fingernails need to be trimmed at the same time, new since AIT. His face is more animated. His most recent portrait done in August shows a smiling, connected little boy, a marked change from the photos taken over the past two years which portray Jason with a blank or vacant stare. If one really knows autism, the signs are still detectable, but no longer is autism the first thing one would notice about Jason.

Jason will be mainstreamed in Head Start commencing in October, a goal we were not sure was appropriate last May. This summer has amazed us all. We plan to continue vision, speech, and occupational therapies but hope to start reducing their frequency. Jason will continue to use his earplug and earmuffs. We're not ready to abandon our climbing gear and hiking boots yet, but we've made great progress on our downward climb from the volcano known as autism. We'll continue to watch for other "eyeball" therapies that might be appropriate for Jason.

To update (June, '94): Jason has completed his year at Head Start. He settled easily into the classroom routine and made friends with his classmates. He has taught himself to read this year, employing both sight reading and phonics techniques. His sound sensitivity has decreased dramatically, and the strength of his prism lenses has been reduced twice since December.

The classroom adaptations (preferential seating and use of an earplug) have proven to be helpful for him. He continues with sensory integration therapy, speech therapy, and vision therapy weekly.

Jason will be mainstreamed into a full–day kindergarten at a private school in the fall. ■

Chapter 2

Michael

by Patty Hartman

The room held the illusion of shrinking in size with each passing moment, as Michael, my three–year–old, in the height of his glory, flitted like a butterfly from object to object. I stood by silently observing as the speech pathologist tried repeatedly to engage him in the most rudimentary dialogue and predetermined tasks designed to assess his speech and language development.

A trusted friend and an experienced speech therapist, I wanted her to tell me that I had nothing to worry about, that my nagging concerns for his lack of speech were unwarranted. I wanted desperately to hear he was simply a late talker and any day now the words would come tumbling out of his mouth. But the expression on Sue's face suggested something entirely different. She turned to me and said, "Patty, this is very serious. He will not outgrow these delays. It will not simply go away by itself and he may have emotional problems as he grows older." She diagnosed him with Atypical Pervasive Developmental Delay. Her words had the impact of someone hitting me in the stomach with a baseball bat.

I stood there motionless and unable to respond, as speechless as my son Michael. Sue went on to explain the urgency of starting speech therapy, but I was no longer processing her words. I only knew that I wanted to get out of that little room as quickly as possible. "Thank you, Sue," I mumbled, and told Michael it was time to go home.

During the entire ride across busy downtown streets, I couldn't help looking at my beautiful, innocent son with his sky–blue eyes and golden–blonde hair. He was a smaller version of my husband, John, and the first Hartman grandson. When he was born the doctor had pronounced him a perfect baby boy. Until this moment, I thought I'd had little reason to believe otherwise. As my mind raced with conflicting thoughts and memories, Michael appeared to be blissfully unaffected by the evaluation and the prognosis. How could he possibly comprehend the significance of this day, and how it would affect the lives of those who loved him?

This was nearly four years ago, but the experience still burns in my memory. Today, Michael is seven years old. He is fully communicative and asks countless questions about the world and the people in his life. Riding his bicycle, swimming, playing baseball, playing computer games at the library, reading, shopping, playing in the park and going to the lake with his family are among the activities he finds enjoyable. He delights in playing pretend games with his brothers, Danny and David, ages five and three. He has begun to make a few friends and eagerly wants to take an active part in their activities.

Academically, he is reading at several levels above his chronological age, spelling with unusual accuracy, adding and subtracting up to ten, telling time to the minute, learning about the solar system, the major organs and bones of the body, the food groups, and a variety of other information that first graders learn. He's currently fascinated with Michael Jordan and the Cincinnati Reds and dinosaurs, among other topics of interest. Most importantly to John and myself is the fact that Michael is happy with himself. He is able to express his opinions and ideas freely, and eagerly seeks out the companionship of family and friends.

John and I attribute the success of Michael's ongoing recovery to a wide variety of factors including good nutrition, vitamin and nutrient supplements, auditory training, vision retraining, a complete biochemical analysis, and the home–based Option Program, which we continue to implement with the help and support of family, friends, and volunteers. We also believe that without the Lord's faithful guidance and the countless prayers said on Michael's behalf, he would not have been able to make his wondrous and continuous movement toward those who love him.

Following Sue's dismal diagnosis on that traumatic day four years ago, I vacillated between denial, anger, sorrow, pity for myself and Michael, and profound sadness for all of us. My visions of a happy family had been shattered, and putting the pieces together seemed an impossible task. None of my college preparation or four years of experience teaching in special education had prepared me for this. Up to this point, it was I who had informed other parents of their child's difficulties and limitations, smiling and giving words of comfort and encouragement. Smiles and words of comfort eluded me as I searched my mind for the answers to the questions racing through my mind. Why me? What did I do wrong? Why is he different from other children? What does the future hold for him, for all of us? I was unable to sleep, unable to eat, and unable to get through the day without tears. I was inconsolable. Relying on John's strength, I poured out my fears as we talked night after night until there were no thoughts or words left to be expressed. Our families offered their support and encouragement also, but nothing could alleviate the sick, aching feeling that gnawed in my stomach.

Two weeks after Michael's visit with Sue, I took her advice and enrolled him in a regular nursery school class. The very fact that I had chosen to remain home full time with my children in order to provide what I considered to be an enriching, nurturing and loving environment became irrelevant at the time. Why I believed Sue, this person who barely knew my son, and sent Michael to school on her recommendation, is still beyond my comprehension. He had little functional speech, he didn't play with other children, he was extremely shy, and he had rarely been separated from his parents. How could I believe my son would be better off in a school setting with people I didn't know and who knew even less about him and the cause of his delays than I did? "Trust the professionals" was something I'd always believed in, and the very fact that I, too, was a professional, and was acting against my own better judgement, was of little significance to me at this point. I had lost so much confidence that I could no longer think of myself as a capable, experienced teacher. I was just the bewildered mother of a child with unexplained developmental delays.

Off he went to school, the place which was supposed to help him in ways I was incapable of doing. He looked so innocent and unknowing as I led him into the classroom and left him in a roomful of strangers. Day after day, as I stood at the observation window of the classroom, tears rolled down my cheeks as I watched him, comparing him to the other children.

The classroom, any child's delight, had a small kitchen area, a dress–up corner, books, puzzles, building blocks and any number of colorful preschool toys. As the other children created and pretended together, Michael rolled cars along the radiator, repeating phrases to himself that were often unintelligible. He did not participate with the other children or follow the teacher's instructions. His eyes constantly wandering, he had great difficulty paying attention for any length of time and was easily distracted. His speech consisted of echolalia and previously learned repetitive phrases. He did not respond to questions such as "What is your name?" "How old are you?" "Are you a boy or a girl?" or "What do you want?" He seemed to have his own agenda, his own purpose for behaving in this odd, disconnected fashion. As I continued to observe, my greatest fears were being realized, Michael did have serious developmental abnormalities. I could no longer deny or explain his atypical behavior. He was not like any child I'd seen before.

Out of sheer desperation, I decided I could no longer blindly follow the advice of others. I knew I had to do something and I had to do it as soon as possible. I began a quest for knowledge with the fervor of an athlete in training. I consumed books, journal articles, and any publication which provided further insight into Michael's unexplained behaviors. I found the label Pervasive Developmental Delay to be inadequate. It was a generic term used to describe children who failed to meet the criteria for other known disabilities. Often it was associated with autism, a term I couldn't even bear to say in the same sentence with my son's name. I associated autism with children who didn't talk, were totally unresponsive, recoiled at another's touch and performed repetitive movements ad infinitum. Michael certainly did not fit this description. He had loved being held and rocked as an infant. Masterfully, he had put together puzzles and enjoyed looking through picture books as a toddler. He was potty trained and feeding himself before the age of three. I simply could not accept autism as a diagnosis. There must be a different, less alarming explanation for his delays, and I was determined to find it.

The fact that I am an outgoing, talkative person proved useful at this time. In my desperate search for answers, I called and talked with anyone, anywhere. Several people suggested taking Michael to an allergist. Their children's behavior had been profoundly affected by the foods they consumed as well as allergens in the air. I familiarized myself with Doris Rapp's books explaining how foods can have a dramatic impact on a child's behavior, and made an appointment with a highly recommended allergist in town. Dr. Brown was thorough in his physical exam of Michael and didn't seem annoyed when Michael wiggled, squirmed, and begged to go home. He ordered blood tests based on the exam and our family's history of food allergies, and suggested that we try the elimination diet with Michael, eliminating corn, wheat, dairy, sugar, artificial colorings, flavorings, and preservatives of any kinds in the foods he ate. The diet produced some positive changes in his behavior. He seemed calmer and less frustrated, and his speech improved slightly. As a result, we planned to continue eliminating the sugar, preservatives, and colorings from his diet while rotating the remaining foods.

In December, four months after the initial diagnosis, I attended an international conference in Washington, D.C., on early intervention for children with handicaps and developmental delays. I carried my notebook, and like a reporter after a lead story, I scribbled names, phone numbers, addresses, anything that might prove useful in helping Michael. In elevators, hallways, and lunchrooms, I approached the experts, taking the opportunity to explain my situation.

Most expressed concern, and offered opinions and suggestions which led to my decision to take him out of school immediately. When I called the director of the preschool to explain my decision, she said, "But we haven't given up on him yet." Was she implying I had? I felt the blood begin to rush toward my face as I gathered my self control and informed her that I had not given up on him either. I explained that her particular program was simply not appropriate for him and was creating too much stress for Michael and myself. I also told her of my newly discovered pregnancy and my desire to eliminate as much stress from my life as possible.

After I hung up the phone, I felt a flood of relief wash over me. I had my child back where I believed he had belonged all along, with his family who loved him.

Resuming our previous routines, I began taking Danny, now eighteen months old, and Michael, now three–and–a–half, to the park, shopping, to the YWCA for swimming. To provide Michael with small groups of children, we visited relatives and friends. I learned new ways of teaching him colors, numbers, letters, and shapes and was able to help him increase his vocabulary. Although he was two years younger, Danny was already putting words and short phrases together. He loved to be read to, and delighted in playing with Playdough, painting, coloring, and building with blocks. Like a sponge, he absorbed and made sense of it all. His curiosity knew no limits and he was quick to respond to me with a smile, hug, kiss, or deep belly laugh.

Michael, on the other hand, sat for long periods of time lining up blocks in perfectly straight rows, and sorting them according to size, shape or color. Spelling was an integral part of his activities also, as he repeatedly pulled the string of a "See and Say" toy just to watch the center spin. He had great difficulty responding to the simplest of questions, and became fixated on the same Sesame Street and Richard Scarey videos. In contrast to Danny, Michael kept his emotions tucked deeply within himself. Often, he laughed at inappropriate times as if he saw and heard things we did not. It was puzzling and confusing for John and me to watch.

Although we were doing everything we knew to enhance and encourage Michael's desire to play with other children, he avoided them and seemed to be driven by his repetitious activities. Spinning objects, banging on nearly every readily available surface, using toys in unusual ways and often breaking them in the process, lining up objects, and crawling into trash cans, were some of his rituals. I was both frustrated and disturbed at the pleasure he received from the repetition of these activities. Despite our efforts to eliminate them, these and many other atypical behaviors increased rather than diminished in intensity. As I made ongoing comparisons to other preschoolers I knew, I could see a widening gap between his development and theirs. Because he was unable to make the simplest connections between actions and consequences, disciplining Michael was often futile. He would say, "I stop, Mommy," and within moments would repeat the behavior. Out of sheer frustration, I turned once again to the educational system for the answers that eluded me.

After consulting several friends and attending local educational workshops, I made arrangements for him to be evaluated by a learning disabilities specialist in January, 1990. As in previous similar situations he had been in, Michael was easily distracted and offered little cooperation during the evaluation. Only a few minutes had passed when Carol, the teacher, turned to me and said, "This is the most distracted, inattentive, hyperactive child I've ever seen in my fifteen years of teaching. Why isn't he taking Ritalin?" Again, I could feel the blood rush to my face, but I resisted the temptation to flee with Michael, and remained silent. She administered the remaining predetermined tasks which Michael found of little use or interest although eventually he did offer his half–hearted cooperation.

In summary, she stated that his perceptual motor skills were very good, his memory skills were excellent, and his ability to identify shapes, colors, numbers, and letters were all age–appropriate. She had serious concerns about his lack of speech and underdeveloped social skills although she did not believe he was learning disabled or autistic. In fact, she even suggested he might be intellectually gifted. Although she felt he could benefit from her classroom for children with learning disabilities, she said he wasn't old enough. She believed I was smothering him and was overprotective, and handed me the names of several books on parenting. As was quickly becoming a habit, I mumbled my thank you's and made a hasty exit. I had put Michael through yet another evaluation that yielded little useful information and further confused me in what to do. I returned home, where Danny and I persisted in our efforts to engage Michael in meaningful, creative play.

Three months later, a trusted friend and colleague suggested another speech therapist for us to see. She was employed at a center owned and operated by a team of neurologists. I made several inquiries and ultimately made an appointment for yet another evaluation. This time, I brought John along for moral support.

Debra was very kind and gentle in her approach with Michael. Using play therapy as opposed to the clinical approach of the previous therapist, she engaged Michael in a variety of activities. Although he responded to her openly and warmly, still he scored in the bottom 1% for his chronological age group. I was devastated. She recommended weekly speech therapy and a complete neurological evaluation to eliminate any physiological, metabolic or genetic reasons for Michael's delays.

Within several weeks, the neurological tests came back negative. The neurologist offered little advice and encouraged us to keep doing what we were doing. When John asked him for a diagnosis, his reply was, "If I had to make a guess, it would be high–functioning autism." He quickly added he would not write this label on any of Michael's records since it could restrict him from obtaining future health insurance. There was that awful word again, the word I could no longer avoid. Staring me in the face, I found it increasingly difficult to deny. However, I could postpone the inevitable as I was eagerly anticipating the birth of my third child and busied myself with the necessary preparations.

David was born in August, 1990. His birth was smooth, quick and uncomplicated. I savored the three days I had with him at my side in the hospital, and basked in the glory of new motherhood. John took care of Michael and Danny while I enjoyed having a respite from household responsibilities. Our family was now complete. We had planned the births of our children closely and now eagerly looked forward to watching them grow. Unfortunately, our dream of being a happy family was far from becoming a reality. Michael's behavior and odd responses in social situations continued to create stress and unhappiness in our daily lives. It was at this time, right after David's homecoming, that I attended a conference on the diagnosis and treatment of autism. I had to find out once and for all if he had this dreaded disorder.

Over a period of four months, including three separate four-hour round trips to Indianapolis for observation, interviews and testing, Michael was finally given the official diagnosis of high–functioning autism. There it was, on paper, in black and white. I read each and every word of the detailed report. At four–and–a–half years old, Michael's developmental scores ranged from two to five years. The doctor had been thorough and meticulous in her diagnosis, and I could no longer avoid or deny it. I finally had my answer, certainly not the one I had hoped and prayed for, but none the less an answer.

I spent many afternoons in the winter of 1991 going to the library with an infant and two preschoolers in tow to follow up on any information which could enlighten me on the subject autism. My moods were often as bleak and gray as the seemingly endless dark, cold days. Several well–meaning people advised me to graciously accept his diagnosis and get on with my life. After all, didn't I have two other children and a husband who also needed my time and attention? I vehemently rejected their advice. My son was not going to become another nameless statistic in a special education journal. Their words, intended to comfort and support me, did neither. How could I give up? My first born son had built a wall brick by brick between himself and the rest of the world and I believed it was up to me alone to penetrate that wall before the mortar solidified, encasing him in a permanent structure. I could not allow autism to shatter the hopes and dreams I had for him and our entire family.

Fortunately, John readily agreed with me. As I sifted through volumes of information, he kept the boys occupied by taking them for bike rides, reading to them, and playing in the back yard with them. I became adept at nursing, rocking and singing to David while simultaneously reading a book on autism. I would mark specific pages and relate the information to John later in the evening. The professionally written material was filled, almost without exception, with dreary prognoses, and offered little hope for recovery. Chronic was the word I read over and over. How dare these people predict the future of any child, especially mine? I desperately sought *help*, not lists of behavioral characteristics or statistics of how many autistic children will never develop meaningful speech, will never have normal reciprocal social relationships, will develop epilepsy in adolescence or will require medication to control their aggression and self-injurious behaviors.

Frustrated and disillusioned, I turned to material written by those living with autism, the parents. To my surprise and delight, many parents were finding answers to their children's odd and previously unexplained behaviors. Feeling as though I'd stumbled on hidden treasure among the vast ruins of a sunken ship, I read and reread the material, constantly amazed at the courage, tenacity and resourcefulness of these dedicated people. Their children were not nameless statistics, but had become delightful, capable, unique and independent individuals who were making decisions for themselves and enjoying life to the fullest. Following two years of evaluations, consultations, and therapies, I finally found the answers I so desperately sought. Now began the arduous task of deciding what methods and treatments to try first, for frequently they involved both expense and travel. We wanted to research each method carefully.

When Michael was four-and-a-half, we enrolled him in preschool for children with learning disabilities. I wanted some additional help with him, and the mornings he was in school gave me the opportunity to spend time with Danny and David. Michael adjusted rather quickly to the highly structured classroom routine. The teachers, Carol and Jean, gave him the time and space he required to make the necessary adjustments. Carol, the same person who'd tested him the previous year, was still not entirely convinced he was autistic, but was willing to help him develop his strengths, and provided opportunities for him to be a part of a group. Many of the children came from situations of abuse or neglect or were labeled at risk for a variety of reasons. They were friendly and fully accepted Michael in the activities, but he still found forming relationships difficult, and preferred to be alone during free time and recess. The teachers patiently encouraged him to participate but never insisted or in any way forced him. The year proved to be a positive one for him and he did not show the signs of stress he'd previously displayed. I also benefitted from the school, making new friends with and receiving support from the other mothers who faced similar circumstances.

At home, Michael's attention span was minimal at best. Still opposed to the use of Ritalin, we tried to lengthen his attention span by using a "whatever works" approach. Danny and I played Candyland, Chutes and Ladders, and simple card games, including Michael as much as possible. Danny was a wonderful role model and maintaining his interest posed no problem. Even David at eighteen months delighted in being a charter member of the Hartman kitchen preschool group. In addition to the games, painting, coloring, and creating with Playdough were regular afternoon activities, but sustaining Michael's interest and attention was challenging. He lacked the ability to focus his gaze or attention in the same way his younger brothers did. He often ran from the room to engage himself in self-stimulating behavior or his favorite routines. Throughout these months, we did, however, notice subtle improvements in Michael's interaction with his family.

Danny became our prized speech therapist as his phrases transformed into sentences and countless questions. Michael seemed to be far more interested in Danny than in any speech therapist we'd taken him to see, and Danny did not charge $40.00 per half–hour session. Since Michael's visual and memory skills had always been a source of strength, we utilized these as we taught him sentence structure. Ironically, he could read with little difficulty, but saying the same words in conversation proved extremely laborious for him. I composed language experience stories on the blackboard and on poster board strips and as we read them aloud together, his ability to talk in sentences improved.

As fate would have it, the National Autism Society Conference was scheduled to be held in Indianapolis in July 1991. The agenda included several speakers whose approaches to the treatment of autism we were eager to learn about. We made arrangements for the boys to stay with relatives, and planned to spend the entire day in Indianapolis without our children, something we hadn't done since Michael's birth. Accustomed as I was to attending educational conferences on my own, it was an added treat to have John with me. Our first day alone in over five years, and we chose to spend it at an autism conference! It may not have been exactly romantic, but at least we were together enjoying each other's company, and the day proved to be enlightening.

A speaker named Steven, from the Option Institute in Massachusetts, had a profound effect on us. His face radiated joy as he talked about his experiences working with autistic children at the Institute. We sat mesmerized as he spoke not of obstacles and hurdles, bur rather of opportunities and the incredible power of a positive attitude. The Institute's program, pioneered by Barry and Samarhia Kaufman with their son Raun in the late 1970's, had become widely known as a result of the book, *SonRise*, later made into a television movie of the same name. The Kaufmans believed in being with their son 100% of the day, interacting with him on the level where he was most comfortable, and encouraging him with constant praise and unconditional love. I was familiar with the book *SonRise* as well its sequel, *A Miracle to Believe In*, but listening to Steven that afternoon brought the words to life in an extraordinarily moving way.

Upon our arrival home, I called the Option Institute and asked them to send more information. I ordered several of their audio cassette series including Special Children/Special Solutions, featuring Samarhia Kaufman. When I was informed they had a nine–month waiting period, and the fee was over $5,000 for one week of training, I was discouraged, but I certainly wasn't ready to abandon the approach entirely. The people I talked with over the phone there were friendly and free with ideas and specific suggestions to try with Michael at home. Annie, an Option staff member, recommended we try to develop his sense of humor by exaggerating our emotions, especially our happiness and joy in being with him. "Autism breeds in routine and repetition," she said. Therefore, we should try to be as spontaneous as possible and vary our routines to discourage his dependence on them. Using happiness, acceptance, and love to draw him towards us rather than to reprimand, discipline, or force compliance, was their preferred approach. It all seemed so simple in theory but proved to be more complicated in its day–to–day application. Nonetheless, we tried to follow her advice for it was in no way harmful to Michael, but rather was the kindest, most gentle approach we'd encountered thus far.

We pursued other leads, including sensory integration as presented in books by Jean Ayres, sensory "isms" as described by Carl Delacato in his book, *The Ultimate Stranger*, and nutritional supplements suggested by Dr. Bernard Rimland of the Autism Research Institute in San Diego. John and I hypothesized that Michael's sporadic hyperactivity was caused by an underactive vestibular system. We located a sensory integration specialist at a local hospital, but when Michael was uncooperative and fearful of her, we decided to create our own personalized therapy program at home.

Each evening for several months, we put Michael in a barrel with open ends and rolled him the entire length of our kitchen and family room, a distance of thirty feet. We also spun him in a net hammock suspended from our garage ceiling, sometimes for as many as two hundred revolutions at a time. We laughed to ourselves as we made sure the garage door was closed during these sessions since we thought our neighbors would neither appreciate nor understand our unorthodox methods of correcting Michael's impaired vestibular system, operating as we were on the theory that the child demonstrating hyperactivity actually craved movement and was simply taking care of his physical needs and imbalances. As Michael gradually began to show signs of dizziness following the nightly sessions, something that had rarely happened before, we decreased the repetitions and within a few months eliminated them altogether. We continued to encourage his swinging on his own, rolling, running, playing chase, hide and seek, and games like the hokey pokey, ring around the rosey, London Bridge, and duck duck goose. Along with Michael, Danny and David delighted in participating in the games, and they became a part of our daily routine.

Although our unorthodox therapy program was not advocated or supported by any doctor or therapist we'd encountered, we none–the–less persisted in our home remedy approach. The alternative was to place our highly intelligent son in a self–contained special education classroom with professionals who offered no hope for recovery.

In the spring of 1992, the school year was drawing to a close and kindergarten loomed like a gray storm cloud. We still harbored grave reservations about Michael's ability to function in a regular classroom. On the other hand, special education seemed far from appropriate for a child who was reading, spelling and writing. As uncertainty and indecision permeated our thoughts, the Lord once again aided us by bringing some special people into our lives. A couple from our church offered their help in whatever capacity we needed. We hesitated at first but ultimately asked them to come to our house and play with Michael, using the Option methods we'd been trying on our own. At precisely the same time, my director at school offered us financial aid to assist us in going to the Option Institute in Massachusetts for formalized training. (I was employed for half a day a week at the time as an infant stimulation teacher for children with handicaps.) Overwhelmed with excitement and anticipation, I called the Institute to get our names on the waiting list. To our amazement, they had a cancellation and were able to see us in merely six weeks. In one short week, we had volunteers willing to spend time with Michael, and the financial assistance we needed to make the trip a reality.

The days we spent at the Institute were incredible and inspiring. We observed as staff members with boundless energy and enthusiasm drew Michael into play. Later, we were observed in the same room and had intense discussions with other staff members on how we could be more effective in getting Michael to play interactively, sustain eye contact, and give us consistent responses to our comments and questions. We had several conversations with Samarhia and her daughter, Bryn, and Steven, our initial contact at Option, and throughout the week we learned to let go of previously held beliefs that had kept us from enjoying Michael as he was. We were given pointers on how to recruit and train volunteers to assist us in our program once we were home again.

For the first time in years, we felt hopeful for the future rather than fearful. The week concluded with a meeting with everyone at the Institute who participated in our family program. Tears filled my eyes as I sat and quietly listened as each person expressed his joy and excitement in playing with Michael and what a delightful little boy he was. Time set aside for brainstorming gave us many concrete suggestions and ideas to implement in our own home program with Michael. As we drove away from the Institute, we were filled with joy and anticipation, feelings we'd seldom shared with each other since Michael was diagnosed with autism.

Fifteen people, from high school students to senior citizens, attended our first volunteer meeting. We summarized our trip and informed everyone of specific techniques we would be using in the playroom with him. We emphasized the significance of a positive, loving, and accepting attitude. We began by imitating Michael's repetitious behaviors, no matter how bizarre or unusual, to show him our unconditional acceptance of him. Our purpose was to slowly demonstrate through our actions that we could be trusted, predictable, and useful, and our world could be even more fun and exciting than the one he'd encased himself in for nearly four years. We wanted to help him develop the motivation to want to be with us, learn from us, laugh with us, play with us, and talk with us. All this was to take place in a small bedroom we'd converted to a playroom stocked with toys, paper, crayons, games, a trampoline, a rocking horse, and other items we could use to invite and encourage his active participation with us. At the conclusion of the meeting, each person signed up for a time to observe either John or myself playing with Michael. As they felt comfortable, they would then spend time alone with Michael as we took notes and made observations to help them be as effective as possible.

Although the home program had just begun and we were all putting a tremendous amount of time and energy into it, I was still on the lookout for new information that could be useful to us. A book called *Rickie*, by Frederick Flach, M.D., was listed in a newsletter from the Georgiana Organization, and I read it with great interest. The author told the story of his daughter's well–documented mental illness which had been treated for many years in mental institutions and hospitals, and which was actually the result of acute visual distortion and biochemical and nutritional imbalances and deficiencies. His vivid account of Rickie's inner battle and ineffective treatment was heart–wrenching. I began thinking of the way Michael had self–stimulated by using his peripheral vision or by watching small items drop to the floor as he repeatedly picked them up and let them fly. He never appeared to tire of a variety of forms of this game: Paper, leaves, tinker toys, blocks, the object itself was secondary to his gazing at its journey to the ground.

I located Dr. Flach's number in New York and called him at his office. He kindly recommended three different behavioral optometrists in Indiana, and after several phone interviews, I decided on Dr. South.

John was skeptical as Michael's strengths had always been with visual perceptual skills. Didn't he prove this to us by learning to put together puzzles with ease, spell at age three and read at age four? However, John didn't see any harm in Michael having a quality eye exam. After an intense hour–and–a–half examination, the doctor concluded that Michael did in fact need glasses. His eye muscles were weaker than normal. "It would be as if Michael, you and I were all running in a marathon together, but instead of running shoes, he wore weighted boots." He said that Michael's ability to track and shift his gaze were underdeveloped. Could this be the reason why he had such poor eye contact, great difficulty in maintaining his focus, and was so easily distracted? Before we left, I gave Dr. South my heartfelt thanks for his gentle and patient approach with Michael. Needless to say, John was surprised at the doctor's findings but it appeared we had discovered one more significant clue in our relentless pursuit of a clear understanding of our son.

When I read Annabel Stehli's remarkable story of her daughter's recovery, I was doubtful Michael would benefit from auditory training for he already had speech and was not totally withdrawn. But after talking with parents from various parts of the country, we decided to pursue it. Since the treatment was still relatively new and only available in selected cities, Michael and I would have to travel to Cincinnati. Leaving John and our two younger children at home was not my first choice, but we believed everyone would be better off with this arrangement. I wrote out detailed schedules so that grandparents and friends could help while we were gone.

Michael's initial audiogram revealed that he was unable to properly process sound. Painful hearing was indicated by three peaks on the graph at different frequencies, and he was unable to hear with the same intensity in both ears. In the ten days to follow, Michael attended two half–hour daily sessions of auditory training, listening to the filtered and randomized music through headphones attached to the AudioKinetron. I stood watching silently through a two–way mirror, amazed at his ability to sit quietly as he listened to this nonsensical music. The entire process still baffled me as to how it could produce evidently astounding life–altering results. Counseling myself not to expect miracles, I secretly hoped for one.

The first indication came during the second week of training as a thunderstorm rumbled outside our hotel room. To my delight and surprise, Michael did not panic and clasp his hands firmly over his ears in his usual fashion. Instead, we read stories together and he quietly fell asleep. Most of the changes we observed were more subtle. The volunteers in our ongoing home program commented as he gradually became more expressive, both in his display of emotions and in his speech. His responsiveness to questions and comments increased as did his fine motor skills. We all noticed he expressed happiness and joy more frequently than he had before receiving the training. Fortunately, he did not display any of the aggressiveness or undesired behaviors often seen in children following auditory training. We attribute this to his gentle nature and to the positive, accepting attitude of his volunteers and the nonthreatening environment we had created for him. Although auditory training didn't cure Michael's autism, it was an extremely valuable tool in helping him be more open to his environment, more inquisitive, and more responsive. The world had became a friendlier, more inviting place for him to be a part of. For these and many other reasons, John and I not only support auditory training, but enthusiastically encourage parents to pursue it.

As winter slowly turned into spring, our Option program kept its forward momentum. Michael eagerly anticipated his sessions, responding with smiles, looks, and laughter, as each volunteer saturated him with love, acceptance, and joy. We challenged him to participate with us in new and different activities ranging from reading books, drawing pictures, acting out stories, playing sports, making train tracks and playing pool, to learning the solar system, the states with their capitals, and that alcohol and tobacco are harmful to your body. Always fine–tuning his goals and objectives, a day rarely passed that didn't include continuous observations and ongoing discussions of Michael's program.

How to be more effective in helping Michael let go of inappropriate behaviors and increase his interest in people and the world became the question uppermost in our thoughts. It affected our decisions about where we ate, which park we went to, and whom we visited. The transition from home to social situations was gradual and well–planned. We waited until we believed he was ready to handle a specific situation without reverting to autistic behaviors to comfort himself before we involved him in deciding whether he should participate. If he wanted to be involved, we would then explain the behavior appropriate for the situation. In some circumstances, we made the decision for him while at other times we asked for his input. For example, Michael wanted to attend the wedding of one of his volunteers, so we repeatedly described in detail what happens at a wedding. We discussed the appropriate behavior we expected from him and when he agreed to conform, we decided to give it a try. I was fully prepared to leave at any given moment during the ceremony, but to my delight, Michael was wonderful and behaved like a perfect gentleman. Pride and joy filled my heart as I watched him sit in his suit and tie so quietly and attentively as the priest performed the ceremony. This approach is the one we've chosen to use and will continue to implement as Michael re–enters a variety of social situations including parties, church attendance, and eventually, school.

In March 1993, Annie, with whom I had developed a close friendship and who was also the mother of a four–year–old boy with developmental delays, gave me an article written by a father from Toronto. He described his son, who at four years old was diagnosed with autism, and was now in sixth grade showing absolutely no signs of his former condition. His amazing recovery was due in large part to the supplemental use of vitamins and the nutrients DMG and octocosanol. After talking to the father on the telephone, and calling a nutritionist to verify the safety and effectiveness of these two food supplements, we decided to add them to Michael's daily nutritional program. The program now included Dr. Rimland's recommended vitamin supplements, limiting sugar and dairy products, preservatives and food colorings, and giving him a variety of fresh fruits, vegetables, meats and grains. It's difficult to determine how much the modified diet and supplements have contributed to Michael's progress, but we believe they are important factors in maintaining a well–balanced, optimally healthy body.

In the spring of 1993, Annie and I continued to share information and trade articles and books we found interesting and helpful since our doctors offered us no additional information. In her reading, she discovered a doctor in New Jersey [now located in Weston, Connecticut—Ed.] who tested children for internal imbalances and deficiencies in their immune and digestive systems.

After further research and discussion, John and I decided I would make the twenty–six–hour round trip with Michael to see Dr. Sidney Baker. The decision was difficult as it involved expense and there were no guarantees or scientific studies supporting Baker's methods. However, as we had previously done with his sensory systems, we wanted to correct any imbalances he might have with his internal systems. This time, my parents volunteered to make the long trip with us, and we were grateful to have their company.

Dr. Baker's office was nestled in the quiet, undisturbed countryside of rural New Jersey, not the setting I'd envisioned for a doctor with his credentials and lifetime experience. He was extremely kind and sensitive in his approach with Michael, putting all of us at ease with his gentle manner. The visit lasted for nearly three hours and included a complete physical for Michael and interviews with myself and my parents about our family history and Michael's medical history. Dr. Baker quietly observed Michael as he played and colored in his office. As we talked, he recorded his opinions, observations, and recommendations for further testing on his lap top computer. He then gave us the complete report along with several prescriptions for lab work. We left with a grocery bag full of vials, containers, and the detailed instructions needed for sending samples of Michael's body fluids to various laboratories.

The results were astounding. As Dr. Baker put it, Michael had several "quirks and peculiarities" in his immune and digestive systems. Among the complex findings were a "leaky gut," and parasites and bacteria present in his intestines which suppressed his immune system. His zinc and copper levels were low and his fatty acid levels were abnormal. Dr. Baker called us and said, "Michael's body is not assimilating food efficiently." He recommended a variety of supplements.

In May 1993, Annie and I attended a conference given by the Georgiana Organization called "Celebration of Breakthroughs." It was wonderful to have a friend as eager as I was to pursue any avenue of help, and once again I was inspired as I saw and talked with other parents. Already familiar with most of the information presented, I was reassured that John and I were in fact doing everything currently known to help Michael. I listened with great interest to the panel of recovered adults who were leading independent, productive and interesting lives.

Getting up at 5:00 A.M. and staying awake until midnight, holding marathon discussions with other excited parents eager to share their stories, created a state of exhilaration and exhaustion. I highly recommend and encourage any parent to attend conferences like this one, to gather information and to offer and receive support.

We are currently preparing Michael for the transition between home and school by visiting the school building, the principal, and the teachers, and familiarizing him with the surroundings in a casual manner. He has a desk with first grade curriculum books from the school he will attend, and together with Danny, we practice classroom etiquette as well as learning the material from the textbooks. Michael is already anxious to go to school, but we want him to be as prepared as possible before he undertakes this significant step. All the while, we are continuing our home Option program.

The intense all–consuming fear I once had for Michael's future has, to my delight, been replaced by joyful anticipation and hope, the same feelings I hold for other my sons, Danny and David. We have won back the dreams we thought were lost forever. Once again, we are finding joy in day–to–day living. We are grateful for the many wonderful people supporting and helping us with their friendship, love and prayers.

Michael's ongoing recovery also would not have been possible if parents like the Kaufmans, Stehlis, Rimlands, and Flachs had not unselfishly shared the valuable information that helped their children. They have all withstood intense criticism from the medical and educational communities in advocating their approaches to the treatment of autism and developmental delays. Words cannot fully express our gratitude and appreciation for their help for parents who, like themselves, relentlessly pursue progress and happiness for their children.

We thank the Lord that the brick wall Michael began constructing between himself and the rest of the world has slowly been disassembled and is being replaced by a bridge linking his world to ours. ■

Chapter 3

Victoria and Katherine

by Chuck and Verna Lashley

W hen we first heard about auditory training, it was associated with being of help to some people with autism. After reading Georgie's story, we hoped it would be as effective for Victoria, our autistic daughter, as it had been for Georgie. I dreamed, and still dream, that Vicki will be the next Georgie.

Vicki

When Vicki was three years old, she was diagnosed as severely retarded by a psychiatrist associated with Johns Hopkins University Hospital. A year later, Dr. Dennis Whitehouse, a considerably more competent doctor, gave us the diagnosis of autism. Through the Child–find Program, Vicki was enrolled in a public school for handicapped and retarded children, a school dedicated to special education for children with special needs. Although there were several other autistic children in the school, Vicki was the only one in her class of ten to twelve children, many of whom were far lower functioning than she. Although she was language–delayed, and did not speak until she was about four–and–a–half, the fact that she could feed herself and was toilet trained put her into the high–functioning category.

In some respects, her high functioning led to her receiving less individual attention from the teachers and their aides than the more limited ones in her classroom. An exception to this general rule was made by Vicki's first teacher, Paula Mackey. In fact, out of this year of common concern grew a deep friendship between her family and ours, and Paula took a strong and deeply personal interest in Vicki. The teachers that followed her were much less involved. Of course, the outward severity of the other children's problems and needs probably overshadowed the needs and potential of the quiet child locked in autism.

With autistic children, there is great concern that meaningful speech occur by five years of age, and although Vicki's words were extremely meaningful to us, by her fifth birthday they were very few in number. Before she was labeled autistic, we suspected and even hoped that her hearing was impaired. With this in mind, when she was two–and–a–half we took her to be evaluated by a duo of Ph.D.'s, an audiologist and a speech pathologist. After an embarrassing ordeal trying to get Vicki to respond to the sounds in the hearing booth, the results indicated no real hearing problem. The two specialists could only recommend that she be evaluated for mental retardation. I don't know of very many labels that can hurt, shock, and devastate parents much more than "retarded."

Vicki had other problems besides her language delay. She was a climber, and would climb on top of tables, up bookcases, and over fences. Once she even climbed out of the second story window and sat on the small roof overhanging our front door— which alarmed our neighbor across the street who telephoned us with panic tempered by reserve in her voice.

When Vicki was a toddler, we had to sell our house because of our in–ground pool. As a magnet draws iron, the pool drew Vicki. Its fence and gate were constantly under siege, and we knew it was only a matter of time before she would scale it, or— one of our greatest fears—someone would forget to lock the gate.

Some of her worst problems were sensory. She suffered from an over–sensitivity—sometimes attraction and sometimes great aversion—to normal sensations like water, heat, coarse clothing, and certain sounds. Music appealed to Vicki. She would dance and often hum, droning along to the melody. The sound of toilets flushing petrified her. She would cover her ears with her hands, scream, and run from the bathroom. We could not have a fire in the wood stove or the fireplace. Once Vicki felt the radiating heat, she would move relentlessly toward it.

In our reports to all the specialists, teachers and doctors who evaluated Vicki, we explained that she had actually developed quite normally for the first eighteen months of her life. She had even spoken several words. One evening we distinctly heard her say "bunny rabbit." She stopped talking soon after that, losing the words she had, and her behavior began to get worse at the same time. During our first meeting with Dr. Whitehouse in 1988, he told us that normal development for up to eighteen months and then a dramatic cessation were classic symptoms of autism in children. He was shocked and apparently disappointed that these facts had escaped the other experts who had evaluated Vicki and misdiagnosed her.

When she was six, we took her out of the county public school against the advice of the principal. He was a fine man, we had come to know and respect his opinion, and there was no doubt in his mind that she needed special education in his school. He was genuinely concerned that if she failed in another setting, her self–esteem would be terribly hurt. We were convinced, however, that their program simply could not tap Vicki's potential. We preferred a school where we felt the staff would have more faith in her ability to progress.

Like most parents, we were sure others had underestimated Vicki, and that she had far more to offer than was generally assumed. Her memory, for instance, had proved to be extraordinary. Almost from the time our daughters were born, Chuck read to them every night at bedtime. When Vicki had begun speaking again, he started reading lines in Dr. Seuss books up to the last word, coaxing the girls to provide the final rhyming word. Vicki caught on quickly. She could only verbalize a word here and there, and although she could fill in blanks, she could not repeat entire phrases or sentences. But it became apparent that she had the books entirely memorized!

When we first considered AIT, Vicki was seven years old and in a special program at Harford Christian School, a private school and a ministry of Harford Methodist Church in Dublin, Maryland. While the school has no formal special education program, it does have what they refer to as an "extended learning" program, with small classes of five or six students and a significant amount of individualized and personal attention. Although we had only been considering Harford Christian School for our younger daughter, Katie, when we discovered their "extended learning" feature, we dared to hope Vicki might go there as well. She failed their entrance test but surprisingly, they still offered to accept her on a trial basis in their kindergarten class. There was no extended learning program in kindergarten, but the teacher, Mrs. Denise McKnight, telephoned us and said that she was interested in working with Vicki. For once someone besides ourselves suspected that this little girl who spoke so little had a lot more to say.

Denise did a great job. Her efforts combined with the grace of God to begin a new life for Vicki. Her language improved slowly, but she developed in other ways more rapidly, quickly catching on to the sign language Denise used simultaneously as she spoke. Vicki mastered the alphabet and its sounds, and reading became one of her strongest abilities.

When we first heard about auditory integration training, we understood that it was not available in the United States. Eventually, when it was offered in Washington, D.C., we made an appointment for Vicki, and went to Washington for the training.

Vicki's autism at times made her seem hyperactive, and the auditory training made her even more so. During the actual time at the AudioKinetron, she settled into the bean bag chair, took off her shoes, covered herself with a blanket, and seemed to enjoy the sessions. Coming home in the car, however, she was extremely hyper for the entire two–hour trip. She remained hyperactive for about six weeks following AIT. Within a week, Vicki's phrases were getting longer and more complete. She was making real strides in language development. Her grades in school prior to AIT were in the lower 80's. By the end of the school year, her marks jumped by an average of ten points, and she was on the honor roll! What a miracle!

During the summer, her language continued to improve. For the first time, she was really dialoguing and asking questions. She does remain in the extended learning program at school, but she is exposed to and expected to accomplish the regular second grade material. The difference is that she still needs extra individual attention due to the restless behavior associated with her autism, although this behavior is diminishing.

We strongly believe Vicki's progress is an answer to prayer. God has worked through the loving, dedicated, and competent staff and faculty at Harford Christian School and an individualized curriculum has been structured for her. Before AIT, Vicki was coming out of her autism with the special attention at school, and AIT has given her an extra boost to accelerate her progress. Much of her hyperactivity is gone. She is calmer, and is able to sit and read for long periods. She loves to read. She continues to maintain her honor roll status.

Katie

When *The Sound of a Miracle* inspired us to research AIT, we gathered all the information we could find. At first reading, it became clear to us that AIT could address not just autism but other disabilities as well. Katherine, our younger daughter, was learning disabled, and with her in mind, we went through all of the information again, highlighting the references to learning disabilities. These references, which had appeared to be so subtle at first, now jumped off the page. We knew that our Katie was a perfect candidate for AIT.

Katie is thirteen months younger than Vicki. Ever since Vicki began school, Katie had also wanted to go to school—just like her big sister. We entered Katie into a three–year–old preschool program at a private Christian school. After three months, Katie showed signs of learning problems. Her teacher phoned and suggested that she repeat the three–year–old program next year. Since that was nine months away, we thought the teacher was too quick in advising us to hold Katie back. Besides, we had never heard of anyone repeating the three–year–old preschool program. We would wait and see how Katie did for the rest of the year, and would work with her at home, especially during the summer.

Reluctantly, the school agreed to allow Katie to start the four–year–old program the following September. That school year was much the same as the prior one, with a telephone call in December suggesting that she repeat the four–year–old program. By this time I could see what the teachers were up against. Working with Katie at home was very frustrating. When the other children parroted "a is for apple," etc., Katie would just draw a blank. Even after she was told the answer, she could not remember it three minutes later. This was the same whether she was learning colors, sizes, letters or numbers. She also showed clear signs of dyslexia, reversing letters long beyond the age when this is considered normal. Katie was also very shy and somewhat backward around people. She was and still is a small, petite girl with a pixie–type face, beautiful blue eyes, and an infectious laugh. She has always been a happy child, but she also knew that she was not doing as well as the other children in her class. She was now becoming so shy she would not join her classmates when they sang as a group in the chapel. When others talked to her at home, she would hide behind me and seldom respond.

Again, for the third year in a row, the school was recommending that Katie repeat the program. This time, we seriously considered complying. Maybe we had pushed her too far. At six she was small for her age, and wouldn't look noticeably older than the other children if she repeated kindergarten and entered first grade at seven.

It was at this point that we decided to transfer Katie to Harwood Christian School, leaving the decision in the hands of the staff there. Katie did not do very well on the entrance exam, but after much discussion with the principal, he agreed to allow her to begin first grade on a conditional basis, with the stipulation that a reassessment be made in December. If she did not demonstrate that she could handle the work, it was back to kindergarten. In the meantime, Katie would go for auditory integration training.

Katie's reaction was different from Vicki's. Instead of being hyperactive after AIT, she usually fell asleep on the return drive. During AIT, again unlike Vicki, she was not settled at all. She often did not want the headphones on, and unlike her sister, preferred my lap to the bean bag chair. On the second day of the training, I noticed that Katie said hello to some strangers in the park. She began to be friendlier towards people and did not seem as shy as she had been. Her marks early in the beginning of first grade clearly indicated problems, with her grades in the 30–50 range. By January, three months after AIT, her teacher reported that although Katie was doing well enough not to have to go back to kindergarten, she would have to repeat first grade next September. She was too far behind to catch up.

After this report, things began to change dramatically. Katie began to bring home papers with much higher grades. She seemed to be exploding with confidence—the confidence that comes from success. Her enthusiasm bubbled over, and by June, she was no longer faced with repeating first grade. She missed the honor roll by only one point—in handwriting—but by the next marking period, she was on it. Our little scholar had essentially accomplished two years' work in one! She was so proud of herself, and was enjoying a degree of confidence we never thought we'd see.

Prior to AIT, Katie rarely completed her work in class. Each day she brought home papers to complete that her classmates had finished in class. She often had to miss recess to stay in and finish a paper. She had been unable to focus on the tasks and was easily distracted. Now she processes information more quickly and completes her work in the allotted time. And she enjoys recess. She is still a cute little pixie with the most wonderful laugh you have ever heard. Now she holds her head up high and moves with poise.

On the bumper of my car is a sticker that reads, "I am the proud parent of a Harford Christian Honor Roll Student." Of course I had to modify it to reflect the plural! This is something I never thought I'd have. Both of our daughters worked hard to earn that bumper sticker. I believe that AIT helped make it possible.

Normal Katie

by Gerri L. Bisignani (a family friend)

Picture a pint–size lightweight, with wispy, feathery brown hair, attaching herself to Mom for shelter and security, eyes to the floor, with a face full of gentleness and innocence. You knew that if she would only meet your eyes and give you a smile and come out of her shell, even for just a brief moment, she would not only capture your heart not for just a split second but take a piece of it forever. Little Katie Lashley.

We met about five years ago. Katie's Mom, Verna, and I have since become close—closer than sisters in many ways. When you share all that comes about from having autistic children, there's a bond that forms that becomes mighty and special—one that only "autistic" mothers can truly share and fully understand. Our meeting and sisterhood came to be as a result of Verna's Vicki and my Evan. Both children are autistic, but so very different. Both are beautiful children who mysteriously and effortlessly draw you to them. Strange how autism brings out a luring specialness in these children. And snuggled in between these two children is Katie. We work hard to make the Katies of the world feel special and important, as they so richly deserve to feel. Seems no matter how hard we try, they still fight hard for their due attention and the normalcy that can't help but be lacking in a handicapped family.

When I first met Katie, and for some time after that, she was extremely shy and somewhat backward. Verna would get annoyed with her at times as she refused to utter so much as a hello. Seems both were equally determined to win the battle, though Katie usually triumphed over Mom. After a while, Verna's attempt to have her daughter cordially speak decreased, and all accepted Katie's shyness. I would say hello, and that would be that. So despite her shyness, Katie's will was stronger. Along with her shyness came other noticeables about Katie. She longed to be a "baby," displaying baby lingo and driving her mother crazy. Verna and I would discuss this from time to time as Katie's behaviors were similar to those of my daughter, Cara. And since Cara was a few years older and I had already been "through" all of this, Verna and I could connect in yet another way. Katie also struggled in school (as did my Cara), both academically and socially, and this was another source of concern for her Mom. For Katie, school was an unwanted necessity that she was forced to tolerate. Her main goal in life was to play. So the fact that she was not doing well simply was not close to the top of her priority list. It seemed that despite all of the problems and worries that she dealt with as a result of Vicki's autism, Verna felt perhaps an even stronger tug because of Katie's problems. We all want our "normal" children to be as "normal" as possible. Couldn't half of our lives just sail along like everyone else's?! The feeling was one I knew so well.

For ten straight days in October of 1992, Verna, Vicki, Katie, Evan and I drove to and from Washington D.C. where all three children underwent auditory training. Without going into great detail, I will say that it was quite an experience for us all. Hopes were high as patience grew thin during the training period. There was one day in particular that I will never forget. I am unable to recall exactly which of the ten days this was, but I am sure that it was somewhere around the seventh or eighth day. Evan had completed his thirty minute session and we had just come out of our room. Verna was with Vicki in their room, their session not yet finished. Katie was finished with her time for that particular part of the day and was talking to the speech pathologist in the lobby area. I walked past them to set my purse down and I stopped abruptly and turned toward them and just stared in amazement. Here was shy, backward, won't–even–say–hello little Katie Lashley talking away a mile–a–minute to someone she barely knew. She was a veritable chatterbox, speaking crisply and precisely, in great detail and at great length to a woman whom she had really only seen wandering through the offices from time to time. Who was this child??! Truly not the same that I had known all this time. I was witnessing a genuine yet unbelievable transformation right before my eyes. When this happens, you can't help but second–guess it all, so I waited until the next day to see if I really was seeing and hearing things. But from that moment on, I knew that Katie had come out of her shell and was truly on her way!

Katie is now seven years old and in the second grade. Aside from continuing to speak independently and say hello, as well as other things when she so chooses, she is an honor roll student. She strives very hard for excellence—no one has to keep on her heels and demand from her—Katie does a thorough job of this on her own, so much so that she refuses to miss even one day from school for any reason. And from what Verna reports to me, she also does well socially. No more does Verna voice concerns about her baby–like, shy, backward daughter. Seems every time she talks about her children, Verna is full of positives. The Lashleys' prayers were truly answered with help and benefits from auditory training. And from what Verna tells me, success continues to come, and it has been more than a year since completing the training.

What makes all of this worth writing about is quite simple . . . auditory training converted "normal with problems" to "normal." No one is without problems, no matter how they are perceived. But how sweet life can be when our problems become less dramatic and distressing, less heart wrenching and overwhelming, and we can sit back and enjoy once again. I am thankful to be able to share in the Lashleys' joys and successes. ■

Chapter 4

Joey

as told to Kendra Marasco

Joey's birth parents were alcoholics, only interested in drinking, who hadn't planned on having a baby (and hadn't planned on not having one either). Irresponsible and unable to make a commitment, Joey's father was dead of acute alcohol poisoning before he would have a chance to be a real father. He died without ever knowing the devastation he had so carelessly created.

Joey's mother, Andrea, was his mother in name only. I'm the only real mother Joey's ever had. Andrea may have given him life, a life of sorts, but because of her neglect of herself and Joey while she was pregnant, much of that life has been filled with pain, tears, and confusion. Knowing the damage she could cause Andrea swore she wouldn't drink while she was pregnant. We had talked about it. She also promised to take prenatal vitamins, but when we sent her the money for them, she spent it at the liquor store. When we confronted her, she was angry and embarrassed, and when we arranged to have the vitamins paid for and waiting for her at the pharmacy, most of the time she was too busy drinking to pick them up.

Andrea's grade school picture of the pretty girl she once was, is on Joey's bedroom wall. He and Andrea are both short and stylish, with dark, shiny, baby–fine hair parted and combed to the side. Their skin is very fair, with a smattering of freckles, and their eyes are at once similar and very different. They are an incredible, wonderful blue, like a clear, stream–fed mountain lake. But Andrea's are huge and round, and Joey's are small, slanted, and wide–set, with a clouded, unfocused look.

Andrea is not like her photograph anymore. She is no longer pretty, and we don't display her more recent pictures. Her hair is straggly and unkempt, her face is puffy, her skin is blotchy and heavily lined, and her eyes are bloodshot. The wonderful blue has faded, leaving redness in its place. I look at her picture and am frightened to see too much of my son there in her smile and in the familiar contours of her face.

His birth parents named him after themselves—Joseph Andrew. He is carrying too much of them around with him every day as it is, without having to bear their names. I wish we'd changed his name. Sometimes the mere mention of their names can make me feel anger and despair.

Joey was small for a full–term baby, only four pounds three ounces, and seventeen inches long. Joey's parents continued their alcoholic drinking after he was born, and after two weeks, Andrea requested foster care. A month later, although they were still drinking, they wanted him back. When the state intervened and made his foster placement mandatory, Andrea called us and asked us to adopt him. Two years after we adopted Joey, we learned that Andrea had been on a binge when she went into labor. The baby had been born in a haze of alcohol with the stench of it filling the room.

In court, social workers told us that Joey was not adoptable, that he was too badly damaged, and that he belonged in an institution. The neurologist said he was deaf, blind, retarded, and partially paralyzed. The lawyer appointed for him by the state argued that since Andrea and I knew each other, and since Andrea had in fact chosen us as godparents, there was a possibility that we might be persuaded to return Joey to his birth mother. Naturally, he felt this would not be in the child's best interests. Our lawyer fought back successfully. "Birth mothers have been arranging homes for the children they couldn't raise since time immemorial . . .long before you johnnie–come–lately social workers came on the scene." When the judge asked me why I was in her courtroom that day, I said,

"This baby is part of my family. My husband, Bob, and I, have accepted the obligation to assist in his religious upbringing willingly, and without reservation. We cannot fulfill those obligations if he is taken away from us. How can we agree to nourish his soul and not his body? We have room in our hearts, and in our home, for another baby. We had been trying to adopt for the four years before Andrea asked us to adopt Joey. We are not going into this blind. We have two other boys, Kevin, age six, and Christopher, four years old. We know what it is to be up all night with a sick baby. In our jobs, we work with children with special needs all the time, and we love our work. He's already a part of our family, and already loved by us. We know what we're getting into."

They let us bring him home the next day, but it turned out we didn't, in fact, know what we were getting into. Joey had been in foster care for all but two weeks of his life. At three months, he was tiny and lightweight, like a vinyl doll with a hollow body. His foster mother said it was due to a milk allergy, and that the several different formulas she had tried hadn't helped. He had continually lost weight. I was convinced that there had been "benign neglect" because the family consisted of so many foster children, two other babies, two toddlers, and their own three preschoolers. I felt certain that with the proper love and attention, he'd be fine. The only thing that really worried me was that he didn't cry. In fact, he made hardly any sound at all. He was too quiet. Why wouldn't a baby cry? A cry is a baby's first communication. Surely only the most severely impaired babies fail to cry.

In some ways, Bob and I thought it was great! We tried gamely to look on the bright side. Who could count the number of hours of sleep we had lost with our other two? Joey wasn't completely quiet, though. In the rare moments when I wasn't already holding him, if he so much as grunted, I came running. By the end of our first day at home, I realized what those brief, single grunts meant, and would change his diaper. My response was immediate, of course, and Joey's grunts became louder and more demanding. He caught on quickly. Within two days of grunting and having me change his diaper, he developed a wonderful, welcome, lusty cry. When he cried, we all came running. He was calling us. He was communicating. He was okay. He would be fine. The neurological was all wrong—he wasn't paralyzed, he just had poor muscle tone. He wasn't blind— anybody could see he was tracking movement with his eyes. He turned his head in my direction when I talked to him his very first day home, so he wasn't deaf either. He could hear, and now he was crying—the sweetest sound I ever heard. It must have been neglect—no one had answered him when he cried, so he had stopped crying, surely it was as simple as that.

We spent hour after hour massaging his muscles and exercising his arms and legs, holding him, and talking to him. We held him upright, supporting his wobbly little head. By the time he had his first pediatric visit, the doctor agreed with me: the early reports were way off–base. There was nothing wrong with this baby that a lot of extra attention and love couldn't fix. Little did we know.

He did a lot of things that surprised us—as toddlers will do—but many of his actions were puzzling. At first, we found it amusing that Daddy's snoring not only woke him up, but made him cry as well. Bob took a lot of ribbing, and of course it was only fair that he get up with Joey then. We didn't think anything of it. When Joey was two, we took him to the zoo, and when the animals were at their loudest at feeding time, he began to scream. But he was little, and it was scary. We didn't feel his reaction was overly inappropriate. The smoke alarm, however, was a puzzle. Yes, it was loud, but he had heard it many times before, and at age five he was still having a reaction of blind hysteria. He would jump up, cover his ears, scream, run, spin around, run, spin around again, and run again. He was panic–stricken. He wanted to get away and didn't know how to get there. As he got older, we would try to prepare him: "We're using the grill, so the smoke alarm will go off. It's loud, but you know it doesn't hurt you." The alarm would go off, and one of us would run to hold him while he screamed and fought to get away. His screaming would continue long after the alarm stopped, and would be followed by uncontrollable, heart–wrenching sobs. He was terrified and couldn't tell us why.

He had many other fears—the dark, the bathroom, the bedroom, the upstairs, the basement. By the age of nine, he was sleeping on the family room sofa most nights, while the rest of the family was upstairs in bed. Had some loud, frightening horror scared him in his first three months of life? Perhaps that was the explanation.

Joey was so reckless that he terrified us. He would charge to the top of the dresser like a squirrel chased by a hound, and dive off head first. Frequently he acquired bruises, bloody knees, and black eyes, and he often required stitches. What was the social worker going to think? One third of his index finger had to be amputated and surgically reattached, and yet he still closed doors by the edge instead of using the door knob. Why wasn't he traumatized by this? We certainly were. Why didn't he learn how to close a door? Why was he afraid of the bathroom, and not of strangers? Why did he insist on calling the same kid to play, every day for two years, when the answer was always no? If he was afraid of his bedroom, why didn't he fear rejection? How could a kid be so social and yet so socially inept? Why did he keep begging to have sleepovers when no kid would stay with him for more than an hour? Why couldn't he grasp the most basic concepts, and why couldn't we reason with him about anything?

Frustration and anger lived in our house. Nothing seemed reasonable to him, nothing was fair. The smallest request led to an outburst. Hours, days, months, and years of daily support and encouragement had no visible effect. The same rules had to be explained again and again and again. He resisted everything we asked. Simple things other parents take for granted, blowing his nose, using toilet paper (surprisingly, toilet training was never a problem), flushing, washing his hands, taking a bath or a shower, every issue of day–to–day life was met with resistance. He was the most oppositional child I had ever known, and the older he got, the worse it got. As I look back, though, his behavior was always the same: petulant, whiny, and incredibly negative. It just seemed much worse because it didn't seem to change as he got older. As his behavior became increasingly inappropriate, our frustration grew and our patience level dropped to below zero. Joey walked around in a fog with a black cloud hanging over his head that enveloped the whole family.

Once, on his birthday, he stubbed his toe coming into the house at the end of a perfect day. It had been a day–long celebration, with breakfast at his favorite restaurant followed by a party with presents where he received everything he'd asked for and more, complete with the Ninja Turtle cake he had to have which I'd completed at 3 A.M. Afterwards, we took him to an amusement park with six neighbor boys where he enjoyed rides, water slides, hamburgers and cotton candy—sun and fun—a glorious day. As we dragged into the house at 8 P.M., after twelve full hours, he stubbed his toe. No blood. No broken bones. He stubbed his toe. And what, with less than four hours of sleep and a full day of chasing after seven wild little boys, did I hear? "I had a terrible day today," Joey said. He was sincere. "It was a terrible day." "But what about breakfast?"

"I stubbed my toe."

"What about your birthday party?"

"But, I stubbed my toe."

"You got so many nice presents, everything you wanted."

"But I stubbed my toe!"

"Don't forget about all the fun you had at the amusement park."

"Don't forget about my toe."

"Don't forget about your toe? I'll remember that damn toe for as long as I live, you rotten, miserable ingrate of a kid." (You rotten, miserable mother of that kid.)

Joey lied constantly—he'd look me right in the eye, and with utmost sincerity would tell me a story right out of Paul Bunyan.

"What have you got on your face?"

"My lips are chapped."

"It looks like lipstick."

"It's not lipstick."

"You can't go to school with lipstick on."

"I don't have any lipstick on. My lips are chapped."

"It came off on my finger and it smells like lipstick."

"It's not lipstick. I'm telling the truth. My lips are chapped."

"Go upstairs and wash the chapped lips off."

His psychologist said he couldn't distinguish between reality and fantasy, truth from fiction. In addition to making it impossible for him to tell the truth, it was also one of the reasons he couldn't learn, and was typical of the fetal alcohol child.

Joey often had a fever for no apparent reason. When his temperature was 102, he acted like a normal kid, mellow, calm, and quiet. We enjoyed his fevers, at least until they'd get up to 104 . . . 106 . . . and they wouldn't respond medically. We spent hours kneeling on the tile next to the tub, giving him sponge baths throughout the night, trying to prevent a seizure. He'd shrivel up like a thin, pale, hundred–year-old man, and we'd both be crying from fear, frustration, and fatigue. Mostly fatigue. The doctor said, "His metabolism is so screwed up, we don't know what's wrong with him." He was put on Ritalin.

Raising Joey was an ongoing story of rising tempers and temperatures, his and ours. He was sneaky and dirty, and among his many bad habits was hoarding food to the point where his bedroom was always a potential bug farm. Sometimes I couldn't stand what he was doing to us. Every time I asked him to do anything, he'd whine and carry on.

"Please put your dish away."

"I don't know where it goes."

"Yes, you do."

"No, I don't know."

"Yes, you do. Think about it." (Joey didn't think anything through. Joey didn't think.)

"I don't know."

"Do we leave them on the table?"

"No."

"Do we put them back in the cupboard?"

"No."

"What do we do with the dirty dishes?"

"I don't know."

"We put them in the dishwasher."

"Oh . . . yeah. I didn't know what you meant."

He was always punishing himself in what I saw as his attempts to punish me.

"Joey, honey, no church clothes for football. Change your clothes, please."

"I don't wanna change. I wanna wear these."

"You can go out as soon as you change your clothes. Everybody's outside playing. The guys are waiting for you."

"If I can't wear these clothes outside I'll just stay in."

"You want to go out, right?"

"Yeah."

"You want to play with all the kids, right?"

"Yeah."

"Change your clothes and you can go out."

"I don't wanna change my clothes."

"Joey, these are your best clothes. If you play football in them, they'll be ruined. So if you want to play football, you have to change your clothes. Understand?"

"Yeah."

"Okay. Better hurry, 'cause the kids aren't going to wait forever."

"I don't want to change. I like these clothes."

Joey didn't change his clothes, and he didn't go out to play. Instead, Joey spent the entire day sitting in the window watching his brothers and all the neighbor kids play football in our yard. He was ornery and cantankerous, the most oppositional child I ever met. If I said red, he'd say green. If I said yes, he'd say no, even when it was something he wanted.

"I wanna go to the zoo."

"Good idea. Let's go."

"I don't wanna go now."

"If we're going, we have to go now. I have to work this afternoon."

"Never mind . . . I don't wanna go."

He'd have ferocious temper tantrums for no apparent reason. He was like an angry tornado whipping through the house and leaving a path of destruction in his wake, clothes and dishes on the floor, drinks spilled and not wiped up, food scraps all over the counter and kitchen floor, and his brothers hollering in annoyance. He was continually disruptive and unreasonable.

"We're going to get new beds, right, Mom?"

"Well, Joey, I don't know about that. Who's going to buy them for us?"

"(Screaming) Don't you know who's going to buy them for us? Why don't you know who's going to buy them for us?" He was out of control, and his behavior made me feel he had control over me and the whole family. Everything we said and did had to be readjusted when he was around—and he was always around us, because nobody else wanted him around them.

By third grade, he was one giant step out of sync with other children his age. He started having trouble in school with kids teasing him, and by fourth grade, he was being tripped, pinched, and beaten up regularly. He had no friends and no one to play with. He wanted to be with other kids, but he didn't know how. Our hearts were breaking for him. Although he was basically kind and could be charming, it was his irritability that made him so unpredictable and difficult to be with, and his inappropriate responses, like laughing at the wrong time, too long and too loud. We wouldn't tolerate other kids hitting Joey, and could control most of that, but we couldn't force them to play with him. I loved Joey, but most of the time, I didn't want to be with him either. For the first fourteen years of our marriage, our house had been filled with laughter and happiness and comparative harmony. In came Joey, and out went harmony, to be replaced with bickering, yelling, and agitation.

Hope appeared on the horizon when my friend Jodi told me Annabel Stehli was coming to do a workshop. Jodi is active in the local Autism Society chapter, and worked diligently to bring Annabel to Rochester. I had worked with autistic children and had read *The Sound of a Miracle*, and was naturally anxious to meet her.

Her presentation wasn't like any workshop I had been to before. It was more like sitting down over a cup of coffee with an intimate friend, laughing and crying together. Over three hundred people attended her talk, and the admission charged raised the funds necessary for training an AIT practitioner and purchasing the equipment. Through my friend, Jodi, and another friend whose autistic son had been through the training, I followed with wonder and excitement the effects of this newly available therapy with increasing wonder and excitement." Evidently it was not just for autistic children. It was for people of all ages, all kinds of people with all kinds of problems, all involving distortions in their hearing. Some of them had an aversion to loud noises (like Joey?). Dyslexia, hyperactivity, attention deficit disorder, stuttering, language delay, expressive language disorder, learning disabilities—all were being helped by auditory integration training. Family after family reported calmer behavior, less agitation, and more appropriate responses to instruction. Reports were coming in from special ed teachers and speech and language pathologists about improvements in the classroom and in communication skills. These were all areas Joey needed help in. Could a fetal alcohol child—with all the damage he had sustained—be a candidate for auditory integration training? We scheduled an evaluation.

The AIT therapist had not treated a fetal alcohol child before, and did not know of anyone in the field who had. But Joey's behavioral problems and his audiogram indicated that he was a likely candidate, and we felt confident that it would help. We asked that he be scheduled immediately, but the program director, an audiologist, insisted that we wait until she conferred with Dr. Bérard, the French otolaryngologist who had developed auditory training. Joey was perhaps the first fetal alcohol candidate, and she wanted Dr. Bérard's expert opinion before agreeing to treat our son.

We knew there were no guarantees. Auditory training couldn't hurt Joey, and it might help him. Dr. Bérard has described the problem AIT candidates have as being akin to a "short circuit: the elements are all there in the brain, but for some reason the connections are not being made." That's fine for a bright, autistic person who started reading at age three, or a child with attention deficit with a high I.Q. But what about Joey? The alcohol was the big question. Having floated for nine months in amniotic fluid laced with alcohol, did he have enough brain cells left to make the connections Dr. Bérard was talking about?

Annabel came to Rochester in September, auditory integration training came in November. When we told Joey AIT would help his hearing so that loud noises wouldn't bother him as much, he was surprisingly agreeable. By January, he was scheduled to begin the training, and the big day arrived.

When he put the headset on, he relaxed into the overstuffed swivel chair provided, and settled down comfortably. For twenty half–hour sessions, he sat sideways in the chair with his feet dangling over one arm while he leaned his head against the other. His chin was resting on one hand or the other most of the time, and he looked mildly bored. But he did it. He sat quietly and calmly, and he listened—mostly. For the first few days, we'd have about two minutes of silence before he'd burst into questions:

"How'm I doin'?"

"You're doing great."

"Is the time up?"

"Not quite yet, Joey. A few minutes more."

"Know what happened on the bus today?"

"Just sit quietly, now. I'll hear all about it later."

"Is it thirty minutes yet?"

"Not quite yet."

"The principal wants you to call her tonight. Don't forget."

"I won't forget." (Don't forget? I've got her home phone number on the refrigerator door.)

Our AIT practitioner told us to watch for exaggerated or atypical behaviors during training. Since that's all we ever got from Joey, was it now going to get worse? For a few terrifying minutes we considered backing out, terrifying because we couldn't imagine what worse behavior could be like, and terrifying because, for a brief moment, we almost gave away our family's chance for a normal life. Our audiologist/AIT therapist reassured us. Negative behavioral changes were temporary, lasting for perhaps a few hours, or a day. Dr. Bérard sees these behaviors as a sign of hope, and encourages acceptance of them as an indication that AIT is working. We were prepared to welcome them, we were ready, his teacher was alerted, and his brothers were warned.

Nothing happened. Nothing. We were prepared for anything —anything except nothing. Nothing. Not one little temper tantrum. No major outbursts. No sleeplessness. No regressive behaviors. No more irritability than usual (then again, how could that increase when he was bumping and tripping his way through life at full–tilt irritability already?). During days six through ten of AIT he quieted down, asking questions every three to four minutes instead of every two to three, not a huge difference. Basically there was no change. It was chaos and confusion as usual. He remained messy, demanding, loud, impulsive, a child who charged through school, the house, our lives—the usual. We watched him carefully, but we didn't know what to say to him, what kind of questions to ask. Joey had always been apathetic, unmotivated, and vague about life, completely uninterested in the details of it. However, he was easily influenced. If his brother Chris had an allergy attack, Joey would start wheezing. If his brother Kevin caught a cold, Joey would start sneezing. He needed attention, an astounding amount of attention. He had to do everything his brothers did, but bigger, louder, and with a lot more suffering. Joey was funny that way. We didn't want to influence his responses (if any) to AIT so we were careful and quiet about it.

When after four weeks of watching for changes, there still weren't any, I couldn't stand it any longer. Other kids were showing changes right during the training sessions. What was the matter with him? Joey had finished two weeks ago. Why wasn't he changing?

"How are you feeling, Joey?"

"Not real good."

"What's the matter?" He gave a long litany of all his woes, injuries and the forces of agony in the world arrayed against him again today.

"How's your hearing?"

"My hearing? Okay."

"Any fire alarms in school lately?" (It was always a sheer disaster when the fire alarm went off.)

"Yeah—one yesterday."

"I'm sorry. It was scary, huh?"

"Mmm . . . no, not really. It was just the fire alarm."

"What do you mean it wasn't scary?"

"I just wasn't scared, that's all . . . Hey, yeah. I forgot. Cool. I didn't *need* to be scared."

"Well, what happened? Did the alarm sound different?"

"Mmm . . . no. It just didn't hurt my ears, that's all."

"Does anything else sound different, Joey?"

"No. Well, something funny happened in school today."

"What happened?"

"I couldn't understand a word Mr. Edward said today." Bob overheard this and clutched his heart, thinking Joey must be getting worse. "I think he has very poor speech," Joey continued. "He mumbles."

Mr. Edward actually does not mumble. He has a big, clear voice and excellent diction, and could easily be heard in the back of the room. I knew because I had spent almost as much time in the class as Joey. Joey sat up front, right next to his teacher. We had known all year that Joey was not only unable to understand a word Mr. Edward said, but often didn't seem to be able to hear him at all. Typically, Joey would insist that Mr. Edward hadn't given him any homework, or that he must have been in the bathroom when the assignment was given out. But now Joey was saying that Mr. Edward mumbled. At least he was acknowledging that Mr. Edward spoke. Could Joey be becoming more focused? Could his hearing in fact be changing? I queried Mr. Edward and he hadn't seen any changes in class. I didn't see any at home, either. But nevertheless, this was new. Joey had realized a new piece of information today. He'd realized that his teacher did speak, and that he didn't understand him. This was new, and it was true. It made us hopeful.

Three weeks later, Joey came home from school. "Joey, how was school today?"

"Okay."

"What did you do?"

"Oh, nothin'."

"Anything new going on in class?"

"No. Oh . . . yeah! I know. Guess what? Today I understood almost everything Mr. Edward said in school!" Joey was excited, his normally apathetic reporting replaced by a new energy.

"I didn't understand everything he said, but I understood almost everything." He was extremely pleased with himself. "I'm so proud of Mr. Edward. He must be taking speech therapy!"

As the school year was coming to a close, we had the usual annual meetings and confrontations with the whole gamut of professionals: teachers, psychologists, counselors, the vision specialist, the principal, and of course, the Committee for Special Education. Four full days of preparation and a physically and emotionally exhausting two–hour conference later, it was agreed that Joey would repeat fifth grade. He would have increased assistance from the vision specialist, add a social skills class, and drop from a mainstream failure into "Option 1," a high–level special class for low–functioning children. Special help would be added for reading, math, and all those other irritating abstractions Joey didn't grasp.

This would ensure that with another year of misery for the whole family dragging to an end, next year would be better. Actually agreement is too strong a word. The committee was not in favor of this. They merely acquiesced. I asked, they argued. I threatened, they countered. I demanded, they demanded. When I called on the powers of the State Education Department and my attorney, they finally gave in, making sure, however, that when "this child is severely emotionally damaged for life by the trauma of being kept back," I would bear the full guilt.

So, I thought, he might be teased about this for the first two weeks at the bus stop. Then some other hapless soul would take the spotlight away from Joey (because he or she was small, or skinny, or wore glasses, or the wrong brand of jeans, or was the new kid). Sorry, folks, but two weeks would be nothing compared to the hundred and eighty agonizingly endless days of getting on a bus and going to school where he would be harassed all day. No one would sit with him in the cafeteria, so he ate lunch alone every day. And if he sat in the wrong seat, Miss Perfect Popularity might dump her tomato–vegetable soup all over his lap. "I don't want you to sit next to me. There's something wrong with you." School was a place where he was continually attacked for being messy, sloppy, slow, stupid, clumsy, and/or ugly. My son had already had a hundred and eighty days times six of the age–level "full inclusion" privileges in this school. No more. No way. No thank you.

As the school year drew to a close, we began to prepare for Joey's brother's graduation. The extended family was coming to town for Kevin, and the house had to be shoveled out to make room for everybody. Semicontrolled chaos reigned, with cleaning, errands, baking, cooking, shopping, a few side trips to the doctor, work, teacher meetings, laundry, deadlines. It was the kind of week that would push Joey to the edge. Not only would he refuse to help, but he would be sure to get in the way, making impossible demands, shirking his responsibilities, never finishing a task, complaining about being hungry, insisting that life wasn't fair.

June 21st was graduation week, and even with all the commotion Joey had always found so agitating, he actually, for the first time in his life, said the word "okay" to me. He was eleven years, ten months and twelve days old, and it was seven o'clock in the evening. I was just getting home from work, and I was an hour behind schedule. Graduation countdown: thirty–six hours. In–laws arriving: twenty–two hours. To say I was exhausted and frazzled would be civilized but understated. The door lock was jammed again and there was no way Bob would get it fixed before tomorrow, so I walked around front to the company door, as Joey called it. There, in the middle of my pale yellow Chinese rug, the only furnishing of any remote value in the house, was my usual greeting: a pair of grubby sneakers and a filthy, originally white, brown sock. For some reason, tonight, it got to me. "I'm not going to have a problem with this tonight," I told myself. "No problem. I'm calm. I'm in control. I'm the mother. I can handle this. Breathe deeply. Again. Again." I would be all right. Everything was all right. "Joey, would you please take your shoes out of the living room and put them in your bedroom where they belong?"

"Okay." ! Chris, Joey's sixteen–year–old brother, witnessed this occasion. We were both equally stunned. It was the first sign of compliance we had ever seen, and Joey actually followed it up by going into the living room and picking up not only the sneakers but the filthy sock. Then he proceeded to take them up the stairs. Chris, staring wide–eyed after his brother, slowly and deliberately took my hand. Joey was reaching the top of the stairs and would no doubt deposit his shoes and sock there. But wait. Joey opened his bedroom door. What was going on here? Keeping his eyes on Joey, Chris lowered his head to my ear. "Who was that, Mom?" he whispered. "It looked just like Joey."

Joey then proceeded to walk into his room and put the shoes in his closet. When he emerged from his room, he pivoted to his left, and made a perfect throw from the three–point line to the laundry basket. The sock. And there was more. He came right back down the stairs, and ignoring Chris (no pushing, no jabbing), he looked right at me. "Anything else you want me to do, Mom?" I experienced personal intermittent tachycardia. This wasn't just a pair of shoes and a sock being picked up, this was congeniality, cooperation, appropriate reaction time, and the absence of oppositional behavior. This was initiating a task and carrying it to completion. This was awareness of others. This was thoughtfulness. This was amazing!

June 22nd arrived, the day before the guests were due. The house was in worse shape now. The laundry room had overflowed into the hallway. The oven, microwave and all four burners were in use. The kitchen was a disaster, with full sinks and counters and flour footprints all over the floor. We were out of time. The guest beds had to be made up—and where was Joey? Hiding out in his bedroom? Across the street at the neighbors'? No, he was right in the thick of things, pitching in, helping out, all day. All day—like a regular member of the family. He was asking for more to do, and doing it. Doing it right. No threats. No supervision. No disappearing acts. No fights. No bickering. No outbursts. Cheerful. Nice. Smiling.

Within five months of AIT, Joey was a different child. The biggest difference was that the tension had gone. We hadn't really considered how we could describe him until he had already changed, but it had been as if he had been balancing on the edge of a steep cliff. Skittish, anxious, frightened, and angry, the least little thing had set him off. Everything had been difficult for him, and that had made his balancing act even harder. Now that the tension was gone, the anxiety had gone with it. He had become calm, congenial, and pleasant—really pleasant. He was a pleasure to be with. My Joey was a pleasure to be with. He was actually good company. The irritability and negativity had evaporated. There was no more whining, pouting, or fussing. If I gave him an explanation or a reason, he accepted it. The sweetest words in the world are not, "I love you." They are, "Okay, Mom."

This year, instead of spending 4th of July in the basement with Joey with his hands clapped over his ears, the whole family went to the fireworks. The noise and excitement were intense, with thousands of people downtown making noise. In addition to the fireworks, there were bands, radios, and people clapping and cheering. Joey was at once excited and nervous. He sat snuggled tightly between Bob and me, with his hands over his ears. As the first fireworks lit up the sky, the look of amazement on his face was not caused by the spectacular light display. As he tentatively uncupped first his left ear, then his right, then both at once, his eyes grew wider. "Why, it's beautiful!" he exclaimed. "It's not scary! Look at the sky. It's beautiful!" All we saw that night was the beauty and wonder on our son's face.

The celebration continues. Joey isn't afraid anymore, and we see many changes. He can follow two–part directions now. When we used to ask him to get his coat and hat, he would bring one or the other. Now he brings both. His attitude has changed, and he is always willing to try. Our family's group dynamics have improved immeasurably. The bickering, tension, and endlessly repeated directions have ended. Joey is happy and calm and we are a real family again. We can relax. Joey can initiate tasks, and he can carry them to completion, one after the other, while we can finish our chores without having to worry about his. Joey can sit down in a chair for more than five minutes, actually for twenty to thirty minutes now, and do his homework. He can follow directions and do the work in the required subject, finding the pages and answering the questions. He requires minimal versus intensive supervision, and we can read the evening paper in peace. He is not jittery or in constant motion, and we wonder if he ran constantly to escape from all the loud, confusing sounds he was hearing.

Joey came in from school today, and with a big, beautiful grin on his face, he announced, "I had a great day today."

"Good news, Joey. What happened?"

"I don't know. I just had a great day today."

"You seem different. You seem a lot happier these days, Joey."

"Yep. I'm happy now, Mom."

"What happened, Joey? Why are you so happy all the time now?"

"I think it was the AIT."

"Why do you think that?"

"Because [cause and effect relationships, drawing conclusions— new, all new] I started feeling different inside after AIT, and now I don't need to be angry anymore. It's not so much work to understand people, and noises don't scare me."

Joey is still brain damaged. There are many things in life that we take for granted that Joey may never experience. He is severely visually impaired. He cannot read easily or well, and he may never drive a car, read a map, or curl up in a chair at a quiet time of day and read for pleasure. He has seizures that are a constant threat. He will probably never be able to live completely on his own without some level of supervision or assistance because he lacks judgment. In fact, he will never be free of his mother's alcohol. We hope and pray, with grief and sadness, that he will never have children. But the new Joey listens, comprehends, and accepts direction. He is comfortable, he is making friends, and one day, he will have a job. He has and will continue to have a better quality of life than we ever could have dreamed of. "I'm happy, now, Mom." Words we never thought we'd hear. ■

Chapter 5

Joshua

by Terry Cooney

Every child is a miracle and every adoption has a wonderful story behind it. Our family has seven exciting "how we got you" tales to tell; but one stands out above the rest in its "believe–it–or–not" quality. This is not the time to recount the details of the ten frantic days we spent between the day we applied for him until the day of Joshua's placement. Suffice it to say that it took nothing short of a miracle (or two) to get through a home study update, an on–site health department inspection, physical exams and TB tests for six people, and two meetings with the caseworker in that time frame. We KNEW this was the child the Lord had for us. The fact that his legal release came through while we were in the office in the midst of placement was the icing on the cake. Joshua was meant to be ours. We had no idea how much that "knowing" would mean to us in the days and years ahead.

At twenty–seven days, our new son was a beautiful, calm baby with a laid–back personality. Having two teens, a busy five–year-old, and a twenty–two–month–old who was the most difficult child we had ever encountered, I was delighted with such a quiet baby. As the days and weeks went by and Joshua continued to be content with eating, sleeping, and lying quietly on a blanket, I rejoiced.

Starting at three months, he developed a severe upper respiratory infection. It wouldn't clear up until our pediatrician put him on a maintenance dose of Bactrum for two months. Joshua was five months old when what started out looking like a digestive virus turned out to be a rare, nearly fatal disease called TEC. His calmness was not his personality! His red blood cells had been slowly dying off and his body was not producing new ones. His red blood cell count and hemoglobin were so low he made the medical books. The hospital staff accurately called him the "miracle baby." A hospital stay, five blood transfusions, and antibiotics (not Bactrum, however; he ended his course of Bactrum when he went into the hospital) started him on the road to recovery and within a month, this child was sitting and creeping. By nine months, he was a bright, lively, busy little boy who toddled all over the house.

This sounds like the place for the "and they lived happily ever after" ending, but this was only the beginning. Joshua developed skin problems and had large, runny sores all over his body that itched horribly. We were so frantically busy nursing his skin and caring for our new baby girl who had come when Josh was twenty months old, that we did not immediately notice the changes that were occurring in him. We would comment that he often looked so sad or that he was so wild, climbing everything. We would note in passing that he never really played with anything; he simply threw things. We talked about his slow speech development and questioned the pediatrician, who saw no reason for concern. His new erratic sleep habits were blamed on the uncomfortable skin condition. There were signs—so many signs—but no one was putting them together.

Then one awful July day, just after his second birthday, in a scratching frenzy, Joshua dug all the skin from a large area on his leg. This crisis sent us running for emergency medical help to a neighborhood doctor. His probing questions about Joshua's development gave credence to our concerns. There were urgent doctor to doctor calls that ended in a recommendation that we rush Joshua to a neurologist. By now we were fully tuned in to our son and we were frightened by what we saw.

Joshua had lost all the brightness in his eyes. They were dull, lifeless, and made contact with no one—not even us. He spent much of his time hand–flapping and carrying wooden spoons around. He said nothing at all. Most of the time he appeared deaf—not responding to his name being called or a book being slammed down beside him. At other times, the slightest sound sent him screaming with hands over his ears. There had been a tremendous regression. The neurologist's diagnosis was mental retardation. A full battery of tests was ordered in an attempt to determine the cause. None could be found. We had no cause, no cure, no treatment. Proper training was the only recommendation. So we enrolled him in the public school intervention program and in a wonderful private preschool called the Preschool Enrichment Program (P.E.P.), for children with developmental delays or behavioral problems.

We already had one of our children in P.E.P. Our three-year-old was the obvious victim of a mother who used drugs, though she denied it. This child was hypersensitive and overloaded. She exploded into long angry tantrums for no apparent reason. She threw herself around, knocking over furniture, urinating as she went and screaming at the top of her lungs. A single tantrum could go on for hours. Yet when she was calm, she was a sweet, loving child. She was doing well at the school. We could only hope it would make a difference in Joshua, too.

Emotionally we struggled. Each night when we collapsed into bed exhausted, huge waves of fear would roll over me, threatening to drown me if I relaxed for even a second. My mind would review our lives. Here we were—a middle-aged couple—with six children, two teens and four under six. The young children were all black or bi-racial individuals. Our dream was to raise them with a pride in their heritage, a love for the Lord, a strong feeling of self-worth, and a good education. Armed and educated, they would be adults who could survive and contribute to society. Now my homemade fairy tale had a huge flaw—there could be no happily ever after ending. What would happen to our precious black mentally retarded son when we were gone?

We lived in the eye of a hurricane. We had a peace in our "knowing" that Joshua was meant for us and this was the best place for him. Somehow, though I couldn't imagine how, God had this all under control. Yet, we went through the grief that every parent must work through when facing a child's disability. Our grief drove us to look for answers. We were sure Joshua had not come to us mentally retarded. The experts assured us the TEC could not have caused it. We had to find out more.

Our faith caused us to grab hold of the scriptures. Over and over we would remind God of His promise in James 1:5 to give wisdom to anyone who asked—and we asked—begged—pleaded. Then one day as I watched Joshua hand-flapping, I knew I had seen another child doing the same thing. Where, God? When? Slowly, the memory came back of watching a movie. The only scene I could recall was one with a mother sitting on the bathroom floor hand-flapping in unison with her autistic son. AUTISM! All it took was a quick reading of the entry in our encyclopedia and I knew we had a diagnosis. Strangely, I felt relief. At least we had named the problem.

We could deal with what we knew. Equally strange was the unwillingness of every professional we dealt with to confirm the diagnosis. We were told over and over that Joshua could not have autism because he remained very affectionate with us and did not recoil from the touch of others. It was almost two years before we located a specialist at a Baltimore hospital who formally diagnosed Joshua as autistic.

As so many parents of autistic children have done, we began a crash course in autism. We researched professional journals and read everything we could get our hands on. God was so good to us as He led us to materials. In the first months, we read the success story of Temple Grandin and the great strides made by the TEACCH program. This fed our optimism and faith. It gave us understanding and techniques. God surrounded us with people of faith who loved us, prayed for us, and who relieved our financial burden by paying the tuition for both of our children to attend P.E.P.

Our family altered our lifestyle so that all of us worked with Joshua as we lived our lives. We included him in everything and took him every place, though it was often very difficult. In the two years following Joshua's regression into autism, we worked incredibly hard and saw very little fruit for our labors. Joshua did not seem to hear most of the time, he never answered a question, he did not respond to his name, he did nothing on command, he rarely spoke, and he continued self–stimming and toe walking as well as carrying unusual objects. He was locked in himself as securely as the people had been locked in the city of Jericho.

Joshua wasn't changing much, but we were. We were always certain that we were not the type of people emotionally equipped to parent special needs children. To our surprise, we were not only surviving, we were doing a good job and finding joy and purpose. Slowly, we came to know that we were to adopt more special needs black children, the most difficult to place in this country.

God powerfully confirmed this to us on March 15, 1991, when we picked up our seventh child, a sweet black baby girl whose face was badly disfigured by several hemangiomas or blood tumors. The one on her right cheek was the size of half a grapefruit. We returned from her placement to find Joshua's teacher (and godmother), Sandy Vanderbeek, wild with excitement. She had been playing beside Joshua at the water table. As she had done a hundred times before, she had held up a small boat saying, "What's this, Josh?" Josh had looked up and said, "A boat." Josh had never—NEVER—answered a question. On this day the walls SLOWLY, ever so slowly, began tumbling down and we praised God for this dramatic sign that we were right where He wanted us.

We had no idea how much we would need that assurance of God's blessing in the eighteen months to come. We soon plunged into our most difficult time in twenty–six years of marriage. Three of our children developed asthma. Two of our daughters had pneumonia twice in six months. Another daughter hemorrhaged violently the week after having her tonsils out. In those two years we had six midnight ambulance rides with children in critical condition. The stress was so great that I developed stomach problems that, at first, seemed symptomatic of a heart condition. This added stress upon stress.

In the midst of all this, Joshua developmentally went into the "terribly twos" at four years of age. Big and strong for his age, he became almost impossible to control when he went into a tantrum. He hit, kicked, screamed, and spat when he did not get his way. Frustration at not being understood caused him to lose all control. During this period, we began to think, for the first time, previously unthinkable thoughts about maybe having to institutionalize Josh for his own safety. Unlike many other autistic children, he was incredibly bonded to us, suffering terribly and sobbing whenever he had to separate from me. Thoughts of having to put him in residential care were unbearable.

It was during this period that Joshua's public school speech therapist asked if I had read the article in *Reader's Digest* about the autistic girl who recovered after some hearing treatment. I had not, and I wasn't even interested. Both the neurologist and an audiologist had declared that Joshua had normal hearing. Though probably a half dozen people mentioned the article within the next couple of months, I didn't bother to investigate —a fact that now seems so strange to me. I am one of those people who leaves no stone unturned when I have a problem.

When Joshua was four, he began going to school for a full day. In the mornings he continued in P.E.P. where his progress was correctly labeled "inconsistent." In the afternoons he went to a brand new experimental public school program for language–disordered children. His teacher was wonderful, but had never worked with an autistic child. She loved Josh, but she took it personally when he had a tantrum or spat at her. Josh quickly got the upper hand and it was a difficult year. We communicated daily through a notebook, and shortly before Christmas, she wrote that she had read a wonderful book about an autistic child, *The Sound of a Miracle*. I was too busy simply surviving to track it down.

Somehow, we did survive that winter. Things always look better in the spring, and Joshua's tantrums seemed fewer and farther between. One day in May, Joshua's teacher at P.E.P. sent home a copy of ADVANCE (a professional journal for audiologists) with a note to read an article called, "Audiologists take on Autism with Auditory Training." As I read the article, I saw descriptions of my Joshua throughout. I read and reread the information and gave it to Jim to read. We talked, prayed, and decided to contact the Georgiana Organization for more information. Peter Stehli answered the phone and talked to me at length. After answering my questions, he asked me a series of questions about Joshua and his reactions to sound. Peter felt Josh was indeed a candidate for auditory training. He promised to put an information packet and list of practitioners in the mail.

A week later, the information had not come. I try to look at circumstances as God opening or closing doors on the path we are to take. Was God trying to say auditory training was not for Joshua? As I pondered the question, the phone rang. My dear friend, Mary Woodard, was calling because her friend had phoned her asking her to get a message to me. The *Sally Jessy Raphael* show that day would deal with autism. So what! Talk shows did not interest me; besides, I had to go to a kindergarten program this morning. Still, Mary's friend had gone to the trouble of tracking me down. I asked my daughter, Christine, to set up the VCR to tape the show. Christine works, but was going in late so that she could attend her baby sister's program. God's perfect timing! I have no idea how to program the VCR, so on any other day the show would have gone untaped. Even so, I wasn't excited to see it and left it unviewed that day and most of the next. Then the much anticipated packet finally arrived in the mail. Among other things, it contained a newsletter with an item about the Stehlis being on the *Sally Jessy Raphael* show—the show we had taped the day before.

God was indeed opening a door. With each passing day it became more obvious that auditory training was HIS plan for Joshua.

Much to our surprise, we found a practitioner just two hours away in Washington, D.C. Though she had a waiting list, she was able to take Josh in August. Again, perfect timing for several reasons. Jim would be off work, so we could make the ten days of commuting together. A young married woman in our church who knew and loved our children would be available to babysit the four young ones being left at home. We had plenty of time to prepare Joshua for the earphones and taking the audiogram. All there was left to do was wait and pray—and pray—and pray for a miracle. It promised to be a long summer.

In June we celebrated our twenty–fifth anniversary. We were certain our two oldest children would plan something, but we were unprepared for the magnitude of the celebration. While our pastor and his wife whisked us away to lunch, Andrew and Christine decorated our home, gathered the food they had prepared and stashed at friends' homes the week before, and received the hundred guests they had invited to share our day. We were overwhelmed at the outpouring of love. Then came the gifts—silver, china, beautiful things to decorate our home. Finally, Andrew and Christine presented us with their gift—an all–expense paid trip to Hawaii. Our life–long dream! Terri, the lady with a word for any occasion, was speechless. Nothing would come but tears. What a gift of love and sacrifice! These two, a college student and a clerk–typist, had each saved $40.00 a month for four years to do this for us. How could we accept? How could we possibly refuse?

Thus the two months' wait for auditory training was gobbled up in planning and then taking a trip to Hawaii. It was the only time since our honeymoon that we had taken a trip alone. It was a blessed opportunity to refresh, to renew, to give thanks, to look back, and to look forward. For the first time in years there were hours to talk and pray without interruption. While sitting and looking out at the magnificent Pacific Ocean during those ten days, we took stock of our lives and saw many things that gave us comfort and encouragement.

We could see with clarity that although the trip was wonderful, we were not travelers. We were enjoying the best money could buy; yet home and life with our seven children was better. Since we were forty–seven and fifty–two, there would probably be no time, after we finished raising this brood, for the retirement middle–class Americans enjoy, but we didn't mind. For us, this was the better portion. In fact, it was in Hawaii that we both came to believe God's plan for us was to adopt yet another special needs child, which we did three months after our return.

Finally, during this period of introspection and prayer, we saw clearly that for our family, having an autistic child was not a tragedy but an opportunity. We have become the local "experts" on autism and get all sorts of calls from hurting parents that afford us the opportunity to share our faith and to encourage them. We have collected a huge library of materials on autism that we share with teachers, doctors, and parents. We have become advocates for autistic children with the school system and fight for programs for them. We speak to groups often and our story has given others the courage to adopt special needs children. Our whole family has developed a sensitivity for "special" people and we work to make them feel loved and accepted. So much good has come from this "tragedy" that we know if given a choice we would do it all again.

We returned from Hawaii with a new joy in our lives, rested, refreshed, and ready to start the auditory training adventure. And an adventure it was. Up and out by 6:00 A.M. to make the hour and a half drive. A dash to the Metro, Washington's subway system, and a twenty–minute ride. A two–block jaunt to the auditory training office. Then after a half hour of auditory training, we had four hours to kill on the streets of Washington. Following our second session of AIT, we reversed the commuting process, getting home in time to feed the tribe and get ready to start it all over. It was exhausting! But it was also exciting. By the third day we were seeing thrilling new developments. Thankfully, I thought to keep a diary during the training and the days following it.

A Diary of Joshua's Development During Auditory Training
August 17–26, 1992

Day 1:   Joshua would not accept the headphones for the audiogram because they looked different from the ones we had practiced with, and were small and uncomfortable. I finally got him to cooperate for about ten minutes and then he would do no more. A discouraging start!

Because they were large, padded, and soft, he accepted the headphones for the actual auditory training. He fell right into the routine. He did want to play with the machine cords and mouth them.

Day 2:   We went to Silver Spring today and parked in a

multi-level garage. When we pulled in, Joshua said, "Sesame Street Live." The last time he had been in such a parking garage was two years ago, when he was three, and we took the kids to a performance of "Sesame Street Live" at the Baltimore Civic Arena. What a memory!

In the restaurant he was too loud and would not calm down, so I got out the tabasco sauce that I use for discipline (one drop on the tongue). I said nothing, just placed the bottle on the table. When he saw it, he quickly and clearly said, "Okay! Okay! You can put it away now. I'll be good." Wow, what a mouthful!

The same afternoon, banging on the door of the practitioner's office, he said, "Somebody open the door and let me in." We had never heard him speak this way before.

Days 3 & 4: Very agitated and moody. Cried easily for no reason. Very tired.

Day 5: His mood is better today. A three-second delay in his response to sound in his left ear was discovered. Joshua accepted the headphones and worked for thirty-five minutes of testing for the audiogram.

Joshua has always screamed when he is bathed. Tonight as I washed him, he said, "Mommy, that hurts me." It is the first time Joshua has ever verbalized and identified a specific hurt.

Day 6: Today the right earphone was louder than the left. Joshua pointed to the right earpiece and said, "This thing hurts me."

Day 7: Joshua has become very independent. He wants to do the subway tickets, escalators, etc., by himself.

I was being goofy, trying to get his attention while waiting for the Metro. He turned to me and said, "What do you want?" This is the first question he ever asked.

He is observing his environment and commenting on it. "There's a butterfly."

Day 8: I called him angel. He said, "No, it's not angel. My name Joshua."

His dad began pushing him in the stroller and stopped abruptly. Joshua looked back and said, "What is the matter?"

We were walking down the street near the playground and he told us, "I want to eat pizza."

Joshua was very interactive at the playground during his AIT break. He initiated play with strange children. He allowed them to touch him. He took turns on the slide, then told us, "I took turns."

He played games of chase and follow the leader with the children.

Joshua did not cover his ears when he heard an ambulance siren as we were walking down the street.

Day 10:   Our new daughter–in–law, Kelly, asked Joshua for a kiss. Josh said, "Josh is too little," and he ran away laughing.

AIT was finished six days ago. We have noticed these things:

–Joshua is MUCH calmer in general.

–He has not had a "hyper" period since he finished. Each day (morning and evening) for as long as we can remember, Joshua has had a hyper period lasting for five or ten minutes when he has run around and bounced on the furniture. This is not happening.

–He follows spoken commands very well and usually the first time we ask. This is brand new.

–He told his sister he was sorry when he hurt her.

–He began riding a two–wheeled bicycle with no practice, no hesitation. He simply got on and took off.

–He fell off in the road and I ran out to help him. He said, "Thank you for being you."

–He has become very aware of the phone, answers it, and talks on it.

–He is very aware of my feelings and cares if I am upset with him. I had just finished changing his bed the other day when he came in and pulled down the covers to climb in. I screamed at him, "Joshua Michael, I just finished making that bed!" He looked at me and said, "What's the matter, Mom?"

–He is waving "Hi" and "Bye." It is a weak wave, but more than he has ever done.

–Joshua told on his sister—something he has never done. She was spitting, which he has been told not to do. He came to me and said, "Sarah spitting."

Two weeks after AIT: September 4th:

Visited Joshua's school today. He found his desk with his name on it. He recognized his teacher, whom he had met last spring. He called her by name. He put away everything he got out. We stopped in the speech therapy room Joshua used a year ago and saw his therapist, whom he had not seen for sixteen months. He said, "Hi, Miss Sue," and went right in. When I was ready to go, I said, "Get your toys and let's go, Joshua." And HE DID!

Dad called when we got home. Joshua answered the phone and

said, "Hello." Then he said, "I went to school today."

September 5th:

We went to the library and McDonald's. Joshua was great. I am counting to five when I help Josh brush his teeth and when I put lotion on him. He no longer screams. He counts to five and says, "All done."

Josh has rough moments, but he is much calmer.

September 7th: Joshua shared a toy with Sarah when she asked him to.

September 8th: Joshua started school. He earned six stars for good behavior. He saw his sister Leanna in the cafeteria and he initiated contact. He waved and said, "Hi, Wenanna." He came home happy, got off the bus, and said, "I'm happy." He was calm and relaxed when he got home, a huge change from last year. Josh went outside while I was on the phone. I went to the door and asked him to come inside until I finished. He did!

Our prayers had been answered. We got our miracle. Joshua is not normal or totally healed, but he is growing and learning. We see that AIT was one piece in Joshua's autism puzzle. It enabled him to cope with his environment and opened him up to learning. As a result, this child that we were afraid we would have to institutionalize is able to be in a Level IV class in public school. He eats in the cafeteria, buying his lunch with the other children. He goes to gym, music, art, and the library and rides the bus. In all, Joshua had a great year, due in great measure to the loving, skillful work of his teacher, Karen Sirkis. His major problem is still his inability to deal appropriately with anger and frustration, but even that is better than it was.

Near the end of the school year, Joshua began to demonstrate a return of his sound sensitivity on a limited basis. We felt it would be beneficial to put him through AIT again, but could not bear the thought of another ten days in Washington. Another AIT mother and I began to pray that somehow we could bring this process to our area. Our prayers were answered wonderfully.

When Annabel Stehli came to Washington to speak last spring, my husband and I took a van load of people to hear her, including our neighbor and friend of twenty-five years, Vicki Whitaker. Vicki is a reading specialist who is dyslexic herself and specializes in helping children who are bright but failing. Vicki has helped us diagnose learning disabilities in two of our very bright children who were struggling to survive in school. She has had a sustained interest in Joshua, following his progress since his birth. After hearing Annabel, Vicki became fascinated with the AIT process.

Soon Vicki, two other mothers, and I began to meet and formulate a plan to bring auditory training to Harford County. In July, 1993, Vicki went to Connecticut to the Georgiana Organization to train with Guy Bérard and is now a certified practitioner.

In August, following another audiogram that showed his hearing to be still hypersensitive, Joshua underwent his second round of auditory training at a new office ten minutes from our home. The process was smooth and uneventful and he cooperated beautifully. We did not see the dramatic changes that we saw last year, but we see many little changes. For instance, he is not covering his ears for sound at all. He has stopped almost all self-stimming except talking to himself, which he still does frequently. He had an initial period of being very agitated and aggressive, but this stopped within a month. His vocabulary has increased and his sentence structure has improved markedly.

His behavior in church and Sunday School is enormously improved. This has always been his most difficult place—too many people, too much noise, too much that is unpredictable. Last month he behaved well, making it through both Sunday School and church nursery without incident. On the days when he does well, we reward him with lunch at McDonald's afterwards. Recently, I was sitting with him in his Sunday School class when he decided he wanted to get up and wander. I told him he had to sit down and listen or he would not be able to go to McDonald's for lunch. He looked right at me and replied, "I want to see my lawyer, Mom." I had a hard time containing my laughter and joy. He has come a long, long way.

It is an interesting aside that after reading Dr. Bérard's book this summer (*Hearing Equals Behavior*), we became convinced that auditory training could help our children with learning disorders. The audiograms done on them showed that they both had severe abnormalities. Our son's hearing was acutely sensitive and he had the two–eight curve in the left ear that is associated with depression. Our daughter has central auditory processing problems along with an audiogram that looked like a mountain range. The audiograms following their auditory training are dramatically changed. It is too soon to see how this will affect their behavior or learning process, but we are optimistic.

My husband also went through AIT this summer. Vicki wanted to put someone through once a day for twenty days to be certain the process would be effective, administered in this way. Additionally, she wanted to have a professional educator experience it in the hopes of securing an advocate with the educational system. Jim became the candidate, though he felt he had no hearing problem. Interestingly enough, he did have some abnormalities in his audiogram. After the third day, he felt he was hearing background noise he had not been hearing. By the end of the session, he knew he was hearing more clearly than before and we all noticed he did not say, "Huh?" nearly so often. The only disadvantage we could see with the once a day for twenty days treatment is that it seemed to all of us that he would never be done. He is pleased with the results, though. So for us, auditory training has become a family affair. We anticipate our two youngest will go through AIT in the next year or two.

Auditory training has not been a miracle "cure" but it has been a valuable tool in freeing Joshua from his autistic prison. At six, he is a happy little boy who will make eye contact, talk in sentences much of the time, and dress and toilet himself independently. Additionally, he knows much of what you would expect from a six–year–old. He plays baseball and hide and seek with the neighborhood kids, rides his bike like a champ, and takes roller skating lessons. Yes, Joshua, our miracle baby, fights a battle with autism, but, thank God, the walls are tumbling down.

When Jim and I speak to groups, we always remind people to accept their child for the person s/he is and to accept the disability, but we urge them never to give up. We encourage them to try to be prepared for the worst, but to live expecting the best. Finally, we ask them to pray and to always—ALWAYS—leave room for a miracle . . . they still happen, you know. ■

Chapter 6

Sharisa

by Annabel Stehli

Sharisa Kochmeister is sixteen. She used to need help to type because she is a nonverbal autistic person with cerebral palsy. Using the controversial technique known as Facilitated Communication, she was only able to hit the right keys if someone supported her hand or wrist. When Sharisa, typing with support, leveled accusations of abuse which ultimately resulted in grave consequences for her mother, her validity as a communicator was placed in doubt, even though her parents were divorced and her father had received custody of her. It was felt that Sharisa's facilitator was making the damaging allegations for her own sick, misguided reasons, not this young girl who couldn't hold a pencil, who made eye contact with great difficulty, and who walked with an awkward gait when she was not in her wheel chair. They didn't think she was capable of communicating honestly on her own or with help.

Sharisa was outraged. Even though it appeared to be neurologically impossible, she taught herself to type independently. Her evidence of abuse was accepted, and resulted in the denial of her mother's visitation rights.

When the television program *Sixty Minutes*, with Morley Safer reporting, was doing a story on Facilitated Communication, a crew came out to Sharisa's house and filmed her typing independently. When the program aired, Facilitation Communication was invalidated. Interestingly, they didn't show the footage of Sharisa, I guess because it would have challenged their premise that FC was a hoax. How sad for the children who are legitimately communicating.

The following is a transcription of part of a conversation with Sharisa when she came to see us in Westport, Connecticut, where we live. We both typed.

Annabel: Are you ready to have a conversation with me?

Sharisa (Her forefinger falls to the keyboard, aiming for the desired key):   Uh–huh.

Annabel: Do you know that I know that you are smarter than I am?

Sharisa: I am smarter than 99.9% of people my age.

Annabel: Do you think the reason people have such a hard time validating Facilitated Communication is because they can't cope with your degree of intelligence?

Sharisa: I think that's a large part of it. I also believe that some, like Dr.—, feel it threatens their livelihood.

Annabel: Don't you think there is a lot of bigotry against autistic people?

Sharisa: I believe there's a lot of bigotry in general, along with fear of diversity.

Annabel: Are you frustrated by the fact that your school doesn't provide an aide trained in facilitation?

Sharisa: It is a pain, but Tammy (her aide in school) is still my friend. I think she finds me a bit bewildering, though.

Annabel: Why doesn't she ask you questions about the things she finds bewildering?

Sharisa: Oh, I think perhaps she's unsure how to phrase them.

Annabel: School is much too easy for you. You must feel underchallenged. We need autistic people's lib. Maybe a group for autistic people would help, where you could get together with other kids with the same issues. [This is now happening, in Westport.—Ed.]

I want to discuss self–esteem and shame and embarrassment with you. Georgie says these were key issues with her when she was little. Your turn.

Sharisa: I have many feelings about these issues.

Annabel: I can imagine. We need a lot of time together. I am thrilled with your ability to communicate intelligently with me. I realize I must have had a demon of doubt lurking somewhere, but he just took off. [Sharisa smiles.] My daughter Sarah, who is fourteen, is embarrassed by us, her parents. Do you feel that way about your dad, too?

Sharisa: I love him, but he's no diplomat.

Dad: And are you one?

Sharisa: I have been known to lack tact at times.

Annabel: What you just typed was diplomatic. Do you feel patronized and underestimated most of the time?

Sharisa: In certain instances. I feel a pleasant camaraderie with you, however. You treat me as I need to be treated—as a sentient being.

Annabel: Are you going to write a book some day?

Sharisa: Several. I need to educate people about disabilities in several different ways.

Annabel: Are you ever bored?

Sharisa: Rarely. I get a lot of entertainment from studying the behavior of myself and others and contemplating the mysteries within and without me.

Annabel: What do you want to be when you grow up?

Sharisa: Rich beyond belief. But seriously folks, I want to write and educate and do public speaking, travel extensively, get married, and be happy. I really enjoy talking to you. I will read your book soon and would like to meet Georgie.

Annabel: I'll be interested to see what you think. Maybe you can review it for the *Advocate* (newsletter of the Autism Society of America) or Rimland's Autism Research Institute newsletter?

Sharisa: I will do that.

Annabel: I think we will be able to collaborate.

Sharisa: I wrote a story about a wicked witch named Autisma. I have two versions—one for younger kids, one for everyone else. I think they'd help people understand. [My fourteen–year–old daughter, Sarah, comes home from school.] Who is this? Hi, Sarah, could we become friends?

Sarah: I'd love to.

Sharisa: Do you write letters?

Sarah: Yes.

Sharisa: So we could correspond.

Sarah: Cool.

Sharisa: Way cool! I'll write first if that's easier for you. I like your outfit and nails.

Sarah: Thanks. I like your outfit. Blue is my favorite color. It would be great if you wrote me.

Sharisa: I would love it. My favorite colors are pink and lavender, but I like violet and blue almost as much. Do you like music?

Sarah: Yes, I play the clarinet in school and I like to sing. Do you like music?

Sharisa: Yes, especially jazz and Eric Clapton.

Sarah: Really? I love Eric Clapton! I also like The Spin Doctors. Have you heard of them?

Sharisa: Yes, but I haven't heard their music.

Sarah: Well, I have their CD upstairs. Would you like to hear it some time?

Sharisa: Uh–huh.

Sarah: Cool.

Sharisa: I'm glad we met.

Sarah: So am I. (She goes upstairs to do her homework.)

Annabel: It's nice to hear your dad say you told him he was cool. You picked the exact right word. To be cool is to be diplomatic. Right?

Sharisa: Right. So is caring about people and life.

Annabel: Two more. Joke: What did the dyslexic say to the agnostic?

Sharisa: There really is a dog.

Annabel: Dad told you that one?

Sharisa: Yea. Why don't I talk more?

Annabel: I don't know. Why?

Sharisa: I am speechless.

Annabel: Sharisa, I have a feeling you will be the pied piper of the nonverbal autistic population.

Sharisa: I will certainly try.

Annabel: There is nothing more wonderful than empowering people, and that's what you're doing when you validate someone's intelligence and insist on his or her having the freedom to communicate and contribute.

Sharisa: Communication is freedom and power and a chance to choose for oneself.

Annabel: I think you are every inch a writer, and will be able to communicate emotion as well as ideas.

Autism and Auditory Integration Training—
My Viewpoint
by Sharisa Joy Kochmeister

Having been viewed as autistic for over twelve years, and having undergone auditory training (AIT) twice since August, 1992, I feel qualified to give my views on both. I hope what I have to say will help shed some light on both, and help increase people's understanding.

First off, I'd like to say that for me, autism wasn't something I think I was born with, and it has been a curse in my life. That having been said, I'd like to share my theory of what autism is. I see autism as a neurochemical disorder that is both difficult to diagnose and impossible to easily understand. I believe that it manifests itself somewhat differently in different people, and that is why it's so incredibly hard to pinpoint, understand, and treat. I don't think the cause(s), degrees of severity are always the same, either. There are, however, as I see it, some definite commonalities among people regarded as autistic.

The commonalities I've observed are as follows:

1. Extreme sensitivity in the areas of sight, sound, touch, taste, and smell.

2. Overly developed brain reactions to stimuli in these areas.

3. Motor planning difficulties and anomalies.

4. Need for structure and resistance to change to avoid confusing already overloaded neural receptors.

5. Excessive motor activity and/or anxiety reactions and/or withdrawal–avoidance behaviors to compensate for and/or adapt to excessive input of information.

6. Great powers of observation and keen powers of recall for visual and/or auditory stimuli.

I would like to say at this point that I disagree with much of what professionals think they know about autism and people with autism. Most of us are not retarded, we do both have and comprehend feelings, we are capable of both imagination and abstract thinking, and we do experience pain, pleasure, sadness, and joy. While it may seem that we don't understand things, this is not true. The real difficulties occur in speed and style of processing, digesting, and responding to what has been presented.

This is largely due to an overabundance of internal communication rather than a lack of it. It is exceedingly difficult to communicate with others when one's time is so taken up with attempts to make sense of a world one finds so confusing. This is the true curse of autism—great ability to absorb coupled with poor ability to process and react.

Several treatment modalities have helped me overcome these difficulties to a huge extent, yet they can still be extremely frustrating. Chief among these is Facilitated Communication. FC gave me a way to communicate that cerebral palsy had denied me. It opened the door to other treatments, such as nutritional and vitamin therapies, occupational therapy to reduce sensitivity and improve motor planning, speech therapy to help overcome oral apraxia in eating and speaking, vision training to help me learn to use my eyes more efficiently and effectively, and AIT to overcome hyper–sensitive hearing and improve processing.

For me, AIT has enabled me to sleep better, be calmer while I'm awake, and understand what I hear more quickly and clearly. I can handle noises which had previously caused me to withdraw or panic. These included applause, sirens, dogs barking, vacuum cleaners, dishwashers, certain voices, the sound of fluorescent lights, piano music, computers, and the sound of the ocean. I believe it also reduced sensitivities in sight, smell, taste, and tactile sensations. I'm much, much happier and much less inclined toward anger. I am, in many ways, a much nicer person to be around. It has also increased my ability to type independently, without hands–on facilitation, and my desire to be independent in many areas. With typing and AIT, I am able to attend regular school for the first time in my life and to make friends. I am truly grateful to FC for getting me started and AIT for enabling me to move forward. I'm eager to see what my future will be. ■

Chapter 7

Charlie

by Christine Goss

When Charlie was born, I was thirty–four, his dad was thirty–five, and his sisters were fourteen and two. My pregnancy was uneventful, but labor was exceptionally difficult, and after seven painful hours where little progress was made, I was given pitocin to speed things up. An epidural anesthetic followed which somehow didn't work at all, and the pain was excruciating. After four more hours, Charlie finally had to be delivered with forceps, and the cord was wrapped around his neck. He suffered some anoxia (oxygen deprivation) and was slightly bluish, but we were reassured by his Apgar scores which at seven and eight were reasonably high.

The day after delivery, my pediatrician visited me and said that something was wrong with one of the blood counts. I questioned him, but he was vague, saying it probably didn't mean anything, and that they would redo it the next day. His circumcision was postponed because of it. I prayed hard that everything would be all right, and when the doctor visited me the next day, I was relieved to hear that the blood count had been retaken, and appeared to be normal.

Charlie developed jaundice on the second day and was placed under lights for treatment. We weren't sure he would be able to leave the hospital with us, but he did, and for several days we had to take him to the pediatrician to check his bilirubin count.

I was able to nurse him only for about a week. I was having problems with breastfeeding, switched him to formula, and from age two months to two years he vomited his formula and milk frequently. I found it unusual that it occurred so often, and it presented a problem when he had to be fed away from home.

Charlie started sleeping through the night when he was three weeks old. He was a light sleeper, and often I would leave on the bathroom exhaust fan so there would be background noise. I can certainly identify with this because I'm a very light sleeper, also. He is still an excellent sleeper, but awakens easily.

At birth, Charlie weighed eight pounds, eleven ounces. By three months, he weighed almost seventeen pounds, and by five months, he was unusually chubby. His face bulged out and he just didn't look quite right, but the doctor wasn't alarmed. I remember my mother being concerned that he was gaining weight too fast.

Charlie met all of his major milestones right on target. Baby and family were progressing well that first year, and we all enjoyed Charlie's pleasant personality. He was an affectionate and contented baby, babbled constantly, and said his first word at fourteen months. Then, between the ages of fifteen and twenty months he experienced recurrent ear infections. He was on a variety of antibiotics, but Ceclor always worked best for him, and was the one most frequently prescribed. I was concerned, not only because he was almost constantly on antibiotics, but also because he had almost completely stopped eating solid food. It just didn't appeal to him anymore. For a period of time, his diet consisted of milk from his bottle and nothing else except vitamins. I was worried about this combination of strong medicine and poor eating habits. Our pediatrician suggested we have him seen by an ear, nose, and throat specialist. At this point, ear tubes were considered, but finally, after seven long months, the ear infections became less frequent and tubes were not needed. It was also recommended that Charlie take a low–dose daily maintenance antibiotic, which usually prevented ear infections, but I was totally against that. In my opinion, he had already had more medicine than most children have during all of their childhood years. As a result of all the antibiotics, Charlie fought a constant battle with yeast infections. His bottom area was so red and sore that he couldn't even wear a diaper. Nystatin cream and medicine were prescribed, but it took many months for his rash to disappear.

It was during this time of sequential ear infections that Charlie's language seemed to slow down and eventually cease completely. He had been saying about six to eight words at fifteen months, but by twenty–one months he had completely stopped talking. We were also concerned about his ability to hear. It was as though he couldn't hear us. We would try to get his attention, but he would completely avoid any contact with us. His behavior at home became very distractable. In addition, he started to play by himself, and would only play with others after overcoming a period of shyness. His eye contact completely disappeared, and he no longer wanted to be held. He became anti–social and aloof. I remember many times sitting on the family room couch trying to hold and cuddle him, but he always avoided my touch. I'd say to him "Charlie, please let me hug you and tell you that I love you," but he would always try to escape any physical affection. This was an emotional time for our family. I cried frequently because I just couldn't seem to reach him. It was as if he was in his own little world, not even acknowledging us when we talked to him. He would cover his ears with his hands when I ran the water in the kitchen sink, while he watched television and someone would scream, and sometimes when someone would sing. He covered them when we rode in the car with the windows down and the air breezing through, or when we tried to sit by the ocean to watch the waves. Until he was five, we just couldn't sit near the sound of the surf very long because Charlie was always running back to the road. Instead of spending a nice, relaxing day at the beach, which we loved to do because Charlie's grandmother lives near the water, we always seemed to be chasing after Charlie. His reaction to noise was confusing, though, because fire engines, barking dogs and vacuum cleaners never seemed to phase him.

When we took him to the mall, which we often did, we would get to the entrance, ready to open the door, and Charlie would start screaming as if he was in pain. Later, we found that he hated the mall because of the background noise there. Apparently, sounds on specific frequencies that wouldn't bother the majority of us sounded very loud and scary to him. I'm sure he was frustrated by not having the appropriate language skills to tell us how he felt. The sound of the ocean, normaly soothing for most people, hurt his ears and frightened him, as did the wind in the car.

From fifteen months to the age of three, Charlie's behavior was hard to control. He was unpredictable and easily annoyed. Because his older sister was a teenager, we would often ask her to baby sit so that we didn't have to take him places. Except for

McDonald's, we never took him to a restaurant until he was much older. Having to adapt to Charlie was difficult for our family, but our strong faith sustained us.

His hearing was clearly sensitive, but there was also something different about his eyes. He squinted a lot, especially when playing with toys. When he played with his beloved matchbox cars, for instance, he would lie down on the floor on his side, roll a car back and forth, and stare and squint at the wheels—sometimes for as long as an hour. Also, when he played outside and ran, he would almost always look sideways and backwards. Once he ran into our parked car in the driveway and hurt himself. Whenever we were riding in the car, he usually would turn his head around to watch out the back window. I always wondered why he couldn't look forward and see, just like everyone else, but the glare might have been too much for him.

Charlie's most alarming symptom was his loss of eye contact with people at around the age of fifteen months, soon after the ear infections began. You just couldn't get him to look at you. He seemed to try, but somehow his eyes couldn't focus. It was as if he were staring into space.

In addition to hearing and sight, his sense of touch had become overly sensitive, and probably explained why he wiggled around in my arms and tried to get down when I tried to hold him. Before he was fifteen months old, he had been a sociable, affectionate and cuddly baby, longing to be held and preferring to be rocked to sleep. I realized that at fifteen months some striving for independence was normal, but his whole demeanor and personality had changed. He just didn't seem to want to be around people very much.

Fortunately, we had a wonderful pediatrician who recognized our concerns and felt the need for early intervention and testing. At age twenty–one months, Charlie was scheduled at Children's Hospital in Baltimore for a speech and hearing test. His hearing was found to be adequate, but the results indicated severe delays in all areas of speech and language development. His speech was at the level of an eleven–month–old. The doctor's diagnosis was communication disorder, and possibly pervasive developmental delay (PDD). I was told later by our speech therapist that PDD is a modern term for mild retardation.

Recommendations included a parent–interactive approach to facilitate attention in language learning and speech therapy. We began hourly, bi–weekly sessions where we would play games, blow bubbles—whatever it took to get Charlie to interact socially and verbally. We also learned some sign language (e.g., more, cookie, stop) which helped us communicate. I filled in a photo album with pictures of Charlie's favorite people and activities, and at home we would go through it and point to familiar faces with the hope that he would repeat names, We also pointed to pictures of familiar surroundings to have him say words. After two months of speech therapy, we saw progress. His eye contact and attention span were improving and Charlie had learned some basic signs. We wanted to be able to continue his speech therapy, and when our insurance coverage expired after two months, we began to seek treatment services through our county public school system.

Just after our last speech therapy session (Charlie was almost two years old), I called his therapist to thank her for her great work and wonderful enthusiasm. It was a conversation that I'll never forget. It was my first introduction to the word "autism." We were having a sincere conversation, and I was asking her for suggestions on how I could help him at home. When I asked her for a professional diagnosis of Charlie after having worked with him, she said, "My personal feeling is that Charlie has pervasive developmental delay (PDD) with autistic characteristics." I immediately researched autism, and indeed found many similarities to Charlie. Later that day, I left for the beach to visit my mother, and I cried nonstop there for three days. It was hard to accept that our normal, healthy baby had somehow regressed and could possibly be autistic or retarded now. Again, it was our deep Christian faith that pulled us through. I called on our family and friends for prayers. People all around the country were praying for him.

A few months later, Charlie was evaluated at school by a special education teacher. She found significant delays in cognition, fine motor skills, language (which was almost nonexistent), and social skills. Home–based services were recommended, and began when Charlie was two and a half. The teacher came to our home for several visits, working on signing, imitation skills, and building his vocabulary by pointing to common objects.

It became obvious to me that Charlie was easily distracted by the familiar surroundings in our home. I asked the teacher if we could meet at school where he wouldn't be so apt to walk away and play with other toys elsewhere. She agreed, and the sessions became much more productive. Observing Charlie and his teacher was excruciating for me. It was so painfully obvious that his behavior made him almost impossible to handle. In order to get Charlie to cooperate and stay on task, his teacher would literally have to hold him down on her lap, which was strenuous exercise for her, and I often complimented her on her excellent physical condition and her strong back. Once she was able to keep him still, she would proceed with the lesson. Her goal was to have Charlie sit directly opposite her on the floor, in order to facilitate teaching him and working together as a team. Little by little she moved away from him until finally, by the fourth class, he was able to cooperate. It was incredibly uncomfortable to have to watch my two–and–a– half–year–old having to be restrained in order to gain his trust and cooperation. However, I feel this was a turning point for Charlie. We were starting to deal effectively with his inappropriate behavior.

In reflecting back, I think Charlie's misbehavior was due to his inability to relate to others and to sense the world and people in a normal way. Stimuli must have bothered him to the point where he was just too frustrated to cooperate with others. If a child's senses are not functioning properly, how can he react normally? Moreover, maybe normal sensory integration was actually painful for him.

During the time we worked with our home–based teacher, I asked her for two things. First, if she knew of any other children similar to Charlie whose moms I could contact. I really needed to share my feelings with someone going through the same thing. She put me in contact with another mother whose child was similar to Charlie. We became friends immediately, and today remain very close. Secondly, I asked the teacher if she had any literature pertaining to Charlie's special needs. She gave me a pamphlet describing autism. That word again—autism. I looked through the checklist and noted some of Charlie's traits: impaired communication and language, impaired social interaction, no eye contact, and taking an adult hand and using it to open a door or turn on a light. Charlie certainly fit some of the criteria.

It is not easy observing your child regress. While other children were going forward and meeting their milestones, Charlie was going backwards. To have a child talking, and then for one whole year not say a meaningful word (other than babbling) is heartbreaking. Just weeks shy of his third birthday, Charlie still could not point to body parts correctly. His cognition, as well as verbal and social skills, had markedly decreased. We kept praying for him.

Our pediatrician referred us to the Director of Clinical Genetics at Children's Hospital in Washington, D.C. Charlie was evaluated there for a possible dysmorphic syndrome. The physical exam demonstrated "a child with expressive language delay in association with possible loss of verbal skills." Blood and urine tests were taken with the following results: urine amino acids screen showed slight elevation of amino acids between tyrosine and phenylalanine, but everything else checked out fine, ruling out possible dysmorphic syndrome. The Fragile X blood test was also negative.

Our next referral was to a pediatric neurologist. Charlie was given an extensive physical exam. The doctor said that since some children like Charlie tend to show physical abnormalities around the skull and facial muscles, he would measure them. Charlie was also tested in the usual cognitive, speech, and motor areas. His conclusion was as follows: "Charlie demonstrated no focal neurologic signs, but did show evidence of age–inappropriate behavior, and was most likely suffering from pervasive development delay. This apparent deterioration in previously accomplished levels of verbal functioning can be a feature of autistic functioning but does raise the question of progressive central nervous system degeneration." He would arrange a head MRI done under intravenous sedation, and monitoring to check for brain abnormalities. He also referred us to the Developmental Neuropsychiatry Department at Johns Hopkins University/ Kennedy Institute in Baltimore.

Charlie's head MRI was taken while he was sedated. This was a terribly upsetting ordeal for all of us because Charlie was not able to understand what was happening and was terrified. The results were negative—no abnormalities were found.

We had to wait for several months to get an appointment at the Kennedy Institute. It was the most thorough examination Charlie had ever had. There was a team of three doctors present during the three–hour examination process. Their diagnosis was "pervasive developmental delay—residual type; with mental retardation (probable)." Their recommendations were a continuation of his special education program through the public school, individual speech therapy services, and a parent support/advocacy group such as the Association for Retarded Citizens (ARC).

Charlie's appointment at the Kennedy Institute took place just two weeks before his third birthday. Two significant changes had just occurred prior to that appointment. First, Charlie had resumed private speech therapy services at Children's Hospital due to an acquired scholarship. Secondly, he had started special preschool everyday. Both of these changes had a positive impact on him. He was again on task with language intervention, and he was involved socially in a class with six other students and three teachers. It was becoming evident that his autistic–like characteristics were slowly diminishing. We were always thankful for any positive changes, and we never gave up hope.

To illustrate how far behind he was in his language skills, just three months before his third birthday, his speech therapist's objectives were: to achieve eye contact while giving and receiving objects; to expand nonverbal communicative intents for gestures for bye–bye, no, me, want; to expand babbling; to follow simple commands such as "give me" and "get the"; and to recognize common objects such as cup and ball. It was as though we were going through a time warp, teaching Charlie everything that he had missed out on for the past year and a half. Everything he was taught we would try to reinforce at home. In particular, I remember trying to get Charlie to repeat after me some variegated babbling; for example, ba da ba pa ba ga, each time emphasizing a different beginning consonant. The whole family worked hard at getting Charlie to repeat sounds, to point to items, and to socially interact. This seemed to bring about a change in Charlie. He seemed to want to learn. It was the first time since he had begun having ear infections that he really enjoyed the learning process. He liked all of our positive reinforcement, our clapping and saying, "Great, Charlie, you did it!" We clapped at everything, no matter how small, and anytime he listened and learned. His cooperation was improving, he began smiling more, and overall he just seemed to be happier.

I have learned that communication is a vital key to being the best advocate for your child. Communication with doctors, therapists, teachers, and other parents with similar children is critical for successful treatment. Charlie's teacher used a notebook to communicate with parents. It was a lifeline for me. Since Charlie couldn't talk, I wouldn't have known what was happening in school without it. When I would also take the school notebook to speech therapy, Charlie's speech therapist would write notes to his school teacher, and vice versa, so that they could each reinforce the same skills. An entry by Charlie's teacher to his speech therapist once read, "It was so good to get your message. Working together WILL make a difference."

Charlie was three, knew about five signs, and was babbling frequently, when suddenly a breakthrough occurred. We were having dinner one evening, when Charlie, unprompted, pointed to his nose, eye, and mouth, and clearly said, "Nose! Eye! Mouth!" in quick succession. I literally almost fell off of my chair. Our previous table conversation hadn't even been about anything similar, so he hadn't been cued. Of course we all clapped and cheered, and he was elated over his achievement. I called his teacher at home and she shared in our happiness. She said that they had been working on that in school. She also said she wasn't surprised, and had great hopes for Charlie.

A few weeks later, we purchased an educational toy manufactured by Texas Instruments called Touch and Tell. A voice interacts with the player, and the goal is to identify objects, letters, etc.. It was the best teaching aid that Charlie had ever had, and his vocabulary increased enormously while using it.

The teachers started hearing much more talking from Charlie. In his school notebook, new words were noted frequently. It was like a miracle to us—Charlie was finally saying words and understanding them. Soon, he progressed to two–word combinations.

At age three–and–a–half, his teacher wrote, "Charlie continues to work hard on articulation." I had the feeling that it was very difficult for him. At times, just knowing how to move his lips, tongue, and mouth seemed so difficult. [This is known as verbal apraxia, and is a common problem with children with communication disorders.—Ed.] We worked at having him repeat his words many times over. We'd always ask him to watch our mouth as a visual cue.

His behavior seemed to be improving somewhat, but change seemed particularly difficult for him at times. We went through a three–month ordeal over his clothing that we thought would never get resolved. He loved his black sweat pants so much that he wanted to wear them every day to school. His teacher and I felt that Charlie shouldn't dictate what he wanted to wear, so we both tried hard to put different pants on him. It got to the point where I would have to hold him down on the floor and force the black sweats off and another pair on. He would fight me, screaming, kicking, and crying. As he was big and strong for his age, with weight and height in the ninety–fifth percentile, it took all my strength. His teacher tried this in school as well. Sometimes she succeeded and sometimes not. She and I were persistent, and it was only through positive reinforcement and rewards (usually a treat), that he finally gave in. He had always hated getting a new coat, or a new hat or gloves—changes in the things that he was used to were hard for him to accept. When spring came and then summer, I feared that he would still be wearing his winter coat. It was often a struggle, but eventually he became much more flexible that year in school.

By the end of the school year, Charlie was spontaneously saying, "See the house. See the tree." His expressive language had grown incredibly, as well as his receptive language. For a time, though, Charlie become echolalic, and often said meaningless phrases. As his comprehension improved, this disappeared. Even though his communication and social skills had leaped ahead, he tested far below age level. Whenever I received written reports of his language skills lagging far behind the norm, I would reassure myself by noting all of his improvements, and refused to dwell on the exact placement of where he fell. It would have been too discouraging to focus on the actual numbers. I always remained positive about Charlie.

I started volunteering at Charlie's school. I wanted to learn more about children with similar needs and discover more teaching strategies. My background was in teaching (regular education), and I was anxious to learn more about special education. As a parent, I always needed to remember that I was my child's first teacher as well as his personal advocate within the special education process.

In his speech therapy class at Children's Hospital, Charlie made considerable progress, and was selected to be in their annual day–long telethon. A videotape of him in one of his sessions was shown in the introduction to the telethon, and Charlie, my husband, and I were interviewed live. This made me nervous because I wasn't sure how Charlie was going to react, but he was good. He answered one quick question and behaved quite well.

Over the summer, Charlie attended a special populations camp for three weeks. The building that was used was quite old and smelled somewhat of mildew. The smell didn't seem to bother any of the children or the counselors, except for the last week when Charlie developed bronchitis. He had never had bronchitis before and hasn't since. He doesn't have any known allergies. It is my opinion that since all of his senses were somewhat distorted, he was probably more sensitive to the smell than the others.

Charlie had wonderful teachers for his second year of school. One of our goals was to obtain dialogue with Charlie. I was concerned about his attaining this skill because his teacher told me that not every child will dialogue. But fortunately, by the middle of the school year, he was responding appropriately to questions. Understanding how to verbalize yes and no to questions was a particularly hard concept for him. He would always say "yes" for "no," and vice versa. Another difficult concept was the proper use of pronouns, especially me and you. It took quite a while for him to understand "me" as referring to himself. For example, he would say, "Give the ball to you," instead of saying, "Give the ball to me." His being able to master these concepts contributed to his successful year.

While attending speech therapy at Children's Hospital, Charlie was placed with another child with similar special needs. Individual speech therapy became group speech therapy. Our goal was to have the two boys interact verbally and socially with each other, and play together appropriately. They needed help with verbal and nonverbal cues, taking turns, and eye contact. Group speech therapy worked well, and Charlie benefitted significantly from it.

Another skill that Charlie acquired was pretend play. It was exciting to see him begin at last to take figures and talk for them.

All of these skills that just normally happen with nonhandicapped children suddenly become gigantic milestones in the lives of our special children.

In his third year of special education, Charlie was in a self–contained classroom again with two terrific teachers. We were thrilled that he was finally able to tell me the names of the other children in his class and that he had begun to understand the concept of time. He latched onto phonics and sounding out letters, and by the end of the year he was reading easy books. He started to blossom with the introduction of academics. He had always been interested in the numbers and letters videos that he watched at home, and I'm sure this helped him to become an early reader.

At the end of kindergarten, Charlie was given the school's standardized psychological tests. His intelligence scores were 91 for the nonverbal, and 71 for the verbal. Normally, the psychologist would have averaged these two numbers to get the final score, but the numbers were so extreme that averaging them would have been meaningless. The scores fascinated me and gave me hope, knowing as I did that the tests are not a true indication of a child's abilities since they are given in a verbal context where language–delayed children are at an enormous disadvantage.

Charlie's speech by age five and a half was still delayed, but he was definitely progressing. His social skills were still somewhat awkward. Often, he would play with children for a short while, but had difficulty in reacting to verbal and nonverbal cues. I remember the first time he asked me if he could go to a neighbor's house to play—I was so thankfully happy that I cried! His sound sensitivities still continued, but as he got older, he seemed to handle them better. I think this was because he had now attained speech, and was less frustrated overall. He had also acquired the ability to block out the painful frequencies somewhat. His worst fear at home was still bath time. Whenever I ran the water for his bath, he would always wait downstairs, far away from the bathroom. And while the water was running, he would be upset, repeatedly yelling upstairs to me, "That's enough water, Mom. That's enough!" I could hardly get an inch or two of water in the tub when he would be demanding that I turn off the tap. Then he would come upstairs, get into the tub, wash quickly, play very little, and get out.

When Charlie was five and a half, he received auditory integration training for his sound sensitivities. This type of auditory integration had just begun to be offered in the United States. In order to prepare him for this ten–day experience, we explained the procedure to him, and let him listen to music at home through headphones. In addition, a few months earlier we had videotaped a report on 20/20 [aired 6/12/92—Ed.] explaining auditory training, and just before Charlie's course of treatment, we replayed it for him to watch, carefully explaining the process. He seemed secure about what we planned to do.

Day one of AIT arrived, and Charlie had his initial audiogram. Our audiologist told me that it was one of the worst audiograms she had ever seen, with jagged peaks and valleys indicating distortion. As I understand it, normal hearing is shown as a slightly wavy horizontal line. Charlie's was scattered with extreme peaks and valleys, and the lines were choppy and almost vertical. I was relieved when I saw it. It was concrete evidence of something physically wrong which might be able to be corrected.

In his first AIT session, Charlie was restless and moving around in his chair, but he never tried to take off the headphones. "Are we done yet?" he kept asking. By second session, though, he hardly moved, and was absorbed in the music. He soon had the procedure down pat, although he became unusually active between the two sessions. I had to hold his hand extra tightly as we walked around Washington D.C. during our interim hours.

On day four, my journal entry reads: "Charlie did super today, too. One thing a little different was that he wanted me to push on his headphones while he was wearing them, pushing them hard into his head. He would put his hands on top of my hands (that were on the headphones), and he would massage the headphones while pushing them into his ears—almost as if to relieve some discomfort. Our audiologist said that it was to massage the sore ear muscles that aren't used to being worked out this way, just as when you are exercising, your muscles hurt if you overdo it. She explained that the inner ear (the cochlea) has small hairs that probably weren't vibrating, and now they are, and it would itch or bother him slightly also."

On Day five, Charlie received his second audiogram; it had started to flatten out somewhat. We were excited about that. Days six through ten proceeded smoothly as well, the only changes still being his hyperactivity between sessions and later at home.

Two days after AIT was completed, we noticed some dramatic changes. Charlie started babbling like a baby. It had been several years since we had heard this from him. He still talked regularly as well, but about half of the time he would say things like, "ba ba da da goo gee," in a sing–song fashion. He started taking my hand to direct me to a particular place, something he hadn't done for years. For example, he would take my hand, and placing it on the pantry door knob he would say, "Can I have a cookie, will you get me a cookie?"

Another sign of regression was his refusal to get dressed independently. I remember many evenings telling him to go upstairs, get his pajamas out of his drawer, and get dressed for bed—something that he had done regularly before. He would tell us that he couldn't do it because he didn't know how. It was a real struggle at every bedtime for about two months.

Our house was fairly near a railroad track, and on one occasion, just after AIT, Charlie got upset and asked his dad to close the door because the train was too loud. It had never bothered him before. Similarly, I noticed that on several mornings Charlie had closed his window during the night. I asked him why he did it and he responded that he just wanted to. He hadn't ever done that before. I feel certain that it was the sounds of the train through the night that seemed louder than usual. Sound–sensitive children have learned how to block out the uncomfortable sounds that bother them. After AIT, they are not able to do that because their hearing starts to normalize; thus for a short time afterward, they hear certain sounds louder until their hearing readjusts.

About a month after AIT, Charlie said, "When I laugh, it doesn't bother me anymore." The implications were profound and I was stunned. I chose my words carefully.

"Did it used to bother you before when you laughed?"

"Yes," he replied. "It used to hurt my ears when I laughed."

"And now it doesn't."

"No," he said. How incredible! Can you imagine your ears hurting when you simply laughed? It was then that I understood the degree of discomfort he had dealt with in many everyday occurrences. He must have learned early in life to block out sound that bothered him in order to survive.

Another breakthrough occurred at about the same time. My journal reads as follows: "The other night Charlie took a bath. It was the first time that he actually stayed in the bathroom while the water was filling up the tub. And he wanted a lot of water this time. Before, he had always wanted a little bit, because he acted afraid of just the sight of the water. Then he actually sat down in the tub while the water was still coming in! He stayed in the tub for about thirty minutes, and played! He had never stayed in for very long. He was even singing Little Mermaid songs." It was the first time he really enjoyed his bath.

And just as surprisingly, Charlie really enjoyed the beach for the first time. When we sat by the water's edge he no longer ran away to the road. He seemed relaxed and happy. How thankful we were for this change as well.

There were many more positive changes in Charlie after AIT. He became inquisitive, asking everyone questions constantly. In fact, he is still curious about everything. His play became noticeably more creative, with lots of fun role playing. He became much more comfortable with his peers, and started initiating dialogue, using higher level language concepts. He seemed to really enjoy going places now, and we finally were able to take him to nice restaurants and feel like a normal family. Everyone who knew Charlie commented on his vast growth and development.

Probably the biggest change in Charlie after AIT was his becoming more aware of himself as a person. It was as if his whole demeanor had changed. He became a much more secure, self–confident five–year–old. It was almost as if a light switch suddenly turned on inside of him, he seemed to be perceiving himself so differently. He was surely happier with himself, and that permeated his everyday activities . We were so grateful.

About ten weeks after AIT, I recorded the following in my journal: "When tucking Charlie in bed tonight, I said, "How do your ears feel now?"

"They don't make that sound anymore," he said. I asked him to explain the sound, and he made a "sh" sound.

"Were your ears noisy before?" I asked.

"Yes," he said. "Inside. Are your ears noisy inside?"

"No," I said.

"They never were?" he asked.

"No," I said. Apparently he thought that everyone heard "sh" sounds at one time or another. He was surprised when I told him that I had never heard like that."

When Charlie had his third and final audiogram, it was much straighter than the first two. There was an amazing difference between before and after.

Charlie started first grade in a new school this year where he began mainstreaming with regular education children in the nonacademic classes. He still received speech therapy, occupational therapy, and motor development classes for his delayed skills.

The weeks and months following AIT proceeded very well. Except for some mild regression and increased activity, Charlie had benefitted enormously. We felt as if we had a new child. He did have one setback, though. About four months after AIT, he began to open and close doors continuously. He would open the door slowly and just watch as if hypnotized as the opening grew wider, and then close it slowly and watch as the opening narrowed. Sometimes he would turn his head sideways and watch, and other times he would watch out of the corners of his eyes. It was happening everywhere we went, wherever there were doors, and he would always insist on opening and closing the door himself. Needless to say, it was bizarre behavior and it drove us crazy. In addition to seeming to enjoy this, he was almost drawn to it. We would ask him why he kept doing it, and his response was always, "I just like watching it." Fortunately, this behavior stopped completely, and has never returned. Strange though it may sound, it is my strong belief that Charlie's fixation was triggered by the antibiotics that he had been taking. Just before this behavior started, he had finished a ten-day supply of antibiotics for strep. This had been the first antibiotic that he had taken since completing AIT. In my networking with other parents who have similar children, I have found it's not unusual for behavior to change due to antibiotics.

During the middle of the school year, I apprehensively enrolled him in a regular education gymnastics class. I'll never forget his very first class. I was watching through the observation window, and as the class proceeded smoothly, and Charlie "fit right in," I couldn't hold back my tears of happiness. It was a true milestone for him.

Nine months after AIT, Charlie (now six–and–a–half) said something else that I considered profound. He took a bath and washed his hair, and instead of pouring water over his head to remove the shampoo, he lay down under the water to rinse his hair. When he emerged, he was alarmed. "I have that noise in my ears again like I used to," he said. "It was the same noise that I had when I was five." We talked about it further and he said he was glad that the noise went away.

At the end of the school year, I attended a special–needs conference. I learned about vitamin therapy, the ear infection/yeast infection link, allergy–induced autism (as it is called in England), nutrition, food allergies, occupational therapy, sensory integration, auditory integration therapy, and something unfamiliar to me— visual training.

Charlie's eyesight, his ability to see things, tested at 20/20. But vision is the ability to interpret what we see. It involves the muscles in our eyes working together efficiently. When a child is not seeing properly, he cannot learn about his environment correctly. And the older he gets, the more he lags behind. Could Charlie's vision have been distorted along with his hearing? Certainly he acted as if something was wrong: his inability to look at us when he was younger, his squinting when playing with toys, his way of looking at things sideways, the odd contortions he would make with his eyes, the way he would try to look at things out of the corners of his eyes, the way he would lie down sideways on the floor and hold onto his Tinker Toys and just stare at them for a long time. We thought it unusual that when he learned how to ride a two–wheeler bike, he just hopped right onto the bike with perfect balance and started riding like a pro, without training wheels. He had some difficulty with steering, though, and we thought it might be related to his vision. In addition, his motor development teacher had mentioned to me that when Charlie was playing T–ball in class, his eyes were not tracking the ball properly as it was being pitched to him.

Besides all of these unusual characteristics, Charlie had started asking me for glasses while he was in first grade. He had been persistent about it, and whenever we'd been near a store that sold glasses, he had vehemently insisted that he needed them, and at times had tried physically to push me into the store. This had occurred for several months. When I had asked him why he needed glasses, he always had the same answer: "I need to see better. I can't see right." I find it incredibly interesting that while Charlie didn't realize that he heard differently, he surely knew that he saw differently.

After a thorough examination by a developmental optometrist, it was determined that glasses would help Charlie with his depth perception and his eye muscle problem. It seemed that his eye muscles were not working together correctly, and the result was that his tracking skills were poor. Glasses would help his blurred peripheral vision as well. Another recommendation given by our doctor was visual training. This would help him visualize correctly, which would improve his comprehension skills and his fine motor skills.

In first and second grade, Charlie mainstreamed into nonacademic classes, including lunch, recess, music, and physical education, and in the second half of second grade, he mainstreamed into reading and writing for two hours a day, with thirty normal children. Charlie received his glasses soon after he began second grade. After wearing them for just a few minutes, he said to me, "Now I can finally see right!" He loves to wear them, and never wants to take them off, even to go to bed. Although our insurance did not cover visual retraining, his present teacher is an expert on the subject of visual perception skills, and has adapted her teaching style to include help in this area for her students.

Charlie has progressed extremely well over the last five years, so much so that his last school testing scores were above grade level in the regular education range. He will be going to a new school next year, completely in regular ed. We plan, and it has been recommended by his teachers, to have him repeat second grade, to ease the transition out of special ed into regular ed.

In conclusion, let me pass along some personal feelings. Charlie's story unfolds like a miracle to me, and for that I am very thankful to God, our family, his teachers and specialists, and the understanding doctors that we met along the way. I believe that early intervention was a big factor in helping Charlie get back on track, and his dedicated teachers and specialists played a major role. Doing all that we possibly could at home certainly helped as well. Also, I believe that his sister, two years older, played a significant role in helping Charlie to improve in many areas. Her unconditional love and willingness to always be there as a playmate and teacher helped him progress enormously. They were and still are best friends. I am especially grateful for the auditory integration training that he received; it normalized his hearing and had a dramatic effect on him. And lastly, I feel fortunate that all of his doctors were especially caring professionals, always open to our opinions.

Why this happened to Charlie is a big mystery to us. Was he correctly labeled PDD with autism and mild retardation? And why, suddenly, after his persistent ear infections, did he regress and lose communication skills? It was such a heartbreaking experience, and although our family was brought closer together by it, many families are not so fortunate, and are split apart by the difficulties that arise.

It is my personal opinion that Charlie's brain stopped developing normally when he started having his constant ear infections and yeast infections. This may have been caused by the strong antibiotics, Tylenol for pain, and poor eating habits. It is also entirely possible that cow's milk may have contributed to his regression and/or ear infections—at twelve months he started drinking cow's milk, and at fourteen months, the ear infections began. Recent studies indicate that some children have definite food allergies which can dramatically affect behavior and learning. Another factor could be the polluted environment in which we live today—maybe Charlie's system was particularly sensitive to chemicals, thus weakening his immune system and contributing to his susceptibility to ear infections.

If some or all of these theories are valid, why wouldn't all children with chronic ear infections develop autistic–like characteristics? My feeling is that this is where genetics plays a major role. Some children may be predisposed to such problems due to heredity. Although most people seem to be able to take antibiotics with no significant side effects, perhaps a small percentage of the population cannot.

In my opinion, when Charlie's brain stopped developing at a normal rate, his ability to sense and relate to the world around him was dramatically altered. In effect, his senses shut down, thereby causing him to appear autistic. In addition, perhaps this led to distortions in all of his senses, particularly affecting Charlie's hearing and vision. It is really not fair to the child and to the family to label him or her as autistic until all the alternative possibilities are considered. In our case, it has taken many years of research, networking with other parents both locally and nationally, attending seminars, journalizing the facts, and constant prayers for guidance. This has been an enormous undertaking for everyone involved, but thankfully, the groundwork has begun, and now parents and professionals are working together to share information and research further.

In reflecting on these last seven years, I certainly have grown as a mother and teacher. Having a special–needs child gave me a greater appreciation for the small, everyday miracles that occur with all children. In addition, I helped establish a national prayer ministry for parents with special–needs children as a way to outreach to others in need.

I'd like to conclude with an interesting observation that was made last month by a family member who hadn't seen Charlie in about two years. She simply said to me, "Charlie really has changed. He just doesn't seem to have that look on his face anymore." I knew exactly what she meant.

To update (December, 1994), Charlie's birthday is in the beginning of November. He was just eight and is repeating second grade this year. He is having a wonderful year. He is doing unbelievably well. He is in the completely regular ed classroom with no resource, no extra help. He moved from Level V to Level 1 in six years, an incredible leap. He just got his very first ever report card, we are out of the IEP (individual educational plan) stage now, a big milestone right there. He got top marks in his academics, did less well in handwriting, and we are still working on his fine motor skills. He also got top marks in behavior and effort, which is critical. He did gymnastics for two years, and T–ball, both in regular ed programs, and he's planning to play soccer in the spring. He has friends and an active social life.

Regarding insurance: We were not able to get insurance, but a friend of ours was more successful, through Travelers (under speech therapy), which at that time routinely covered anything related to autism. ■

Chapter 8

Tammy

by Jody Koegler,
as told to Kendra Marasco

Tammy and her twin were preemies, and only Tammy survived. Although she weighed only 2 lb. 9 oz. at birth and spent her first three months in a neonatal unit, she seemed to develop normally. Her mother died when she was three–and–a–half, and her father remarried: I am her stepmother.

When Tammy entered kindergarten, it became evident as the year went on that she had an auditory processing problem. It was difficult for her to absorb preliminary information in any subject, and spelling was impossible for her. Throughout kindergarten she couldn't remember the name of even one child in the class, and at the end of the year, when she was obviously not ready for first grade, it was recommended that she go to "pre–first." This class, with only two teachers, two student teachers, and fifty children needing individual attention, was inadequately staffed. Tammy needed far more than the little one–on–one she received. By the end of the year, her handwriting and math skills were negligible, she still couldn't read, and she had to repeat the class the following year.

When she continued to have problems, Tammy was placed in special ed in a self–contained classroom, with only eleven other children, a special ed teacher, and an aide. Here she received speech and counselling, and with adequate individual attention, she gradually began to read. She was able to mainstream for music and art.

Tammy remained in special ed for several grades. By the end of third grade, she was reading only on first grade level, and that, in fact, was a generous assumption. Her math was a problem for her as well. She couldn't seem to retain information, had great difficulty memorizing, and was able only to read words she had memorized. She couldn't sound out words, and hesitated painstakingly over anything that she was required to read aloud. She would see the first letter of a word, and would try to guess what the rest of it was. A good percentage of the time she was not reading what was actually on the page.

When I would put my finger on the word I wanted her to read, quite frequently she would try to read the word above it. Even after repeatedly pointing to the word and saying, "What does this word say?" she would read the sentence above it. For compound words we had to slow it way down, dividing up the word, putting a hand over half of it and saying, "Sound this part out." If she was able to do that, and we tried the same process for the rest of the word, it was almost impossible for her to put the two together.

Because she continually reversed words and letters, we suspected dyslexia. She would often say things backwards, and in reading would read "on" for "no," for example. After three years, I saw no ability as far as reading new material was concerned. She just could not do it. Her only real achievement was the fact that she had increased the number of words she had memorized and was able to put together. My younger daughter, in second grade, was way ahead of her in reading because she was able to sound out words. Requiring Tammy to do this only caused confusion and embarrassment. In addition, Tammy didn't appear to comprehend words spoken too quickly, or multiple concepts in one sentence. "Hang up your coat and take your seat, Tammy," was too much for her. She could cope only with one thing at a time.

To compensate for her disabilities in the academic area, Tammy tried to be the absolute best helper and the nicest kid in the class. As far as behavior went, she didn't have too many problems in school.

Tammy's brother, Zachary, is autistic. Although most of Tammy's traits are associated with auditory processing problems and dyslexia, some of them can be related to autism. She has a need for sameness, for example, and once at a family dinner, when her dad sat in a different place at the table, she fell apart.

I had been considering auditory integration training for Zachary. What little speech he had was sporadic, one word at a time, and rarely appropriate, and the fact that he was always trying to block sound by putting his finger in his ear was another indication that AIT would be helpful. Because I associated AIT only with the treatment of autism, I hadn't thought of it for

Tammy's dyslexia, but the more I found out about it, the more I found myself thinking maybe this could help Tammy.

When she was small, she had shown signs of hypersensitive hearing, but she appeared to have adjusted, no longer covering her ears, for instance, when I turned on the hair dryer. As I thought it over, I could see that she had reacted inappropriately to many sounds. I wondered why she would get so hysterical when we would get upset with her: could it be that our raised voices had made it impossible for her to even understand what was going on, and we just hadn't realized it?

Just before Christmas, when Tammy was in the third grade, she began AIT. Five days into the therapy, we went to the grocery store, and as we walked into the store, Tammy said, "Mom, does that sign say 'Employees Only'? I was shocked.

"How did you do that?" I asked.

"I read it, it was easy." As we drove through town toward home, she started reading more and more. She read street signs as we drove by them. "Mom, does that say 'No Outlet?' I thought to myself, "Gee, a week ago she couldn't put a compound word together without putting her hand over it, and now she's looking at it as we're driving by."

The next day, I told Tammy's AIT practitioner that she was reading a lot better, markedly, dramatically, better than the week before. Tammy's initial audiogram showed she was hearing at minus ten in the hyperacute area, on several frequencies. Her midpoint audiogram showed that her hearing was starting to level out.

The next day, we were in the bathroom, and I was blow–drying Tammy's hair. We had been practicing some Spanish. Tammy's sister was being a clown and saying nonsense words in Tammy's one ear while I was talking to her in the other. Suddenly Tammy stopped and said, "Mom, I can listen now!"

"What do you mean, Tammy?" I had a feeling I knew what she meant, but I wanted to hear her explain. It surprised me that she could express what she was feeling.

"You know it used to be that I had a hard time listening to people. You're talking in one ear, and Emily is talking in the other ear, and you're using the hair dryer, and I can still listen to you. I can still understand you!" For the first time, she seemed able to focus on one conversation and tune out the background noise.

Tammy began to make quantum leaps in her reading. I saw great improvement, as did several other people. My mother hadn't seen Tammy for a few months, and when she stayed overnight at her house, she called me the next day."I can't believe the difference in Tammy's reading," she said. "I mean, she read a book to me, and I just couldn't believe the difference in her." Other relatives and friends also remarked on the changes in Tammy.

During AIT, we kept Tammy out of school. Her teacher had supplied us with a full page of class work and homework, and Tammy read the letter without hesitating. She finished AIT on Sunday, and returned to school on Monday fully prepared.

I asked her teacher to keep a record of her progress, and she called me a week later. "I have some really good news for you," she said. "We have seen an improvement in Tammy's ability to read." Her special ed teacher contacted me saying that all the other kids in Tammy's class read at first grade level, and Tammy was now the best reader in the class. They sent her to the self–contained fourth through sixth grade special ed classroom, and the teacher found that Tammy was easily reading at third grade level. Basically, she had gone, in one week, from reading at first grade level to reading at third grade level. Everyone was really impressed.

From the time Tammy completed AIT at Christmastime until the end of the year, everything else started falling into place. Her teachers reported that she was participating much more actively in class. Instead of holding off and waiting to be called on, she was shooting up her hand as soon as a question was asked. Her self–confidence was growing, and her interaction with the other kids was improving as well. She was much better able to tolerate other children, and even made friends with one little boy who always had driven her crazy. She was actually starting to carry on friendships during classtime, and needed to be spoken to about maybe settling down a little bit.

Some of the changes have been very subtle. Although she has always been well–behaved, she has a new intuitive sense about social situations. She is able to express herself better, with thoughts and words that indicate much greater maturity than I had thought was there. It stuns me when she uses long words. Before AIT, for instance, she could never get it straight than an "air conditioner" shouldn't be called a "cold heater." She would often drop the first syllable of a word, calling a computer a "puter" for example.

Other signs of progress became evident as time went on. Her teachers noticed that her response time to questions had shortened. Her sense of humor improved. I think she had always had her father's wry sense of humor, but she appeared to be better able to express it. Some of the things she comes out with now are pretty funny.

Tammy, and everyone who knows her, is thrilled with all the wonderful and amazing changes we have seen. So thank you, Dr. Bérard. Thank you, Annabel. And thank you, Kendra (Tammy's AIT practitioner). I will be in touch because I'd like to set up an appointment for Zachary for AIT and maybe me, since my attention deficit is driving me crazy! Maybe this would help me too. ■

Chapter 9

Nicholas

by Sally Bober

I am a professional in the field of auditory integration training, and have missed opportunities to help my own child! I didn't realize that Nicholas had listened to my many conversations. Of course NOW I know that he heard much more than the conversations that took place in our house. Sometimes it's hard to realize just how much your kids process.

Our life has truly been an emotional roller coaster ride for the past nine months. Our sons noticed that Mom was traveling and talking on the phone for countless hours. At that point, there were so few people doing auditory training that we had to travel far and wide to investigate it. We were in the "let's look and see" stage, so we talked to anyone and flew anywhere to learn whatever we could about this method. Beverly, my partner in our large private speech pathology practice in East Texas, was one of the first six people in the world to be trained by Dr. Bérard to be an auditory training practitioner, and I was in the first class trained in America at the Georgiana Foundation. The excitement, turmoil, joys and fears surrounding this new treatment were touching all of our lives when Nicholas came out of school one day and said, "Mom, I think I want to do auditory training. Beverly just came back from training (with Dr. Bérard) and learned some new things. I think I need the training . . . do you want me to tell you why ?"

"Really ?" I replied. I was flabbergasted at the amount he had already absorbed about AIT without my even realizing it. "I think I have it figured out," Nicholas confidently continued. "I've been thinking about all of this since Beverly came back. Do you want to know my analysis ?"

My mind was spinning with all kind of thoughts and notions. "Yeah, tell your "expert" Mom what you think." I could feel myself start to sweat, and guilt begin to well up inside as I said to myself,

"I have not figured out my OWN child !!!" Sensing that Nicholas was getting ready to tell me something that was really going to amaze me, I tried to get a grip on my emotions.

"You keep telling me that I don't try hard enough in school. Why do you think that I do so well on my achievement tests each year ?" (He received perfect scores on three quarters of his achievement tests, but is diagnosed with ADD.)

"I don't know," I said. "You tell me. " And I continued to listen. He began to explain to me that the testing time is the one time in the classroom that the teacher demands quiet. You can't shuffle your feet, move your hands or move your desk. If you do, someone will come by and make you be quiet. Also, all of the directions are short and the answers are short, so you don't have to pay attention for very long at a time. You can "click on and off" as you go along and answer the questions. His teacher would later report that he would click on and off as many as two or three hundred times in a class. This would account for the fact that he appears fully attentive one moment and lost in his own thoughts or "daydreaming" the next. INTERESTING!!!

"Why," Nicholas asked, "do you think I argued with you for a solid year until you allowed me to play fast-paced music to help keep me on task when I study? The information you gave me about classical music being the best to play because it works the limbic system of the brain and helps attention—well, it just never worked for me. So you finally allowed me to decide on my own what works best for ME." His last comment really hit me. How many times do we parents tell our children what to do and how to do it, without allowing them any say so in the matter. Nor do we allow them to tell us what they think works best for them. I was already thinking that we had really blown it. Especially since these kids with sensory differences know their bodies better than anyone else possibly can.

All these thoughts kept cropping up in my head, jumbled with Nicholas' revelations. "LISTEN ! LISTEN ! LISTEN !," my heart kept reminding me, but my brain was running wild trying to problem-solve with each word he uttered.

"Why do you think I have so much trouble paying attention in the classroom?" I didn't even try to answer that one. He continued very confidently, "I hear everything that goes on—every phone call that the principal makes in her office; every single time an eighteen-wheeler truck gears down on the highway three blocks away. I HEAR IT! I HEAR EVERYTHING! I hear people talking outside the school building, and I can understand their conversations. There are so many noises in my head that I can't concentrate on what Mrs. Weaver tries to say. I can't focus and pay attention to the teacher's spoken words—I'm too distracted. AND, why do you think I'm tired all the time? It takes so much energy to pay attention that I am worn out. I TRY SO HARD, AND I JUST CAN'T DO IT!!!"

Oh my gosh, I couldn't begin to comprehend what he was trying to describe to me. I remembered Dr. Bérard explaining that these children have phenomenal coping mechanisms. It's as though they are "trying to concentrate on calculus in the middle of the expressway." Because they are distracted by the traffic, they cannot sustain the attention to work on the calculus problems. Now this story is coming to life in my OWN FAMILY! Dr. Bérard's story that Beverly had related had been right in front of my nose and I had never realized it.

I asked Nicholas to try to tell me more so that I could understand. Did he hear things louder or different or what? He really couldn't describe it. Now I know that, much like Georgie, Nicholas was unable to describe the difference in his PERCEPTION of sounds. I thought of the example of a child who gets glasses for the first time and looks at the blackboard and comments, "Oh, that's what it's supposed to look like?" Perception is unique to each individual. We cannot know how someone else sees or hears. MORE FOOD FOR THOUGHT—HMMMMMMMMMM!!!

I asked Nicholas what sound disturbed him the most, hoping that by rephrasing the question, I could help him tell me more. He instantly answered, "That's easy, the ceiling fan in my room. And it really bugs me if the chain hangs down and makes that awful noise. Now that really drives me crazy."

I asked him to describe the noise of the fan—to mimic it for me. When he did, it not only sounded louder than I would have described the swirling air from a ceiling fan, but his "sound" did not match the sound that I would have made.

I didn't really know where I was heading with these questions. Remember, this was the first individual that had ever told me these kinds of things, so all of his words were a shocking revelation. I desperately wanted to keep this line of communication open. I kept assuring Nicholas that he was going to be able to help not only himself, but also many others by his willingness to share his innermost thoughts. Nicholas said that he didn't think he has ever known silence, that there were always noises in his head. The thought that he never had any relief from the noise disturbed and overwhelmed me. OSHA (Occupational Safety and Health Association) requires that there be so much on–time and off–time in factories where there is a lot of noise. Aside from audiological damage, the noise will literally cause medical problems in people. WAIT, what was that thought? Noise could cause medical problems in people? Of course it could. How about the effect of constant noise on Nicholas? What about his headaches, stomach aches and allergies?

I wanted to pursue this subject more, but both Nicholas and I were so emotionally drained that we couldn't handle another thought. We sat in the car and cried bucket of tears. Nicholas cried out of frustration and a determination to figure himself out, and I cried out of guilt. As a parent I am supposed to protect and guide my child, and to have or find the answers to help my child. I had been going through my life with my eyes closed and had missed so many things about my own son. Or, had my eyes been so wide open and full of wonder at the prospect of helping to light candles for so many children and adults with special needs that I didn't dream that my own child could be suffering from auditory anomalies?

I was so proud of Nicholas for taking the risk to say some of these things . . . the risk that some adults might say, "That's hogwash!" He is so bright that he needed to thoroughly analyze it himself before presenting it to me.

I came home and told my husband, Phil, every word of my conversation with Nicholas. After I had read *The Sound of a Miracle*, I woke him up at 3 A.M. to talk about it, and he said lovingly, "Sally, it makes sense to me!" This was his reassuring reply to me for a second time. He did not allow himself to enter into the guilt and self–beating that I felt. I felt so sad . . . sad that we had not helped Nicholas when he begged for it in so many subtle ways . . . sad that I had not known any of these things about my child. And sad most of all that we had called him an "underachiever" which is really one of the ugliest things you can possibly say to a child. But when you have two "overachieving" parents, the possibility of an underachieving child was very confusing and frustrating. BOY, HAD WE MISSED THE BOAT!

Phil brought it all into perspective for me, and for us as a family. We really can do that for one another . . . when I am weak, he is the strong one, and vice versa. He was so excited by this new-found information that he went to Nicholas and had a wonderful conversation with him. He experienced a new closeness in understanding Nicholas for the first time. We had learned so much about our son that day! Now we could move forward to help him!

"Get off your sad guilt trip, Sally," I said to myself. "Today is the first day of the rest of Nicholas' life. Don't dwell on what we didn't do to help Nicholas, forge ahead to learn more about him, and then figure out the strategies to help him. YEAH!"

Why do parents, mothers especially, fall for the guilt? In the age of Dr. Bruno Bettleheim, mothers blamed themselves because "they didn't love their babies enough and made them autistic!" Those poor "refrigerator Moms." I needed to heed what my sweet spouse was saying. "Don't worry about yesterday, we have no control over that . . . focus on tomorrow."

The thought that Nicholas had never known **silence** really puzzled me, and I wanted to question him more. I got him up at 6 A.M. the next morning and took him to the back yard. We live on a golf course in the piney woods of East Texas . . . literally in a forest. I said, "Okay, this is as close to silence as I can find. Dad and I like to come out here early in the morning, get into the hot tub, and enjoy the quiet, the silence of the forest. I'm going to stand next to you and tell you what I hear or don't hear. Remember that what you are describing to me is not a difference in the sound, but a difference in your perception of the sound. When I stand next to you, if there is a sound, we will both hear it. The incoming sound will be the same for both of us, but our perception of the sound makes us hear it differently."

I stood next to him and said, "I hear nothing. I do not perceive any sound. It is quiet to me." Nicholas just laughed and laughed!!!!

"You're kidding me," he said.

"No, I'm not kidding. I hear silence. What do you hear?" Everything that Nicholas told me shocked me. Again I had that old feeling of disbelief that we had not figured any of this out for ourselves. He mimicked seven different kinds of bird calls that he could hear in the trees that morning. He told me about the conversations of people walking in the neighborhood out of sight. Leaves were falling from a tree in my view. I said, "What does that sound like to you?" as I pointed in the direction of the falling leaves.

He quickly answered, "Maracas!" He looked at me puzzled and said, "Well, what did it sound like to you?" I replied that the leaves did not make a sound . . . I merely saw them fall. I perceive no sound at all. He looked at me as if to say, "Mom, you are really strange!"

I had finally begun to ask the right questions, and the answers were there. We had not known what to ask, therefore we were not getting the information we needed to understand the perceptual differences in these children. AND we had not been listening to the answers.

We learned that Nicholas had other sensory differences as well. If I wanted to have a serious conversation, he would never look at me. He wanted to sit on the floor and rub the carpet. It was his way of concentrating but we didn't know it at the time. The rubbing made a noise that masked out distracting noises. We never knew that fabric and clothing, particularly socks, really bothered him. He didn't like the feel of the material on his skin.

Nicholas has a very different pain threshold and can tolerate extremes of heat and cold. He can walk barefoot on coral that would cut my hand without feeling any pain on the bottom of his feet. You can scratch his arms and legs until he bleeds and he doesn't feel it. BUT, the beds of his toenails and fingernails are extremely sensitive. It is a combination of hyper- and hypo-sensitive skin receptors.

One day Nicholas brought me a paperback book he had been reading and said, "I can't read this cheap book—I need to get the hardbound copy." When I asked why, he said that he could see the words from the other side of the page coming through the page he was trying to read. HE COULD READ BACKWARDS AND FORWARDS FROM BOTH PAGES! It made me wonder how many individuals in the world have been labeled dyslexic who may, in fact, have hypersensitive vision and other sensory differences.

One wonderful aspect of Nicholas' hypersensitive vision is his ability to work puzzles. He can work a thousand–piece puzzle with no difficulty. He tells me that he can see the edges of the pieces so precisely that it's very easy to find where to place them.

Nicholas' Sensory Integration Occupational Therapist says that Nicholas requires a lot of vestibular stimulation. He can ride all amusement park rides ten or twelve times. It was discovered that swinging in the school playground for thirty minutes helped to calm him and enabled him to focus better in the afternoon.

We discovered that crowded restaurants were a nightmare for him. He could hear the alarms, the fluorescent lights, and noises from the kitchen. He didn't like the noise of people chewing their food or the scraping noise of utensils on dishes.

Nicholas went through AIT training in April, 1993. We kept a diary so we wouldn't forget ANYTHING.

Two weeks after training he was sleeping better and read two hundred and fifty pages of a book for pleasure. Before, there had always been distractions when he tried to read at night. He began to join in more family activities, and answered the first time we called him. He ran track during training and almost broke the city record. His coach, who knew nothing about the training, said, "I can't believe this is the same child! Not only did he win, but he listened to me for the first time in his life." When I asked Nicholas what was different, he said, "No one told me that Coach was trying to give me instructions. All I could ever hear was the air blowing through my ears when I ran."

We had not told the school what we were doing until we could get some unbiased comments. One teacher commented that he had an "inner calmness" that was different. Another teacher said, "He's paying attention, what's the deal?" They had known Nicholas for so long that they noticed these subtle differences right away.

Three months after training, Nicholas was more responsive to the world. He was less fidgety, and read eighteen hundred pages of books for pleasure. He was able to sleep in the car for the first time. Before training, the mobile phone antenna and the rear window defrost sounded like wind chimes to him, so he would pretend to be asleep.

Family members noticed changes in his facial features and commented that he was so much more relaxed and comfortable with people. He had never wanted to go to his brother's baseball games before because of the noise. Now, he not only went, he sat in the scorekeepers' cage, kept the score, and announced the players.

At six months his classroom performance and homework were showing more consistent learning. When his teacher praised his poetry as "phenomenal," Nicholas said, "I've always had those good words in my head, I just couldn't get them down on paper." He continues to show an increased interest in reading and an overall positive attitude.

Nine months after training we went on a cruise and Nicholas tolerated noise that even I had trouble with. His teachers report that he is paying better attention in the classroom, staying on task, and keeping his desk cleaner.

Both as a professional and a parent, I had a lot to learn about "aftercare." I thought that after AIT things would just kind of fall into place, that we would just wait and see what happened. I had talked to other parents and counseled them about aftercare, but until you experience AIT in your family you don't realize how much work is left to do.

A lot of the work involved educating the teachers that what they perceive as behavior problems are really perceptual differences. My husband and I stayed in touch with Nicholas' teachers, and were active in his classes, to show our support and willingness to help.

The things we wanted to work on were increased and sustained attention, increasing appropriate behavior, and improving Nicholas' organizational ability both at school and at home. We also wanted to work on improving Nicholas' self–image. Although he had used his amazing coping strategies to compensate successfully for thirteen years, we wanted to see a curriculum based on success, not failure. Simple, effective modifications were made that allowed Nicholas to be successful, using the skills that were his strong points.

Auditory Training opened the first door for Nicholas. It was our responsibility to make sure that that door led to a hallway with lots of other doors (tutoring, speech pathology, behavior training, etc.) If the door opens onto a broom closet filled with junk, we have done no service for our child.

In addition to his sports, social, and academic progress, Nicholas has developed a natural musical ability with the guitar. His teacher says that his skill cannot be taught, you either have it or you don't. His music teacher reports that he has developed what she calls "perfect pitch," and believes he never could have achieved it without AIT!

It has become perfectly clear, as we put it all into perspective, that God had placed Nicholas in our home so that we could light a candle of hope in his life, learn from him, and help him and many others like him. (And, of course, so that we could practice on him!!!)

We now feel that we have achieved, as much as we possibly could, consistent learning. In our continuing commitment to help those who learn to a different drummer, I would like to share this poem entitled:

Learning to a Different Drummer

How will I ever get any better,
If no one has the time to teach?
If I sit on the sidelines all my life,
What goals will I ever reach?
I can't keep up with the kids in my class,
Don't compare me to my brothers.
Just give me a chance to grow at my pace,
Without competing with the others.
Wish someone would try to teach me,
Though I can't learn like the rest.
If someone cared enough to reach me,
I promise, I'd really do my best! ∎

Chapter 10

Jessica

by Kate Pius

"Congratulations! you're having a baby." When the nurse told me I was pregnant at the obstetrician's office, I wasn't surprised. I had known from the moment our baby was conceived. At twenty–three, with a secure life, a new home, and a growing family, this period of my life was matched by no other. It had a dreamlike quality, and was almost too wonderful to be true.

Except for gestational diabetes which was controlled by a proper diet, my pregnancy was without complications. I was vigilant about the doctors' recommendations, and avoided all nasty substances like caffeine, nicotine, and alcohol. I walked every day, and during the walk would pray to God that if there were to be any suffering involved in the pregnancy, to let it be mine.

Dawn, one of my dearest friends, coached me through labor, waiting for the greatest moment for any mother, bringing new life into the world. After twenty–nine hours, it was nearing delivery time, and the doctor, half asleep, examined me and walked out of the room. Confused and worried, I asked Dawn, "What's wrong?" She said she heard the doctor say,

"She's too small, she won't be able to deliver this baby. We're going to have to do a C–Section." I was ready to wring his neck because he could have determined this hours ago. Another doctor who had arrived to assist, examined me and disagreed.

"It'll be some work, but you can do this," he said.

"Hey! When is this going to get bad?" I said to Dawn.

"Are you crazy? This is bad now," she replied. After four hours of pushing, the baby was almost born when the doctor, obviously scared, told me to stop. The umbilical cord was around the baby's neck. As soon as he removed it, she was born. I caught a glimpse of her and felt joy and the most perfect love. But she didn't cry.

"Why isn't she crying?" I asked, grabbing Dawn's arm.

"She's not breathing!"

"She's going to breathe," the doctor reassured me. He laid her on a table and put his hands against the side of her head near her ears. Immediately she pulled her knees up and the horrible silence that had blanketed the room was broken by her cry. February 23, 1990, at 12:53 A.M., and she was finally here safely. I remembered my walks and thought, smiling, 'Okay, Lord, it worked out as we planned it,' and I fell asleep.

Jessica was happy and so very beautiful and normal. As she grew, however, I wondered why she didn't do the things all other babies did. I felt awkward when she wouldn't make eye contact, or coo and laugh at times when other babies seemed to. In terms of "rankings" and "percentiles" she was big and healthy–looking, so people around me would agree with me that she was just quiet, it was just her personality. After all, she laughed and giggled when we bounced her on our knees and played with her. What did I know? The doctor always said she was healthy.

At five months, Jessica played with all her rattles and gadgets for hours at a time with her full attention. My husband thought this was a godsend. Who could ask for anything better? She could entertain herself for hours.

Her sleep patterns were irregular, and getting her to sleep was a chore. She would be up for five hours at a time, and was almost always awake very early in the morning. Sometimes she would sleep in the car, but otherwise, she would cry for the duration of the drive unless I gave her toys to play with. I thought this was normal, she wanted something to do. What child doesn't? Nothing seemed to be out of the ordinary. All babies are fussy at times, have tempers, and want their way. At least she wasn't a picky eater. She always wanted to eat and weighed thirty pounds by her first birthday.

At eighteen months everything was fine and the doctor said she was physically healthy, but he asked me to come into his office and close the door. I thought this was odd. He told me I should spend more time with Jessica, and that if that didn't solve the problem, she should be evaluated by a child psychologist. I was furious. She was always in the care of either my husband or myself. She was never neglected in any way. When I repeated the doctor's comments to my husband and family they thought they were preposterous.

Life went on with the question in the back of mind, 'Is my child okay?' When I saw children the same age as Jessica interacting and talking, I thought, 'Jessica is just not talking, she'll talk soon.' Relatives tried to reassure me with stories of distant cousins who didn't say a word until they were five, but I was alarmed.

I worried about the way she played with toys, stacking them up, organizing them, or grabbing them and throwing them, but not understanding how they were meant to be used. Instead of scribbling with crayons, for instance, she just lined them up. She put everything in her mouth. I tried not to think it was abnormal, I wanted to believe it was just child's play.

When we went to the beach, she would bury her head in the sand. To prevent her from doing this, I had to carry her, thirty pounds of Jessica and a full gadget bag. I hoped she would walk soon.

By the end of the summer, Jessica was becoming more and more stubborn, harder to please, and less interested in things around her. People who "knew" told me the terrible twos were coming. She would take out all the pots, pans, Tupperware, and canned goods, and really make a mess. This was on the borderline of cute, and I'd seen it before in other kids, but not to this degree.

I didn't want to shut her out, and getting meals on the table while keeping her constantly amused and interacting was hectic. Since she didn't comprehend that I needed time to do things, I had to catch up after she went to sleep.

Things didn't get easier as the holidays approached. Shopping with her in the stroller was impossible because she always demanded my undivided attention and wouldn't stop crying until she got it. When I tried to explain away her behavior, ignore it, and continue to shop, I would wind up giving in because I couldn't stand to see her cry.

My younger brother and his girlfriend went out to Ohio to visit my older brother, and when they came back they told me that my nephew, only two months older than Jessica, was talking and playing like a "little person." I felt Jessica was missing out. I thought maybe she wasn't talking because she constantly had ear infections. Sometimes she would say a word and never say it again, it was almost comical. Every time, I was sure she would soon begin to chatter away, but it didn't happen. It was upsetting that she didn't interact even with friends and family members who were familiar to her. She would sit on my lap for only ten seconds, even if I tried to play with her, and it seemed she just didn't care about the people around her and didn't warm up to anyone.

When she was almost two, I made an appointment with a school psychologist at an early learning center. After we got there, Jessica climbed all over the waiting room, and during the hour–long evaluation, she wouldn't greet anyone, neither the psychologist nor the other two people present. She just sat on a chair playing with the vertical blinds. When she was shown how to put pegs into holes, she lined them up on the floor instead. I tried to defend her, explaining that her ear infections made her grumpy.

The psychologist devastated me when he gave me his diagnosis: Jessica was autistic and needed to be enrolled in a special program. I was completely incredulous and started to cry. Although I knew the term autistic and knew it was a horrible fate, I had no idea what it really meant. "Do you mean she's like Rain Man?" I asked, all the while thinking that my daughter was beautiful and healthy, not severely handicapped. I managed to make an appointment to come back with my husband, grabbed Jessica, and left. I will never forget that day. I brought Jessica to the car and kept staring at her, thinking about what it would mean if this were true, and what to do next. I drove home feeling numb, deep in thought, going back and forth in my mind between what to do now and insisting that they must be wrong.

My husband called his parents, told me to talk to his mother, and went to give Jessica a bath. In my mother–in–law's objective and intelligent way, she didn't dismiss the diagnosis, and said she had always been concerned about Jessica's lack of eye contact. We cried together as we agreed that we both knew something was wrong. I thought I was going to die. None of us knew what all this meant, or how we even felt about autism except that it hurt. The heaviness of the grief and loss was dominating our lives. I still couldn't believe it.

None of this pity was any good for me. I wasn't strong enough to detach from the pain, but I knew I wanted to do anything I could to improve the situation, and hopefully to prove that the psychologist was wrong. I could feel my husband's pain, also, although he didn't talk about it openly.

That first weekend was a horror. I cried a lot, trying to deal with my anger and sorrow. At the end of the week I finally brought myself to make an appointment with my pediatrician. She didn't make a diagnosis, but she advised me that something was wrong, and I decided to make an appointment with a pediatric neurologist recommended to me by my mother–in–law. He was a highly regarded specialist in his field, and two and a half months later, when he could finally see us, he gave Jessica an MRI. We went back and forth for months, waiting for the results, it was nothing short of a horrible, expensive, unprofessional joke. I'll share what I learned from his expertise: "Relative to prognosis, with the significant impairment in communication and a complicating autistic behavior, it is anticipated that there will be improvement in function, but ultimate prognosis must be guarded." This man was useless! All he could recommend was that she be enrolled in an early intervention program. We wanted to know what *we* could do for Jessica, how we could help her. We had no idea, and it was terrible to feel so helpless. I didn't know what to tell people, how to explain it. The more I thought about how much I loved her, the more I wanted to help and the more I hurt.

I took Jessica everywhere I went. We travelled to Ohio to visit her cousin, and I could compare them face to face and feel a weight of sadness, she was so far behind him. We went to the supermarket, and for her it was like a giant kitchen. If I took my eyes off her for a second, she'd be grabbing cans.

Researching autism was like digging in quicksand, I read everything I could and nobody could tell me what to do or what to expect that was positive. Nothing made any sense to me. I didn't have any hope until I read *The Sound of a Miracle* and began to understand why Jessica pulled my ears and other people's, why she didn't like music, why she had tantrums, banged her head, and hummed. It seemed so obvious that her hearing was abnormal. Through friends I had heard about an audiologist named Shelley Francis who practiced auditory training nearby, and I couldn't wait to see her.

I tried to convince Jessica's behavior modification therapist that Jessica had a problem with sound. I described AIT and urged her to take a serious look at it. I was ranting and raving about it, people thought I was nuts. Good for them! They cautioned me that it was not a well–known therapy, which I knew well, and they reminded me that Jessica was happy and didn't know what autism was, and that the label didn't have to stick. They said she would come out of it. In spite of their opinions, I wasn't about to sit back and wait when I knew I was on the verge of a good change in Jessica's life.

Jessica was twenty–seven months old when we arrived at Shelley's office in East Meadow, Long Island, for our first session of auditory integration training. Jessica's head was sensitive, she had always resisted putting on a hat, or having her hair combed or washed, and loud music had also annoyed her. We had to restrain her for the first session, as she struggled to break free of the headphones, screaming and crying as if to ask why she had to endure so much discomfort. I questioned why I was causing my child such pain, and wondered if it could be worth it.

After the first session was over, she seemed calmer in the car, less fussy than she had ever been. When we returned later that afternoon, dreading the second session, she tugged on her left ear, looked at Shelley, walked into the sound–proof booth, and sat down. I had never seen her so intent on doing something, she seemed determined to continue with AIT all on her own initiative. It was too much to grasp at one time, and I didn't want to read anything into it too deeply, but I was on cloud nine. Both Shelley and I were amazed. With each passing session. Jessica's resistance dwindled, and by the last day she put on the head phones herself, sat by herself, and smiled when the music came on. Because we couldn't obtain an audiogram, we weren't sure if all the hypersensitivity was excised, but there were clearly changes in her behavior from the beginning.

Her contact and interaction with people improved, and her ability to understand. When we were getting ready for a session and she actually brought me her comb and allowed me to put her hair in a pony tail, I was completely surprised. She had always enjoyed watching me feed the ducks but had had no interest in throwing bread to them herself. Now she took it from me when I offered it, broke it, and gave it to the ducks. The only difference in our trips to the ducks was the fact that when she fed the ducks herself, it was post therapy. Another change was that she was able to recognize things, people, and places. I would tell her I saw a tree, and when I asked, "Where's the tree?" she would point to it. I had always tried to get her to do this, explaining, talking, showing, and waiting for a reply, and now, for the first time, I was getting responses. She began to play with toys appropriately. A doll was now a little person to be treated kindly, not thrown on the floor. A car was not something that flew through the air, it rolled. She went to bed more easily and at a regular bedtime. She stopped biting, kicking and punching, and seemed more at peace. She would walk beside me instead of my having to carry her. Most importantly, she would listen. Before AIT, you could call her name and she would ignore you. Now she would look at you and give you her attention. Sometimes she would do as she was asked, not always, but at least sometimes. She started trying to use sounds in response to questions, instead of staring blankly or humming.

In some areas she didn't respond as well. She still cringed at the sound of music, washing her hair continued to be a problem, and her attention span was still short. But all her therapists and teachers commented on how much she had improved.

Just before her three–month follow–up visit to Shelley, Jessica seemed to regress. Her stubbornness and aggressiveness towards others returned, and she would grab peoples' ears, pull hard, and pinch them. She seemed to plateau in her growth, and I thought she needed a second round of AIT. Shelley wanted to wait six months, and when she had completed the last session of her second round of AIT, Jessica was finally able to listen to music on the car radio on the way home, and to watch television for the first time as well.

It is nine months later, and she has made great progress. She is potty trained, puts words together creatively, and understands what she says. She can draw recognizable pictures. She knows where she is and where she is going, and expresses interest in going places. Socially, she has come alive. Her gregariousness is remarkable. She asks for her friends with excitement and love. She shares and plays and has become a leader in the sense that she makes certain everybody is in on playtime. She knows how to count, knows how old she is (three), recognizes the name of her home town, talks to people on the phone, asks for people she hasn't seen in a while, and remembers people, places and things almost photographically. When I told her we were going to Uncle John's house, she thought I meant my brother, whom we had visited in Ohio before AIT. She kept saying, "Sue, Philip, and baby Joey." She was visibly confused when we arrived at Uncle John's house and it was a different Uncle John, my uncle, her great–uncle, whom she had never met. Even though she had been barely two and practically nonverbal, she had remembered the names of everyone in the family in Ohio.

She listens now, and understands instructions, realizing she can't always have her own way and has to answer to authority. The happiest thing for me is that people don't treat her differently. Strangers don't think her behavior is unusual, and treat her like the happy, developing, loving, beautiful child she is. I can't over-emphasize just how happy I believe she is.

I now understand autism to be a sensory integration disorder. Vision therapy is our next project, another therapy many professionals discount as too new, along with AIT and vitamins. Many professionals haven't even heard of these therapies. I strongly believe that at times you must follow your heart and judgment by never locking doors you haven't even opened. Many times prior to Shelley's diagnosis, for instance, I'd had Jessica's tested by an audiologist, and she always checked out fine. This was misleading, but I couldn't let it lead to a dead end.

In retrospect, although speech therapy, occupational therapy, and sensory integration were useful, AIT jump-started Jessica's development in a miraculous way. I'm not qualified to prescribe it, and don't wish to overglorify it, but I feel strongly that it should be taken seriously and not overlooked by health-care professionals.

I truly know that my daughter has been given a new life where she is not in her own world but can function as an integral part of our society. I thank God for all the help she has received, and most of all, I thank Him for leading me to a Miracle! ∎

Chapter 11

Steven

by Bonnie Glow

Dan and I were married in September, 1980. A talented musician, he developed a home music business and shop which I eventually helped him run. We had Steven in 1985, and because he was in a breech position, he was born by planned Caesarian section. There were no complications, and Dan, elated with his first child, eagerly took care of him while I breastfed and recovered slowly from surgery. He proved to be an unusually dedicated father, then and later.

Steven weighed 7 lb. 10 oz., had good Apgar scores, and was a contented, quiet baby. He slept well between feedings, and was sleeping through the night by eight weeks. He made happy cooing noises, and his big brown eyes sparkled when he smiled. While he was still a baby, Dan began a ritual of reading to him every day.

During the first year of his development, he appeared to be normal, although he liked to roll across the room in addition to sitting up and crawling. At ten months we took him on a camping trip and he was extremely sociable with the people we met. Every kind of food appealed to him, and the doctor was pleased with his growth. He had only one ear infection, treated with antibiotics for ten days, and had no adverse reactions to the standard vaccinations.

As his language developed, single words were intermingled with a variety of indistinguishable sounds. Unlike most toddlers, he didn't get into everything, wasn't particularly curious, and was agile and graceful, with exceptional gross motor development. He was oblivious to other children his age. He was only mildly interested in the construction equipment when we put an addition on our house, and was upset when we moved him into his new bedroom. I questioned his language development and was reassured by the pediatrician that he would soon have a lot to say. By the time he was two, Steven could recognize and recite the alphabet and count forward and backward to ten, but he didn't converse.

Friends of ours had a family day care center, and Dan and I felt a few mornings a week there would help Steven's social development. He warmed up to the adults, but didn't interact with the other children. He either scattered toys or played with them inappropriately. Our friends advised us to call the town's educational service director. The director of special education there suggested we wait for an evaluation until our new baby was born, in hopes that the excitement of having a sibling might help his language development.

Lisa was born when Steven was two–and–a–half, a beautiful, healthy eight–pound baby girl whom Steven completely ignored. I told Dan I didn't think he even knew she existed. Our pediatrician continued to be oblivious. If I set fire to his office he wouldn't notice. He acted as if I was the one with a problem.

When we went on a camping trip in August in our mini–motorhome, Steven rode contentedly for hours in his car seat, but his behavior in public places made us uneasy. He would pace around the perimeter everywhere we went, never touching anything, and seemingly unaware of his surroundings. People gave us strange looks. One young woman took me aside. "My younger brother behaved like your son," she said. I looked pleadingly at her.

"What's he like now?" I asked.

"Oh, he's in high school now, in special ed, but he can read near grade level."

"Is he social? Does he talk much? Does he have friends?"

"Well, he really prefers to be by himself, but he's come a long way."

"Thanks for the encouragement," I said sincerely. I still had no idea what I was dealing with.

Steven was three in October, and although the pediatrician still maintained he was developing normally, he was uninterested in toilet training and began rejecting almost all the foods he had previously liked. Thinking he was bored at home with his mom and dad and still unacknowledged sister, we sent him to nursery school three mornings a week. When his teacher noticed that he played inappropriately, was unable to interact socially, and was obviously language delayed, she suggested he be evaluated by special ed professionals. A psychologist observed Steven several times, both at school and at home. "There is nothing in Steven's environment that would have caused his problems," she said, which was not only a relief, but also a surprise since it had never entered my mind that we could be regarded as unfit parents.

In January, he was placed in our areas's regional school for children with special needs. His teacher accepted him where he was, built on his strengths, and was patient and loving. Steven took to her, allowing her to redirect his aggressive behavior. His speech continued to be almost unintelligible, and he had almost no eye contact. Unable to focus in a group, he preferred to be alone or with an aide. On the plus side, he could do unusually complex puzzles, operate a VCR, count to thirty, and recognize many printed words.

To cope with Steven's finicky eating, I had to be creative. I mixed dried barley grass (a powdered form of green vegetables) with peanut butter, put eggs in milkshakes, and mixed finely chopped meat or chicken with soft cheese.

Toilet training Steven continued to elude us. He began smearing the contents of his diaper in his hair, on the floor, on the walls, or on his clothes, and did the same with food. When we tried keeping him in overalls, he soon learned to unfasten them. Cleaning him up was a challenge. He yelled and screamed in the shower as if in pain, and would turn the water off whenever we tried to fill the bathtub. This negative behavior was balanced by some progress socially. Once, while listening to music in school, he got up and went over to the toys and picked out a toy bus for himself. Sitting down next to a boy with Down's Syndrome, he noticed him, got up again, and returned with a toy bus for him, too.

When Lisa was six months old, we hired a babysitter to work for three afternoons a week while I helped Dan in the store. Robyn was gregarious, fun and physical, she made everything a game, and Steven's difficult behavior and toileting habits didn't phase her. Soon he was expanding his repertoire of memorized songs and amusing jingles, initiating some speech, and playing with his outgoing little sister. We were fortunate to have Robyn's devotion and guidance for the next two years, aided by frequent visits from two wonderfully helpful girls, sitters–in–training, who lived across the street.

Although I felt God was far away from me and my problems, at the urging of a friend who had helped deliver Lisa, I began to go to a Bible Study at her church. I was depressed, but was able to draw strength and comfort from the group, and they taught me to begin to trust in the Lord for all things. Through listening to their stories of divine intervention in all kinds of hardships, I began to believe that He could turn any bad situation into a triumphant one.

By the time Lisa was eighteen months old, she had surpassed her four–year–old brother in language development. Although he appeared to be intelligent and was a strong visual learner, he wanted nothing to do with auditory learning. A neurologist we consulted in Hartford diagnosed him as either autistic, PDD, or language–delayed. "He may never learn to talk correctly, and he could be mentally retarded although his abnormal brain development won't appear on a brain scan." She had come to her conclusions in five minutes, and had offered her diagnosis with the finesse of Attila the Hun, leaving us in a state of anger and confusion, and adding to my depression. My friend, Helen, consoled me: "The mother knows the child," she said, reinforcing the hope I'd always had for Steven.

At last we found a caring, kind pediatrician, Dr. Gregory Runkel, who speculated that Steven was mildly autistic, and who felt that the right education would be extremely important. Steven began attending school for a full day. His teacher was competent, cheerful, and firm, and Steven made progress in all areas including toilet training and accepting a wider variety of foods.

At Sunday school, I was reassured that Steven was welcome and loved unconditionally. My depression miraculously lifted when our pastor and the elders anointed us with oil and prayed over us. When I prayed quietly one night, "Lord, please help Steven to say his own prayers himself," a voice, clear and audible, assured me, "It won't be that long." I turned around to see who was there, and there was no one.

The summer he was five, Steven finally became toilet trained. Camping, hiking, and swimming were favorite activities, along with amusement park rides, and going to the college farm nearby to pet and feed the animals. Steven played and interacted to some extent with Lisa, and they developed games like "house" and "picnic." The games lasted for only a few minutes, but they represented a big improvement. He began calling us Mommy and Daddy.

In school his teacher felt he could be mainstreamed into day care for part of the day in preparation for kindergarten next year. We were thrilled when he found himself a "girlfriend" who held his hand. Although he still acted out destructively and aggressively in the classroom sometimes, we were optimistic, and Dr. Runkel was amazed at his progress. "Keep up the good work because it's working," he said.

When Steven began kindergarten, he was mainstreamed with an aide for both morning and afternoon sessions. Although he couldn't say more than a couple of words at a time, his memory for vocabulary words was impressive. The other children thought Steven was smart, but he couldn't interact with them because of his language deficits. He could only engage in parallel play and didn't talk to anyone his age. He loved kindergarten because of his energetic, fun–loving teacher, Nancy Rucker. She capitalized on his skills by bringing out a large assortment of wooden building blocks and encouraging Steven to make a roadway with bridges and curves which encompassed the room. She took pictures of it. Steven's aide, who was experienced with nonverbal children, encouraged him to draw, and he was finally able to make his first drawing of a simple face with a smile on it.

Dr. Fein, a neuropsychologist who had evaluated him before, saw him again and was amazed at his progress, especially in reading. "He should not be able to read at all because of his language problems," she said. "I can't understand it." She didn't think he was autistic or PDD, and I was in no hurry for a label since whatever it was, the treatment would be the same.

Steven's speech therapist was friendly and patient, and helped him become proficient at the computer. He adored her. She used a small computer, a Zygo Macaw, to help build his speech, where he could push a button with a picture on it to get a sentence he wanted to say. It helped him learn to find appropriate words on his own, and his spontaneous language grew to two and three word sentences although he still couldn't use pronouns or answer yes–no questions with much accuracy.

My friend Helen continued to be a steady, positive and spiritual influence in my life. Her cheerfulness, hope and certainty helped me feel grounded. When her youngest daughter was married and Dan was unable to attend the ceremony, I went to the church alone, and sitting there, I imagined Lisa's wedding. I wondered if Steven would ever come that far. As I watched the bride and groom at the altar with their backs to me, I rubbed and blinked my eyes. The bride's auburn hair became dark, long and wavy, and the attendants faded away until there was a glow around the bride and groom. The groom's tuxedo became light silver–gray and he became taller, his blond hair turning to light brown. I couldn't see his face until he turned to his bride to speak to her, smiling and looking down as his hair fell across his forehead. It was my own son Steven. The vision was to remain vivid and real in my mind.

As I had been led to expect, Steven began to say his own prayers at bedtime, in language that had improved although it still wasn't very clear. At home he was basically compliant, and tried hard to please, but in school he was sometimes aggressive, occasionally hitting his aide and his classmates and squeezing their necks. Sometimes he would find his own behavior hilarious and would even put himself in time–out, laughing from his chair. His classmates avoided him, and he began to regress in his toilet training. Thinking he might have imbalances in his body chemistry which were contributing to his problems, a naturopathic doctor suggested an organic acids test. A sample of Steven's urine was frozen and sent to the lab.

Dr. Fein visited the school to observe Steven. She witnessed his stubborn and disruptive behavior firsthand along with the great strides he had made academically, where he was reading simple books, writing short sentences, and excelling at the computer. The following month she gave us a diagnosis of severe receptive language disorder with attention deficit hyperactivity disorder (ADHD) as a secondary problem. Her recommendations for first grade were to mainstream him for lunch, recess, and gym, and possibly some art and music, with intensive remedial work and speech therapy and a small contained class of two or three children for academics.

Terry Fers, his speech therapist, feeling as we did that his frustration was related to language, challenged us with the idea that his hearing might have some distortions, making language difficult to learn. He still called himself "Steben" for example, because he couldn't articulate a "v" sound. We found it both a relief and a let down when his standard audiogram was normal.

I got some added insight into Steven's hearing when I watched Annabel and Georgie's appearance on the *Sally Jessy Raphael* show. I was amazed to see Georgie draw a map of Africa in its entirety from memory, with all the countries properly named. She was obviously brilliant, and yet she'd had far more problems than Steven. Here she was an honors college graduate, a talented artist, socially normal and happily married. Annabel said, "Georgie heard normally according to a standard audiogram which was useless in her diagnosis of hypersensitive hearing." When she said, "AIT has moved autistic children into the learning disabled (LD) category, and LD kids into the normal category," I became driven as never before to find this therapy for my son. I tracked Annabel down. She gave me the names of parents whose children had had AIT, and some of the practitioners trained in the procedure. With every phone call I made, I became more certain that Steven could be helped, and that my prayers had been answered.

Steven's Planning and Placement Team meeting (PPT) was coming up in a few days, and I was excited about sharing my new and promising information on AIT. Terry, Steven's speech pathologist, was enthusiastic, but Dr. Fein said she didn't think it really worked and that she wouldn't waste her time and money on it. Undaunted, I called an AIT practitioner whose office was an hour away, and although she had a waiting list, an appointment soon opened up.

Four days into the AIT program, Steven began using pronouns correctly and speaking in longer spontaneous sentences. His speech became clearer. He was able to replace v's with b's and pronounced Steven properly. We witnessed the emergence of a much calmer, more verbal and social little boy. He made his first self-initiated verbal contact with another boy his age on the last day of the training. He no longer had a problem with toilet training, and he began to enjoy taking showers and running a bath. When we realized combing his hair was no longer a problem, we decided to risk taking him to the barber, an unthinkable action in the past. "This is the best behaved child I've had all day," said the barber. Sally, our practitioner, explained that before AIT the shower and the bath running had sounded overwhelmingly loud to Steven, and the comb and scissors next to his ears had been deafening.

We could see a significant change in his comprehension. He responded better to questions and simple directions and improved in his ability to focus and sustain attention. He and Lisa had more fun together, and developed a horse and rider game where Steven was the horse. They were able to share coloring books and crayons for the first time, all the more amazing since Steven had never enjoyed coloring before. Regressions involving new behavior such as refusing to go outside or wandering around the house shaking a toy truck, were short–lived.

"Mommy, are you okay?" he asked with concern after I fell off my bike on a family mountain bike expedition. He had never before shown such an appropriate response to someone else's pain. Usually he had laughed when someone got hurt. Dan and I looked at each other with delight.

Six weeks after AIT, Steven happily entered first grade. Although I knew the teachers were prepared for the aggressive and destructive behavior and extremely short attention span of last year, Dan and I had seen so much improvement that we were optimistic. Steven's teacher right away picked up on his intelligence in math and recommended him for the gifted math program. His attention span and concentration had improved so much that he was able to keep up with the class, and soon was above grade level in reading and spelling. Unbothered by the noise and disturbances of the classroom, he was absorbing academics like a sponge.

With the help of his little socialite sister who included him in her play, Steven began to learn some appropriate social behavior. At his seventh birthday party in October, he had his first peer party ever, with classmates whom he invited himself. He played games with them, opened presents, shared toys, and even led a game of "Simon Says." Dan and I were overjoyed.

Our homeopathic doctor recommended B6 and magnesium supplements for Steven, and they seemed to calm him down and make him more focused. When he went without them for two weeks, his teachers, although they didn't know he was off the supplements, found him to be less cooperative.

When Steven's organic acid test results were in, we went to the doctor's office to discuss them. He had found two test results. I had asked him to postpone the original test until after Steven's AIT, and evidently the lab had neglected to cancel it, and had tested the urine given both pre and post AIT. The results of the first test, at 343 and 463, showed the extremely elevated levels of homovanillate (HVA) and vanillymandelate (VMA) normally associated with autism. (HVA and VMA are two organic by–products of adrenal hormones, norepinephrine and epinephrine, which stimulate the nervous system.) Post AIT, his levels were down to normal, at 97 and 125, proof on paper that AIT worked. Steven's nervous system had obviously been on sensory overload, with emotional shutdown the typical reaction. AIT, in reducing the overload, evidently allowed the brain to relax and function more efficiently. No wonder Steven had attention, language, comprehension, and social problems.

After school started, Steven had some additional temporary regression. He hit his aide and his father, making the other children afraid of him, but within a few months the hitting stopped, and Steven's classmates were forgiving and friendly again. Once more he was holding hands with the girls. A small baby was a frequent visitor to the school, and Steven tried to hold the baby, gently touching his face, stroking his hair and hugging him. He had missed this with Lisa.

Steven advanced academically at a rapid rate, impressing everyone with fast, accurate work. He was learning about money and time, which had never interested him before. Because of his exceptional visual memory, he could read at second grade level and spell at third grade level. His writing was neat, his memory for vocabulary was excellent, and he was especially talented on the computer. Although he still struggled with language, most of his work had become age appropriate and creative. His hyperactivity levels were down, which I associated with the change in his hearing. His drawing skill became age appropriate. By the middle of first grade, he was spending three quarters of his day in the classroom, leaving only for speech therapy, reading group and math enrichment. His wonderfully competent first grade teacher believed in his capabilities and pushed him to excel.

The message of AIT is spreading, but I could so easily have missed it, and I feel an urgency to make other parents aware of it. Dan and I had no indication of any sound sensitivities in Steven. He hadn't appeared to block out noises. We never would have guessed that his irritability, hyperactivity, inappropriate speech and odd behaviors were in any way sound–related.

I am so grateful to all Steven's dedicated caregivers, his teachers, aides, grandparents, babysitters, doctors, our friends, and those associated with AIT. Most of all, we give thanks to the Lord for putting people in Steven's life who brought about his remarkable shift to success. Once I was able to rediscover Him at my church and in my Bible Study group, I felt His presence through it all, and know that His love, mercy and glory is where it all begins and ends. ∎

Chapter 12

Asia

by Adair Renning

Both of our daughters were born in Korea. How they came to be part of our family through the process of adoption is no less amazing or miraculous than giving birth.

Jerry and I always knew that we would adopt. For us, it was never a question of "American made" versus "the imports," after all, this is a baby we're talking about here, not a car, and a baby is a baby is a baby. They all laugh and cry the same, need love the same, and have to have their diapers changed.

Our first visit to St. Louis County Social Services in Duluth, Minnesota, where we lived at the time, left us deeply depressed. We were placed at the bottom of a waiting list of a hundred and thirty-five families and told that we could not realistically expect the placement of a "homegrown" child (either black, white, bi-racial, or American Indian) for five to seven years. Although they didn't handle foreign adoptions, they referred us to several agencies who did. Ultimately we decided on Children's Home Society of Minnesota, in St. Paul. Children's Home Society had come into being as the end of the line for the Orphan Train, which brought children from the East coast to the Midwest in the late 1800's. Children's Home Society places children from several countries as well as the U.S., but proportionately arranges for the adoption of more Korean children than any other.

In March of 1980, during an intensive two-day pre-adoption counseling session with our social worker, Mary Abbett, we were shown referral packets for several children, to familiarize us with the information we would be receiving when a child was available for us.

Now let me explain here that I am Irish, which genetically predisposes me to premonition, intuition, mysticism, and comfortable acceptance of psychic phenomena. But nothing prepared me for my reaction to the second picture in the stack. Kim, Hee Young, born November 22, 1979. Fine black hair in a halo around her head made her look like a dandelion going to seed, a cupid's bow mouth and sparkling black eyes. Something inside me began to vibrate like a tuning fork, and I KNEW that this was our daughter. The signs were in the referral, too. Last name Kim (Jerry's sister's name is Kim). Her given name, Hee Young, means "she will be pretty like flowers and could share happiness to all." We worked in a greenhouse/florist. Her birthday was the day before Jerry's sister Kim's. I was right, of course, she was, and is our daughter, we named her Meghann, and the story of her adoption and arrival and first two years is part of another story. So let's fast forward to 1982.

Jerry and I knew we wanted to adopt more children, and although our name was moving up on the list at St. Louis County Social Services, we wanted another child from Korea. Because so many of the children available for adoption have physical, mental or emotional challenges, Children's Home Society of Minnesota (C.H.S.M) is always looking for parents for the Special Needs Kids. Jerry and I had discussed what challenges we felt we, as a family, could deal with. We agreed that we certainly could handle a condition which could be treated by surgery or therapy. I had often told Jerry that I had always felt drawn to autistic children, and thought that our home would be a good environment to provide the stimulation an autistic child would need. But, instinctively, I knew that I would KNOW the child immediately, as I had Meghann, and the medical condition would be secondary.

Our local adoptive parents support group, part of a national association (OURS), was busy planning a T.V. special in celebration of National Adoption week. This is traditionally held every year during Thanksgiving week. In preparation for the event, the nation headquarters had sent us much literature, balloons, past issues of their bi-monthly magazine, plus several copies of their 15th anniversary issue, the first with a glossy cover.

As usual, all work stopped when the magazine came, and as I thumbed through, one article caught my attention: "The Children of PACT Need you." PACT is an acronym for Partners Aiding Children Today, an organization which locates children with special needs whose prognosis is questionable, arranges for financial sponsors until the extent of their diagnosis is known, provides foster care, and if the child is an orphan, helps in finding their Forever Family.

All three beautiful children on the first page of the article were appealing, and all were in need of the time and care that PACT could provide for them. Turn the page . . . Child #5. She was described as a beautiful eighteen–month–old girl with Hirschprung's disease, which is a failure of the nerve endings at lower end of the colon to develop properly. A stoma (artificial anus) was created shortly after birth. Her emotional development was of more concern to Teri Bacall, the social worker, than her physical problems.

The paragraph went on to say that due to her special needs (the colostomy), she had been placed in a "baby home" until a foster mother could be found for her. She had not adjusted well to the orphanage and Teri was asking for sponsors to support her to see if time and stimulation in a loving foster home would help her to adjust.

My heart was pounding, it was happening again..THIS WAS OUR CHILD!!! I had no doubts about her, only my ability to convince everyone that I still had both oars in the water. The first step, as the smaller, logical side of my mind took over, was to call Children's Home Society, talk to Teri Bacall, the PACT social worker who had found Kyung Hee, and find out everything I could about sponsoring her. Since Teri was in Korea at the time, Bobbie Wiggins, another social worker at C.H.S.M., was able to give me some more information. Correct name (not the same as in the picture) was Oh, Kyung Hee. D.O.B. 4/4/81. She was a C–section baby whose mother had died a month later due to complications in childbirth. Her distraught father sent her two older brothers to live with relatives and neighbors and left Kyung Hee with Social Welfare Society for adoption because of her medical problems. She had been ill for most of the last eighteen months, Bobbie said, suffering from a variety of skin problems, eye infections, diarrhea and measles.

She was described as very fussy, with slow physical and behavioral development. At eighteen months old, a time when most toddlers are into everything, learning to talk, and generally a bundle of live wires, Kyung Hee was only beginning to roll over onto her stomach, could not sit up without support, and did not play with toys with her hands. Teri noted that Kyung Hee was "very irritable, with autistic–like symptoms and a possibility of retardation." Bobbie suggested that I call back in two weeks after Teri's return from Korea.

I was convinced that there was nothing wrong with that little girl that time, her surgery, and a loving family, complete with Mom, Dad, sister, two dogs and an assortment of birds and fish, plus good food couldn't cure.

Planning for the taping of the National Adoption Week TV special on November 6th managed to keep me busy, but part of my mind was racing with thoughts of Kyung Hee. Jerry and I agreed to make a few phone calls to our insurance company about coverage and our family doctor about her condition "just in case . . . " My mother arrived on November 16th in time for Meghann's third birthday, which we were celebrating on Thanksgiving Day. She took the news very well, that is, she didn't scream or cry or faint. She just looked at me as though I'd lost the last remaining shred of sanity I had left home with. Where would we get the money? (I didn't know yet, but we would.) What if she was retarded? (She wasn't.) What if the surgery didn't correct her condition? (It would, and if it didn't, we'd deal with it.) After two days of positive bombardment, my mother was a little less sure that I was crazy and a lot more attached to the picture of Kyung Hee.

November 22, 1982, was Meghann's third birthday. Teri had returned from Korea and left an update on Kyung Hee's condition with Bobbie. At that time, thanks to Teri and PACT'S efforts, she had been in a foster home for about six weeks and had made remarkable progress. She was described as a fat little girl who smiled easily. Her skin conditions had cleared and she was responding well to her foster mother. She could shake hands, wave bye–bye and clap. The main concern, still, was her inability to play with toys with her hands. She would drop or throw things down and then push them along with her index finger. Teri also felt that she was ready for permanent placement with a family that understood and could accept her developmental delays and health problems. And now for the kicker . . . our social worker, Mary Abbett, would be in Duluth on Wednesday with all available information. Would we be available to talk with her about the possibility of placing Kyung Hee with us? OH MY GOD!! Now we had to face the money hurdle immediately, instead of in two–three months. Well, this then, was the real test. IF we were meant to be the parents of this beautiful little girl, somehow the money part would be worked out. COME ON, MARY! The pictures Mary brought with her reminded me of Third World children who are severely malnourished with distended stomach, extremely thin arms and legs, and for the most part either expressionless or crying. In one picture, taken the day Kyung Hee left with her foster mother, her head had been shaved in an attempt to cure the continuous boils and skin disease. Mary said that the Korean agency was reluctant to place her, fearing that she would never be able to bond to a family. I just sat and cried.

Mary agreed to give us two weeks to figure out how to jump "THE MONEY HURDLE," and left with her car loaded with medical supplies we had collected to send to Korea.

The story of Meghann's adoption and arrival was born of an attempt to raise the money, and it was that story and the plight of Kyung Hee, who so desperately needed a family, that reached a group of business men who wished to remain anonymous, who were going to take care of the financial arrangements in the form of a long term, no interest loan. These total strangers knocked down the single largest barrier to our adoption. The only way we could ever thank them (besides paying them back, of course) was by proving them right in their assessment of us as a family. We immediately made an appointment for December 14th to sign the placement agreement and start in motion the wheels that would bring our daughter home.

The next ten days were spent in preparation for Jerry's parents' and grandparents' arrival for Christmas. The mail brought four new color pictures of Kyung Hee that Teri had taken in November. The changes were nothing short of remarkable. Her cheeks were rosy, her eyes sparkled, and there was even a picture of a smiling Kyung Hee, the best present of all. Early in January, Jerry and I received four more pictures and updated information, all positive. According to the Korean social worker's statement, she was "bright and responsive and no longer had a feeble, vacant expression." Clearly family life had been just what she needed.

We spent the rest of January calling physical and occupational therapists and surgeons in an attempt to learn everything we could about Kyung Hee's various challenges. I managed to locate a local family with a child with Hirschprung's disease, to get the Mom's perspective on day to day management and care.

It was time to choose a name. We decided to name her in honor of the single most important person in her life at the time, her foster mother, Mrs. Ae Ja Choi. We changed the spelling to Asia and kept Kyung Hee for her middle name. She became Asia Michaela Kyung Hee Renning.

Finally, on March 21, 1983, Mary called to tell us that Asia would be arriving at the Minneapolis–St. Paul Airport on Saturday, March 26th. I had a mental picture of Mary, holding the phone away from her ear to avoid the scream that followed.

We met our flight aide, Barb Dalley, at the airport at 4 P.M. We had thirty–three excited "Baby Greeters" in our party alone, and there were eight other children arriving, all with their own welcoming committees. Barb waved to me as she went on the plane to bring Asia off. As Barb handed her to me, all that really registered was the incredibly pained expression and huge black eyes of the child in my arms. She was absolutely terrified of the strange looking people, bright lights and loud noises. Korean–speaking friends tried to introduce her to us in Korean. Friends were pushing closer and cameras were flashing, and Asia began to cry. It was then that we learned that despite their best efforts, her escorts had not been able to locate colostomy bags for Asia. In Korea, a cloth diaper had been used to cover the stoma, held in place by a three–laced binder, similar to an old–fashioned corset. Because the colostomy has no sphincter muscles, it was functioning constantly, and if not cleaned immediately, her body's digestive enzymes would begin to irritate her skin. We had no bags either, and could get none until Monday, so we tried to make do with disposable diapers until we got home.

Dressed and dry, Asia appeared to rally a bit, but I was a complete wreck as I tried to mix a bottle for her. She was so much more frail than we had ever imagined. Her arms and legs were so thin and her muscle tone was so poor that when we picked her up under the arms, her arms would fly up over her head. There was no resistance at all in her shoulder muscles. All ten fingers were constantly crossing and uncrossing in all sorts of impossible combinations. She made strange, croaking noises in the back of her throat and ground her teeth together. She had no interest in the bottle or toys, and was comfortable only when Jerry's mother was rocking her.

Despite all warnings of bad weather and offers of places to stay for the night, Jerry and I were determined to make it back to Duluth. The blizzard turned a three–hour trip into five, with Meghann and me singing "Twinkle Twinkle Little Star" in Korean to comfort Asia. At least one person in the car (Meghann) "looked right" to Asia.

We arrived home around midnight, but we were all so wound up that sleep was impossible until nearly 2 A.M. We spent the time carrying Asia through the house and letting the dogs get to know her. They seemed to sense in that uncanny way of animals, that there was something a little different about this " human puppy," and were especially gentle with her.

We had set up the crib in Meghann's room, and finally got both girls settled in and collapsed into the waterbed, only to be awakened one hour later by Asia's terrified screams. She was completely disoriented, needed a diaper change in the worst way, and was absolutely terrified of me. I tried to fashion something similar to the binder she had worn out of old cloth diapers. I made a bed for the two of us on the living room floor. She would doze for a few minutes, then wake up screaming and thrashing on the floor, making a complete circle with her head at the center and her feet beating a path on the floor around her. Morning brought a new torture. Because of a pre–flight paperwork mix–up, we had no idea what Asia was used to eating, but I thought I'd be safe with warm baby food cereal. WRONG!! She screamed and threw her head back until the vile stuff dripped out of her mouth, then resolutely clamped her lips shut. It would be several days before we realized that this was her first experience with any other food or method of feeding but formula from a bottle.

We already knew from prior information that she hated taking a bath, but hate is much too mild a word for what Asia felt about bath–time. Screaming continuously, she alternated between total rigidity and complete limpness, sometimes rolling her eyes back in her head as if going into shock. She resolutely refused to get her hands in the water, and screamed even louder if they accidentally got wet. Somehow we managed to finish bathing her and drying her hair, but dressing her was like trying to stuff cooked spaghetti into clothes. Her feet were so small and limp that we had to hold her socks on with loose Velcro strips.

Later that day after about an hour nap, Asia woke screaming and clawing herself, her neck covered with hives. Our family doctor called in a prescription, which helped somewhat, and we tried to get to bed early. But once again, Asia woke in pain and panic, and we spent another fitful night on the living room floor.

First stop on Monday morning was with Margaret, the enterostomal therapist for colostomy bag fitting and instructions on the care and feeding of a child with a colostomy. So far in Asia's young life people in white were the enemy, so she expected nothing different from this young woman. But Margaret knew how to work with panic–stricken children, and quickly and efficiently measured and fitted Asia with her first colostomy appliance.

Shortly after dinner Monday evening, Asia woke from a nap so badly covered with hives that her face was hardly recognizable. Her eyes were swollen shut and her neck was swelled even with her ears. She was clawing herself with her hands and feet and it took Jerry and me both to try to restrain her. While I bundled her into a snowsuit, Jerry called St. Mary's Hospital emergency room.

Two shots of adrenaline later, one fast acting and one long lasting, Asia's face began to regain it's shape, as if by magic. She became a little giddy and was flirting with the nurses before she fell asleep.

But we weren't out of the woods yet. On Tuesday, Asia not only refused to eat, she rejected her bottle as well. By late afternoon, when my friend Cindy arrived, she still had had nothing to eat, despite sleeping most of the day. While I held Asia, Cindy looked in Asia's mouth and found her gums and cheeks covered with sores. Her mouth was so tender that even the nipple to her bottle hurt. Cindy, Jerry and I took turns feeding Asia eight ounces of formula with an eyedropper, to keep her from becoming dehydrated.

Because it was impossible to keep Asia from scratching, the nurses fashioned tiny mittens from soft elastic bandages and taped them on her hands. Asia's fingers had been her only toys for so long that she was lost without them. Every few hours I'd remove one mitten at a time, and she was overjoyed to have her "friends" back.. When the rash had cleared, both mittens were removed, and she spent hours crossing and re–crossing her fingers and matching the two hands.

The colostomy bags made a tremendous difference in Asia's disposition: for the first time in her life, she was pain free. Although her six months in Mrs. Choi's loving care had begun to crack the "institutional shell," we still had a long way to go. Asia was terrified of any new experience, terrified of being left with strangers, and adamantly refused any food until we play acted with Meghann as "the Queen's Taster." After Meghann pronounced it fit to eat, Asia would try it, but everything was still baby food consistency.

Because Asia's stomach muscles were nearly nonexistent, she developed a very unusual way of getting into a sitting position. She would roll onto her stomach, and then with both legs stretched behind her, she would push up with her hands. Then she would bring her legs around, one on either side, completely flat on the floor, full circle, until they were in front of her and she was sitting up. This feat, combined with the constant crossing and uncrossing of her fingers, convinced us that she was double–jointed. She refused to hold toys and would scream and throw them down as though they were electric. And she still made the croaking noises in her throat and ground her teeth. Occasionally Asia would "blank out" or spend a lot of time waving her fingers in front of her eyes or rocking from side to side in the walker. We believed that many of these actions were born as a means of survival and possibly protection from pain.

Therapists at United Developmental Achievement Center theorized that her inability to grasp and hold objects stemmed from hyper–sensitive nerve endings in her hands. Because she had been confined to a crib during so many illnesses, she had not learned to crawl and toughen the palms of her hands. This also accounted for the nonexistent shoulder muscles. Time to toss out the walker and get her back on the floor!! But she still made no effort to speak, in either Korean or imitating our speech.

We finally conquered the resistance to hold objects by offering her a small clear bottle with a picture of my mother in it. She had been fascinated with the larger version of the same picture since her arrival, and simply couldn't resist this one of her very own. Cross one milestone!

As Asia's strength grew, she began to crawl more and lie on the floor less. We devised all sorts of exercises to strengthen and tone the muscles that were weak from lack of use. Although her progress in four short weeks was astonishing, there were still several areas that concerned us. Asia appeared to have no idea how to chew food. In fact, the very consistency and textures of certain foods seemed to bother her. She showed no interest in feeding herself with her fingers. She made no attempt to imitate sounds, and would only stare at us blankly if we tried to encourage her to speak. Her only voluntary forms of communication were screaming and crying if she was hungry, tired or wet, much as a newborn would do. Bath time still terrified her and she seemed afraid to get her hands dirty or wet. She would willingly handle a very few objects for a very short time, then throw them down and play with her fingers.

We arranged to have Asia's development evaluated by Physical and Occupational Therapists at Nat Polinsky Rehabilitation Center. For all Asia knew, the two therapists were just playing with her, but all the while, the quality of every movement was being noted and assessed. The therapists felt that Asia, now two years old, had the overall development of a seven–nine month–old child. However, because of the quality and variety of her movement patterns, they believed that her delays were the result of lack of stimulation, rather than a permanent condition. Although her behavioral and physical development was significantly behind her age level, the prognosis for normal development in all areas was good.

Asia began to blossom. Her eagerness to keep up with her sister soon had her pulling herself up by the sofa and taking a few tentative sideways steps. She was genuinely happy most of the time and became a hopeless flirt. Her progress amazed friends who only saw her every few weeks. She was adjusting so well that we decided to investigate the possibility of starting her surgery early in the summer. The surgery, we were told, involved two separate operations; the first to remove the section of the colon with no nerve endings and re–attach it to the rectum, and the second about a month later to close the stoma.

The surgery was scheduled for May 25th. My mother arrived a week earlier to keep home and hearth together while I stayed in the hospital with Asia. As it turned out, the surgeon was able to perform both procedures at once, and Asia was released a week later. It wasn't until the second day home that we began to see the terrible psychological toll the surgery had taken on Asia. She almost completely reverted to the nearly autistic child who had arrived from Korea two months before. She would lie on the floor with her back to us, rejecting us completely. She refused to smile, and steadfastly ignored any attempt to play and retreated into the security of her finger play, teeth grinding and her bottle. We hoped that this was her way of handling an incredibly painful situation, and when she was ready to, she would come back to us. By Saturday, Asia began to show a little interest in Jerry and Meghann wrestling, and on Sunday morning, when she pulled on my thumbs and wanted to play "Rock Rock" we knew we had our daughter back.

After a wonderful vacation with friends in Colorado, as we made the last two turns to our house, Asia, from her car seat perspective, recognized the trees by the side of the road, and squealed and clapped her hands. It was another breakthrough for her. She had left two weeks earlier, stayed in many different homes, slept in many different beds, but always with Jerry, Meghann and me. And now, we all four were coming home together.

On August 20, 1983, Asia stood up in the middle of the floor and started walking. She walked to the kitchen and back several times and then decided to try right hand turns and sudden stops and starts, laughing all the way. She walked continuously for two hours, with her arms up and her hands curved as if holding onto an invisible bar, and never fell once. Time to call all the friends and relatives again!!

Learning to walk opened both physical and mental doors. She was constantly on the move, and if Meghann was busy, Asia would run laps from the living room to the kitchen.

We encouraged Asia to ask for things instead of crying for them. She was required to say "Up" or in her case "Puh" to get out of bed in the mornings or after a nap. Once she had mastered the word and knew what it meant, only once did she refuse to say it. It was her way of testing to see if we were as strong willed as she was, and I have to admit there were times when I wondered that myself. Fortunately we didn't have to go anywhere that day, so she stayed in her crib until 2 P.M. Her meals were brought to her, but no toys. It was time, we decided, for Asia to begin to take some of the responsibility for her daily existence, and she resented it. We didn't expect volumes of words at once, but we did want some response when we asked a question. Blank, vacant looks were no longer acceptable.

Our second visit to Polinsky was in early September, and we were thrilled to find that she had gained eight months in development in just four months' time. Although her future development could not realistically be predicted, Jerry and I felt that there were no limits to what she could achieve. We learned to gear down our expectations, and be grateful for accomplishments that others would take in stride.

Asia's abject terror of doctors' visits knew no bounds, and we constantly had to come up with new routes to take to get there. Once Asia knew the way, she would recognize landmarks and begin screaming miles before we were there. This did have one slight advantage, however, if you're into sick humor. We NEVER had to wait in the waiting rooms. The drawback, however, was that no one ever listened to me when I tried to tell them that Asia's few attempts at speech were not clear, and that I felt that something was wrong with her hearing. They would look in her ears and confidently tell me," Well, yes, her ears are red, but that's because she's screaming. I'm sure her speech will clear up as soon as she adjusts a little more." Meanwhile, her teeth grinding habit was beginning to drive us crazy. It had escalated in both frequency and volume, and no amount of behavior modification could control it. Not "Asia, please don't grind your teeth," or "Asia, thank you for not grinding your teeth," or "Asia, if you have to grind your teeth, please go in the other room." Sometimes you could hear her from the other room anyway.

Finally, at the risk of being called a neurotic, doctor–hopping mother, I took Asia to another pediatrician. In order to thoroughly examine Asia's ears, the nurse strapped her to a "papoose board" and flushed out bloody earwax that looked like Grape–Nuts. She had a galloping ear infection and much fluid behind her eardrum. She was put on amoxicillin for eight months, on and off, and not only was the ear infection cleared, but the teeth grinding miraculously disappeared. And, she began to speak. Because of Asia's intense fear of anything resembling a doctor's office, normal hearing tests were out of the question, but, under a mild oral anesthesia, a brain stem audiogram was done, and Asia's hearing tested "10% better than normal." Now I have a better understanding of what that really means. It was about this time that I realized something which other mothers out there may identify with. None of the letters after a doctor's name spell GOD. But we have allowed ourselves to be intimidated by them to the point of reverence, and it began to make me sick. I found that doctors were threatened if I spoke in words of more than two syllables, especially if I were able to pronounce any of the words pertaining to Asia's condition correctly, and they became downright hostile if I knew what they meant!!! I learned to be discriminating about the doctors we chose. If they talked *with* me, gave me credit for having more than half a brain, and allowed for the remote possibility that I could read, they passed. Otherwise, it was more doctor–hopping.

For Christmas that year, we had gotten Asia "Touch and Tell" by Texas Instruments. The basic module, called "All About Me" has clothing, body parts, a scene with a house, truck, tree, car, dog and cat. When you touch a picture, the voice module says, "Yes, that is the red truck." Incorrect responses bring, "No, that is the red barn. Can you find the brown dog?" And so on. For months, Asia had randomly touched the pictures and made no attempt to learn, in spite of all our efforts to help. We guessed it must be too advanced for her yet. One afternoon after the ear infections had been taken care of, suddenly all the answers were correct. "Yes, that's the green tree. Yes, that's the blue truck," and on and on and on. Asia finally got it, or it got her. I quickly put another page in, this time parts of a face. One try around, and she had it mastered.

United Development Achievement Center arranged for an occupational therapist to come to the house to work with Asia once a week, to help bring her up to speed. One of the first things was to help with the tactile hypersensitivity. Since Asia loved small cars, Barb would bury them in ice cream buckets of cotton balls, pinto beans, popcorn..as many different textures as possible. Asia had to dig through the bucket to get the treasured car. For large motor skills, and also because a friend who was into holistic medicine suggested it, we got Asia a small exercise trampoline. The theory was that not only would it strengthen the muscles in her legs, but would increase the oxygen supply to her brain. At first we held her hands while she jumped. Soon, she would wear out one person, and we would switch. Before long, if we had company, we all took turns holding her hands, sometimes for a thousand or more jumps. She totally wore out the adults, and didn't even start breathing hard herself.

In addition to doctors, Asia had many other fears, among them, loud noises, riding in the car after dark, small enclosed spaces, and sleeping all night. At first we thought she feared the crib. We suspected she had been physically restrained to keep her from hurting herself, because there were red marks on her wrists and ankles when she had arrived from Korea. For eighteen months she woke two to four times every night screaming, terror stricken, not even knowing I was there. Even if she had known I was there, she had no language to tell us of her fears. For eighteen months, no one could help us. Finally, a child behavior specialist asked if she had ever slept through the night anywhere. I remembered a time when she had fallen asleep on the living room floor, covered with a quilt. What did we have to lose? We bought her a child's sleeping bag and promptly at 9 P.M. she went to sleep. We tip-toed to bed and awoke to the alarm the next morning thinking she must be dead. My first full night's sleep in a year and a half.

In 1985, Northern Minnesota's bitter winters were taking their toll on my asthma, and we were all ready for more than one month with no frost, so Jerry began interviewing for a job anywhere south. He was hired by a greenhouse supply company with an office between Detroit and Ann Arbor, Michigan, and left in August to start work and find a home for us. Meghann, Asia and I stayed in Duluth to arrange for movers. It was our first experience having someone else move us, and I was apprehensive myself, but Asia looked on horrified as most of her belongings were packed away, and all the furniture taken out. It was three days later in Milan, Michigan, when Asia relaxed as she saw familiar things unpacked.

School had been in session for about a month when we got Meghann settled into kindergarten, and began evaluations to determine the program best suited to Asia's needs. The school's psychologist, Joellen Gutterman, was thorough, patient and kind with Asia and me, and recommended a school in a small town nearby with a program for pre-primary impaired. Asia would have to take a bus. A BUS!!? She'd never even ridden in anyone else's car, much less on a bus. But the bus drivers were outstanding, and Asia came to love them.

Asia loved school, but tended to play on the fringes of the group, not really interacting. She preferred to spin the wheels of cars or gently flick corners of paper against her cheek or lips.

She was nearly five years old and still spoke in one–word responses. She had made many gains in development, but there was still a huge gap between her chronological age and her developmental age. She still refused to bite or chew her food. Her appetite was phenomenal, she could eat more than any two of us put together, but because she has the metabolism of a hummingbird, she stayed reed thin. I swore that she was born without a "Full" gauge. Everything had to be cut into bite–sized pieces, because it went down the way it went in. She fed herself with a fork or spoon, actually preferring not to touch the food with her hands. One night, the Irish in me took over. I had visions of Asia at fifteen, still swallowing everything whole and never having eaten corn on the cob. Time to change. I fixed chicken noodle soup and grilled cheese sandwiches, but told her she could have the soup after she had eaten the sandwich. It was not cut up, so she had to pick it up and bite it, something she had never done before. It took about two hours. We had all finished, and her soup was long since cold when she finally, angrily, but hungrily, ate the sandwich, and was rewarded with the soup. We took pictures and then called all the relatives.

In 1986, after many visits to Mott Children's Hospital at the University of Michigan, Asia had colostomy surgery performed again. The first hook up just wasn't working the way it should, and the colostomy was the only way to avoid giving her three to five enemas a day to keep her bowel from swelling like a circus balloon. The surgery was a setback, but not as severe as previous ones.

Jerry and Asia started Tae Kwon Do in 1986, and in one year, Asia had her yellow belt. She and Jerry went twice a week and practiced their forms faithfully every day.

If I were to be brutally honest, Asia's school career was highlighted by minimal achievements and punctuated with unacceptable behavior. Even with a full time aide beside her, she interrupted the class, gazelle–leaped in the hallways, and continually tried to touch the teacher or other students. She had the attention span of a gnat. The noisy classroom was sometimes too much for her, so she and her aide would go into another room. While at Paddock Elementary School, her teacher, Mrs. Vollink, and her aide, Marsha Adams, were both candidates for sainthood.

In addition to the distraction in the classroom, we began to notice that other noises bothered Asia; the slamming of the baby seat on the grocery cart, the vacuum cleaner, train whistles, dogs barking, fireworks, the toilet flushing, the list goes on. She would cover her ears, or press one ear to her shoulder while covering the other. Her gentle flicking of paper against her lips progressed to her eyes, and then from flicking paper to pencils. When upset, she would dig holes in her fingers . . . the ring fingers on both hands are permanently calloused. She began having more absence–type spells . . . the lights were on but no one was home.

We contacted a psychiatrist, who shall remain nameless, and faithfully kept our appointments for every week for four months. During that time she might have actually seen Asia for 45 minutes . . . maybe. Based on second and third hand information, she diagnosed Asia as having attention deficit disorder and prescribed Imipramine. We started her at 10 mg. and increased by 10 mg. twice a week. At 60 mg. there was no change, no better, no worse. At 70 mg. we had zombie child. Good bye, Dr. You–know–who–you–are, good–bye Imipramine.

In 1991, the self–injurious behaviors, zero attention span and nonexistent impulse control continued. We contacted a psychologist who actually spent the fifty minute sessions with Asia (what a novelty). He suggested that she be seen by a neurologist who ordered an EEG and CAT scan of her brain, and also an audiological exam. None revealed anything. She was diagnosed with pervasive developmental delays and given Ritalin. We were assured that any negative effects would disappear if and when the Ritalin was discontinued. The first day was incredible . . . conversation, spelling, drawing, helping. The second day she began to cry uncontrollably about an hour after being given the Ritalin, literally turning herself into a pretzel, wringing her hands and digging her nails into her palms. She was inconsolable and out of control. These spells would last about four hours. It was unbelievably horrible to watch helplessly. Afterwards she would seem OK until the next pill. We tried half doses, quarter doses, every other day, but nothing worked. We couldn't stand it and neither could she. The worst that would happen if we took her off "cold turkey" was mild flu–like symptoms. That we could live with, but this we could not. Good–

bye psychologist, neurologist and Ritalin. But not, unfortunately, good–bye facial tics. Richter scale sometimes.

In early 1991 Asia's teacher sent home a copy of the *Reader's Digest* condensed version of *The Sound of a Miracle*, by Annabel Stehli. I was ready to try anything that didn't involve drugs, so I spent days on the telephone trying to track down a clinic that performed the therapy that had been so successful with Annabel's daughter Georgie. No one at the University, Michigan State, or the Autism Society knew anything. I managed to track down Dr. Stephen Edelson in Oregon and spoke with his wife. His grant study was already full, with 1,000 on the waiting list.

In the fall of 1991, Dr. Doris Rapp, an allergist who specialized in hidden food allergies which caused behavior problems in children appeared on the *Sally Jessy Raphael* show. Listening to the mothers was like listening to myself. My mother–in–law gave me the book *Is This Your Child?* by Dr. Rapp, for my birthday, and by using the food elimination diet described in the book, we immediately began to discover that Asia had many food allergies, among them corn, oats, wheat, eggs, and milk. Because this comes under the heading of "experimental medicine" (read VOODOO) by much of the medical profession, it took a while to find an allergist who subscribed to Dr. Rapp's theories. Traditional allergists tend to believe that if it doesn't make you cough, hack, sneeze, wheeze, throw up, or break out in hives, then you're not allergic to it. We were fortunate to find Dr. C.F. Derrick, in Trenton, MI, whose testing confirmed what we had found by eliminating certain foods, and who was able to give neutralizing drops to counteract the effects of the offending foods. Asia was even sensitive to the air in her school, and had drops for there as well. Her improvement was immediate, and noticed at home, school and church. It was as though the Gypsies had switched children on us in the night. But it was a good switch, a *great* switch.

In September, 1993, Asia entered the 5th grade in Milan Middle School. In order to have her aide, Marsha Adams, with her, her classification was changed to Autism. I had fought it for ten years, because I feared what images the label *autistic* would conjure up in teachers' minds. I was afraid that they would look at the label, not the child, and immediately think "plate spinner," and never expect any more of her than that. But we knew that there was/is an intelligent child with a remarkable memory hiding in there somewhere, looking for the door out. Without an aide, however, she would have both literally and figuratively fallen through the cracks. Because she has no impulse control and literally has never met a stranger, she was/is a walking target. It was a rough transition, but without Marsha it would have been impossible.

Back at Dr. Derrick's in January of 1994, we discovered allergies to perfume, formaldehyde, chlorine and apples. Asia's facial tics were getting worse and we asked Dr. Derrick's help. He recommended magnesium taurate, which we picked up at a pharmacy near the office. The pharmacist also recommended DMG (Di–methylglycine) and Vitamin B6, all of which we bought. He gave me several articles from the Autism Society which mentioned several other vitamins which had been helpful for many autistic children. No dosages were given, however, so I began a phone calling marathon to find how much of each to give Asia. It was during one of these phone calls that I happened to talk to a mother whose child had had auditory integration training, the treatment Annabel Stehli's daughter had had. This mother was full of enthusiastic reports about what the training had done for her son. She gave me two numbers of a husband and wife who did AIT at two separate facilities. I couldn't dial fast enough. While waiting for the information to arrive, we began experimenting with dosages of the many vitamins, and immediately began to see positive results. The most visible was that the facial tics completely disappeared. GONE. It was amazing. Any time of the day or night I could look at Asia's face and it was calm, not jumping, CALM. There were other changes as well. The quality of her speech improved. She spoke in more complete sentences. She was able to stay on task for longer periods. She has always had an incredible memory, and now it worked for her in spelling . . . totally fifth grade words. Asia loves to draw, and she collects names the way some people collect stamps, sometimes categorizing them by first names. Yes, it still took work, but it paid off. Her aide noticed, her other teachers noticed, my mother noticed. We were thrilled.

And then we started getting ready to embark on yet another adventure. Ken Wilson at Innovative Therapy had tested Asia and determined her to be a good candidate for AIT, which we began in early June. In the meantime, he recommended soft foam earplugs to help with some of the inevitable noises, such as lockers slamming and kids screaming in school. Now she can walk down the hall with her arms swinging, instead of her hands covering her ears.

Last Saturday Asia told Jerry, "Dad, please put the glass down softly, it hurts my ears." As we stared at each other, our chins hit our chests, and we raced to get the cork coasters. This is another beginning; another key to yet another lock to one more door to the wonderful mystery that is Asia. The more we learn, the more we realize how much more there is to learn. But learn we will, and we won't stop trying until we've unlocked as many doors as there are keys for.

It has now been five months since Asia completed Auditory Integration Training. After the initial burst of positive signs, Asia experienced her AIT practitioner's predicted regression. I was confident that I was prepared for this, and had repeatedly assured him. But after two weeks of wonderful progress, to watch Asia go back to where she had been and even further was difficult, to say the least. The regression lasted about two weeks, and just when Jerry and I were beginning to think that we had imagined that there had been any progress at all, suddenly, she was climbing out of the pit again.

School started at the end of August, and we were anxiously waiting for locker assignments, to see if the slamming of doors and the bustle of the kids in the hallways would still bother Asia. For the first few days, we had to remind her that "Ken (her AIT practitioner) had fixed her ears." Now she dashes through the halls, arms swinging, without even flinching at the noise.

Many of the teachers who knew her last year commented at the recent teachers conferences that Asia was much calmer, more in control and more independent. She is able to work for longer periods of time without her aide. The spelling words she brings home are the same ones the others in her class bring home, and she usually has them mastered the first night.

We had friends over a few weekends ago, several who had not seen Asia since AIT. Picture their shock when she came up to them and said, "Hi, Janice, how was your summer?" instead of the usual "What color is Mom's hair?" or a similar phrase which meant nothing to anyone but her. Friends have commented that her speech is much clearer, and for many, I no longer have to translate from "Asia" to English.

Yes, there has been much progress, some that is apparent only to those who know her best, but some that is measurable as well. At the four month point, I decided to have Ken repeat the expressive/receptive language test he had done with Asia prior to AIT. The results were astonishing. In just three months, with no other treatment of any kind, Asia had gained in all areas. The lowest gain was one year seven months, but in two areas she gained three years!! *Three years' gain in three months!!* I was flying!! Ken thinks, and I agree, that this is not new knowledge that she has gained, but information that has been there that she is now able to access. Who knows how much more is in there, just waiting to spill out and surprise us all? When I called Ken to have the test repeated at the six–month mark, he said it was no longer appropriate for her, that she had gone beyond it.

We don't think for a minute that we've seen the end of the progress. We take every gain and run with it. There is still a lot of the "old Asia," and parts of her that I wouldn't change for anything. We will continue chipping away at the blocks and unlocking the doors as long as we can continue to find new keys. Stay tuned!! You haven't heard the last of Asia yet.

Editor's note: The following is a memo recently received from Adair Renning just after Oliver Sachs's piece on autism appeared in *The New Yorker* ("A Neurologist's Notebook, Prodigies," 1/9/95, pp. 44–65). I had commented to her on a part of the article about Stephen Wiltshire, an autistic savant and the main subject of the piece. Stephen's five–year relationship with a favorite teacher had just ended with the teacher's transfer to another school. Dr. Sachs writes: "A normal child would be deeply distressed at the loss of someone who had been so close for many years, but no such distress was apparent in Stephen. I wondered if he was repressing painful feelings, or distancing himself from them, but I was not sure whether, *in his autistic way, he had any personal emotion here at all.*" (Italics mine.) In reading this, I was reminded of Georgie's reaction when her eight–year–old sister died. Georgie was six and appeared to have no reaction at all. When she was twenty–four, she read the manuscript of *The Sound of a Miracle*, and after finishing Part I, which ends with the death of her sister, she put the book down and "cried for a week."

Georgie said all the emotion was there but she hadn't been able to express it. Along the same lines, I asked her a few years ago why she had never told me she loved me when she was little, and she said, "It never occurred to me. I knew you knew."

Adair's memo of 1/4/95 reads: To help dispel the myth that autistic children have no emotions, I would like to share this recent event:

We spent Christmas in North Carolina with my family, the first time we'd all been home in seven years. There were many aunts, uncles, cousins—even second and third cousins that none of us had met. Asia remembered EVERYONE from the previous visit seven years ago [what Sachs refers to as "eidetic" memory— Ed.], when we had no idea how much information was being processed and saved, and how much was just flying around in her head, looking for a place to land.

We spent the evening with forty or so relatives, feasting on wonderful Southern home cooking, taking videos and pictures, and catching up. All the while, Asia was able to play appropriately with the other children, something that would not have been possible a year ago. The house was filled with the sound of children's laughter, and Asia was radiant. When we left, she sat quietly in the back of the van for a while, and then we heard the sound of quiet sniffling. "Honey, what's wrong?" I asked.

"Mom, can I be sad?" was Asia's reply.

"Why are you sad, honey?"

"Can I miss all the people?"

"Of course you can, honey, but we'll see them again, soon."

"Can I miss them and still miss our house in Michigan?"

"Sure, but we'll see our home in Michigan soon."

"These are happy tears too, Mom. I love the people."

"I know, honey."

Asia cried quietly all the way home. She kept saying, "Look Mom, look at my eyes. I still have tears."

Six months ago, this conversation would never have occurred because Asia would not have been able to tell us WHY she was crying. She has such a deep well of feeling for everything, and it can surface spontaneously and be triggered by the music at a concert, a movie, or simply a visitor leaving. The difference is that now she has the gift of language to express these deep emotions. We expect to see her begin to express many more of these emotions, gain from them, and then release them. We always knew that emotions were there just under the surface, but she used to express them in self–abuse, scratching, clawing her arms, and digging holes in her fingers. She simply couldn't tell us why she was upset. ■

Chapter 13

James

by Joan Matthews

[Author's Note: This article was originally written for Mothering, *a magazine which advocates controversial practices such as home birth, extended breastfeeding into the toddler and even preschool years, the family bed, and home schooling.* Mothering *ultimately turned the essay down, but Annabel offered to include it in this anthology, even though the piece is addressed to women who have normal children and who are probably unfamiliar with the characteristics of a developmental disorder.]*

Mothers like us [i.e., the readers of *Mothering* magazine] are often criticized for our parenting practices. Extended nursing, attachment parenting, and the family bed are seen as the cause of every tantrum, every imperfection in our child's character. Frequently, we are given dire predictions of the outcome of our foolishness: "You're ruining him for life." Or we're told of our selfishness—how we're using our children to satisfy some pathological drive in our own psyche.

To counter the criticisms, most of my friends have developed an array of responses. I'm sure you have your own repertoire. For example, when your aunt criticizes you for "still nursing" your one (two/three/four)–year–old, you can point out how healthy she is, and how she hasn't had a single ear infection or bout of diarrhea.

If you are criticized for feeding your child "on demand," you can point out how satisfied he is with his food—unlike you were as an infant (and then you can tell the story your mother tells, of how you'd scream for the half–hour before each scheduled feeding).

When your mother is scandalized by your family bed, you can tell her that your son goes to sleep each night with nary a whimper.

When your doctor tells you that you're stifling your daughter's independence by taking her everywhere rather than leaving her with a sitter—or by "catering to her every need"— you can note how little separation anxiety she displays, how independent she is on the playground, how intelligent and social, how well–adjusted and settled she is.

But what if you can say none of the above things about your child? What if your breastfed, nurtured, family–bedded child is unpleasant, unlikable, unteachable, unresponsive, antisocial, rigid, difficult about food and sleep and toileting, sick all the time, self–destructive, or worse, violent toward others? What if he is turning out miserably, not because of anything you did but because of a serious, pervasive developmental disorder?

How do you help him? And how do you counter the chorus of "I told you so's," who repeatedly blame you for something that was prenatally (and perhaps genetically) predetermined?

If you're a first–time parent, and hence have never witnessed the miracle of normal child development, you may go through years of confusion as you sift through the bad advice and figure out what's actually wrong, then develop a plan to really help your child. Along the way, everything you do will be held up by somebody or other as the root of your child's problems. The viciousness with which others (particularly "experts" and relatives from the older generation) attack you will be quite surprising, and you may wonder whether the mother of a leukemia victim gets similarly accused.

In fact, defending your child, and yourself, will be the hardest part of the struggle. But follow your instincts—not the experts—and you will do what's best for your difficult child.

Disorders Often Show Up at Eighteen Months

My son, James, was relatively normal until he was about eighteen months old. Then he underwent a baffling personality change. (Eighteen months is a common age for autism and other developmental disorders to emerge after a normal first year.) Although he always enjoyed music, he quickly became obsessed with having some kind of music on from dawn to dusk. Simultaneously, he started to withdraw from other people, particularly children his own age. Kids he'd been around since birth suddenly made him scream. During social visits to familiar houses, he'd cling to his stroller and scream until we left.

If we took him to a public place such as a museum, he would have a fierce tantrum, lying on the floor kicking and crying until we left. Sometimes, instead of a tantrum, he would go into a coma–like state, sitting motionless in his stroller, his eyes out of focus. He would make no response to anyone who approached him— he'd act blind, deaf, and mute. He also loathed any kind of physical exercise, and if we forced him to take a walk, he would simply lie down on the sidewalk and refuse to budge. Often I would have to carry him home like a heavy sack of groceries.

At home, he spent most of his time either playing his tape recorder or watching videotapes. He had almost no language. His voracious nursing (one or two times an hour during the day and every two hours at night since birth) intensified. Sometimes he wanted to nurse every fifteen minutes. But as he turned two and beyond, there was something unsettling about his nursing—he rarely made eye contact anymore; he'd nurse as if he were drinking from a stone fountain, then abruptly stop and walk off; I felt used.

If anyone new came into our apartment, either the screaming and tantrums or the coma would be James's response. He was most upset by visits from children.

My chorus of critics (particularly my mother and my family doctor, the father of six, who had once advised me that I should barricade my newborn in his crib and simply go out whenever I felt like it— "Crying won't hurt him") blamed James's withdrawn behavior on me. I had spoiled him, and this was the result. My pediatrician blamed the nursing and urged me to wean him. "Put distance between you and your son," he advised.

Two Years Old

As a two–year–old, James still did not show the growth spurt in language that his peers were showing. He was using single words but did not know his name, didn't know "yes," and when he was baffled but knew a response was required of him, he would simply repeat whatever had been said to him ("echolalia"). He also displayed little of what I would term "gusto" for life. He didn't imitate much; he was obsessed by a few things, primarily his tape and electronic machines in general, but didn't want to learn new skills. In fact, he feared learning, feared new things, feared change. It was as if he were a crotchety old man in the final years of his life.

Interestingly, though, James became intensely fascinated by the alphabet. Although he acted like an uneducable dolt most of the time, when it came to the alphabet, he seemed like a budding genius. He worshipped letters, and I used to remark that he considered them to be twenty–six little gods. He knew the alphabet by sight at two, and by three, he could recognize many words on flash cards. (By five, he could sound out words such as "monoammonium glycyrrhizinate" and could read aloud with the fluency of an adult.) Plastic letter sets were his favorite toys; he'd watch alphabet videotapes repeatedly; the alphabet song sometimes moved him to tears; he'd watch "Wheel of Fortune" with the focus of a Zen master. Although he couldn't draw pictures and was deficient in fine motor skills, he taught himself to write with the precision of a draftsman. While other kids were drawing houses and trees, James was writing out the names of cars in sturdy block letters. His love of letters suggested a competent, passionate mind, and we hoped it indicated that he was not retarded or profoundly learning disabled.

He also began displaying an extraordinary visual memory —by three, he knew most of the countries of the world by glancing at their shape on a map or a puzzle, and he could identify puzzle pieces of countries and states whether they were upside down or backwards. Although he seemed like a vegetable as I pushed him in his stroller, he would later remember complex routes that we had journeyed only once (another aspect of visual memory) or remember where a pleasantly shaped pothole was over a mile from our apartment. Often he would jump out of the stroller to show me a drain pipe or piece of litter that had caught his attention—at times, the thing he'd spotted was down a flight of stairs, or across the street, or through a third–floor window.

He became intensely fascinated by geometric shapes, too, and at one point insisted that his cheese be cut in letters and intricate geometric shapes or he would not eat. Once when he'd asked for an isosceles triangle and I mistakenly cut a right triangle, he shoved the piece back at me angrily. As he approached his third birthday, he easily picked up words like "equilateral" and "triangle," but still couldn't use "hello," "good–bye," or "yes," utter a complete, original sentence, or say his name when asked. He couldn't draw a house but he could draw perfect diamonds, triangles, and rectangles.

During the first three and a half years of James's life, we lived in Manhattan, and I spent much of my time during his depressing toddler years trying to find activities that he could tolerate. Since he could not stand other children, playgroups were out. La Leche meetings were unbearable for him. The few times I tried going to one, James clung to his stroller screaming and choking as if he were being tortured. The only playground activity that interested him was the swing, but in our neighborhood there were only two swings in the overcrowded playground, and a child was limited to a five–minute ride. Hence, we went late at night, in the rain, during a snowstorm, etc., and I would swing my detached child, positioning his ubiquitous tape recorder under the swing so he could listen to the same music repeatedly, his face frozen, his eyes out of focus. Occasionally, I would take him to a deserted playground in Central Park where even the drug pushers feared to go. The bums and crack addicts would eye me as if I were crazy.

The few other activities James tolerated were as mindless, repetitive, and obsessive as the swing. Although he generally rejected anything new, once he accepted a given activity, he'd sometimes fixate on it, and we would have to repeat it endlessly. During the summer before he turned three, I fed hundreds of quarters into the mechanical duck ride on Broadway while James would ride listlessly for often an hour at a time. When people would smile at him (or stare disapprovingly at me), James didn't even see them. We also spent hours riding the elevators and escalators at the Columbia Law School, silently going up and down, up and down. It was as if I had become Sisyphus and James was my stone. These were some of the most dismal and isolated days of my life.

During one two–week period when I couldn't nurse him because I was taking tetracycline, James became obsessed with lollipops. The two weeks passed, he resumed his round–the–clock attack on my body, but the lust for lollipops remained. Soon we were spending a part of each day in search of the elusive "perfect" lollipop. He quickly learned where every candy store was in the neighborhood, and who sold what kind of lollipop. It was almost impossible to set limits on the number of lollipops he could get during one day. We finally settled on two to four, despite the tantrums.

In the various stores, James would finger every lollipop, sometimes spending an hour or more deciding on the right one. Lollipops with cracks or flaws in the color, or with a creased wrapper, were rejected. If a given store was out of the one he wanted, we'd wander the street till we found an acceptable substitute. But he would rarely eat his lollipops, preferring to arrange them on his otherwise unused activity table. When normal kids came to the house, they generally attacked James's candy table, while James would hide (usually crying) in another room.

This state of affairs became increasingly difficult for me to endure. I lost contact with all my old friends, except via the telephone; I could invite no one over; I could go over to no one's house; I had a child who sat like a zombie in his stroller, coming out of his coma only when we passed a candy store; and I was criticized, chided, joked about, and harassed by seemingly everyone. Even my husband Doug, who staunchly defended me to his mother and my mother, and who stalwartly put up with being kicked and disturbed in our family bed, would sometimes snap and become just one more critic.

Meanwhile, all the neighborhood kids—including the ones who'd been bottle–fed, tossed into cribs to cry themselves to sleep at night, and dumped into day care—were turning into charming, loquacious little people. Every day I'd hear stories of toddlers who had weaned themselves, who were brushing their own teeth, speaking in paragraphs, learning to skate, wearing underpants after "toilet–training themselves," and in a word *growing*. James was stagnating—obsessively interested in music, lollipops, and the alphabet, but not in joining the real world. Words such as "autism" began hovering in the minds of people who observed him, and indeed at home, he often engaged in various "autistic" behaviors such as turning light switches on and off repeatedly, staring into flashlights, manipulating his fingers before his eyes, and lining cards up on the floor. When we tried to teach him something, he'd either stare right through us or have a tantrum in protest. He was generally unteachable, and we sometimes wondered if he understood anything we said.

Punishment to force compliant behavior was usually ineffective unless extreme (such as putting his tape recorder on the highest shelf, near the ceiling, until he obeyed us). Starving him would not get him to eat a balanced diet (he showed little interest in sustenance besides nursing); his only alternative beverage was apple juice, and extreme thirst could not get him to drink water.

Compounding my overall problems with James at two was the fact that I was forty and determined to have another child before my time ran out. But his round–the–clock nursing was throwing my periods off. When James became two and a half, I stopped nursing him at night to help my fertility problems. I expected him to cry and complain for a week at most. Seven months later, he was still waking in the night, still begging for "na–na". I spent a portion of almost every night sitting up with him while he gulped apple juice because I'd refused to nurse him. (Recently he told me that apple juice tastes like na–na.) I would be sitting at the kitchen table with him night after night in an exhausted rage, sometimes worrying that I wouldn't ovulate because of the stress. Every time I got my period, I would blame his nursing for "killing" my unborn child.

Oh, and I should mention that James was still utterly incapable of falling asleep by himself. His body simply couldn't wind down at the end of the day. Usually I could nurse him down, but if that failed, my husband had to walk James around like a newborn—sometimes until 2 A.M. I still remember the rage in Doug's eyes when he once returned home at 1:30 A.M.—with wide–awake, thirty–five pound James strapped into a backpack. Doug had walked the wintry streets of Manhattan for an hour while the snow and wind had whipped his skin, but sleep still hadn't come to his stubborn son.

Three Years Old

When I took James for his three–year–old checkup, my pediatrician was aghast that I was still nursing (we hadn't seen him since the two–year–old checkup—after all, breastfed kids don't get sick). He was also appalled at James's lack of speech, warning me of possible brain damage, and he urged me to get some kind of speech therapy. Oh, and he blamed me for being lackadaisical about toilet–training—how could I explain to him that James had no awareness of that area of life, couldn't dress or undress himself, and could barely understand spoken directions?

I left the doctor's office enraged, but decided to take James's problems a little more seriously. After all, we could no longer blame the terrible two's. Thus began a new phase in James's life —enter the therapists. Of course, the blame for James's condition was put squarely on me—James had an "environmental" disorder, caused by too much mothering and too much nursing. (A decade ago, disorders like James's were blamed on parental *neglect* and the "refrigerator mother" syndrome.) He hadn't learned to talk because I was too responsive to him—by "anticipating his needs," I had sabotaged his motivation to learn to ask for things in words. According to one speech therapist, children learn to talk "out of frustration and need," and since I had deprived him of both, James had remained mute. "You take him everywhere, feed him all day, and sleep with him at night," the therapist said. "He's got it made. He doesn't *need* to grow." (Note: Even though I was a first–time parent, I immediately discounted such baloney.)

As far as my excessive nursing was concerned, I was told by one well–meaning therapist that I was overfeeding James because my own mother had bottle–fed me on a schedule, had allowed me to cry night after night in my crib, and had even peppered my thumb when I tried to suck it. The expert's conclusion: I was really nursing the "ghost baby" inside me, and James was the victim of my own inner problems. I was forcing him to nurse to feed myself.

Except that I had grown to utterly despise nursing him as I began my fourth year of it. With James's lack of eye contact or concern for my feelings, I felt like a rape victim. I would have stopped in an instant if I'd thought he could handle it. As it was, I finally got pregnant when James was three, and the abruptly milk dried up. Undaunted, he kept on asking for na–na, and I continued to let him suckle on my dry nipples until I went into preterm labor at thirty–one weeks. I hated it so much that I would harbor thoughts of slitting his throat as he tortured my pregnant–sore nipples. I continued this self–torture, though, because I felt nursing was one of the few connections to other people he had. (My husband indulged him in other respects because we were the only two people he was close to.)

Our experience with the therapists did not last very long, because existing therapies these days, it seems, are primarily behavior modification, using seal–training methods. You reward and punish until you get the desired behavior. Often a therapist would simply start shouting at James when he couldn't understand, following a normal human impulse that says if I just speak louder, my listener will catch on (James didn't). And hovering inside every therapy room was the notion that James would not respond because he was naughty and undisciplined, that he wasn't trying hard enough, that he was a bad boy who *needed* to be punished. James would sense this and try to leave.

I can imagine the anger I must be engendering in any well–meaning therapists who are reading this. After all, the American way to treat any problem is to go see a specialist rather than try to tackle it yourself. But therapy for a child like James was an utter waste because a child who does not understand spoken language *is* like a seal. Before speech therapy, you may have a child who cannot speak, understand, or follow directions, but *after* therapy, you have a child who still cannot speak, understand, or follow directions but who also has low self–esteem and perhaps an utter terror of leaving the house or being confined in a small room with a stranger.

At one point, James became obsessed with calendars, making me write out our entire schedule a month in advance. It took me a while to realize that he wanted to know in advance which trips were merely to the store and which ones were to some therapist or doctor, hence trips to be feared.

At the age of three, James's developmental problems were further compounded by physical problems. All the critics who told me that nursing was unhealthy for him were utterly and absolutely wrong. In retrospect, nursing was the only thing that kept him physically healthy during the first three years of his life. The week my milk dried up, James got his first bout of sinusitis. Green phlegm flowed for three months. (Children with developmental disorders are more prone to illness, perhaps because of the stress of living in a world that is passing them by, perhaps because their disorder has its origin in a weak or oversensitive immune system. His runny nose cleared up for a month, then the "normal" kid from upstairs came over for a visit, bringing his array of day–care diseases. James spent the afternoon crying in his stroller, and got sick a few days later. The green phlegm oozed for four months this time, pouring out all day faster than we could get a kleenex to his nose, and cleared up only intermittently in the summer months.

Four Years Old

My daughter, Lauren, was born just before James turned four, and we moved to Illinois in search of the good life. In no time, we'd found a house and a yard and a preschool that would accept our son. What miracles! My new Midwestern pediatrician assured me that all of James's problems would resolve as soon as I "let go of him" and let him make his own way in school.

Two weeks before school started, we got serious about toilet training. We were tired of diapering a forty–five–pound child, particularly when we had a newborn who also needed our attention. For months we'd been kind and patient, waiting until

James was ready, evoking the name of Sigmund Freud every time we were tempted to pressure him. With school approaching, though, we couldn't wait any longer. James would be trained, and to hell with Freud.

If I took him to the toilet every fifteen minutes, James would use it. Otherwise, he'd simply soil his pants. One day James soiled his underpants three times. Doug responded with his own form of "toilet–training in one day". We both had had enough. Sitting James down, Doug started yelling at him. "I am *angry*," Doug shouted. "You will *never* do this again, do you hear? You will use the toilet from now on, and you will *never ever* go in your pants *again, never, never, never* . . . " James was reduced to sobbing, and we were disturbed by the whole incident. I feel that James is just getting over the shock of what we did to him, though he never had an accident from then on. (A year later, a social worker would commend us for finally "getting serious" with James.)

Preschool—The Big Mistake

I asked that James be put in the three–year–old class because of his language and social problems. Despite a patient, loving teacher who had special ed experience, James hated school from the very first day. He either went into his coma state, or tried to leave the classroom. He was nonverbal and hostile toward the other children. At first, the teachers couldn't get through to him, but I suggested they spell out words rather than say them (a trick we'd learned at home), and they made some minimal contact. After I picked him up each day, he'd spend the afternoon in an intensely obsessive unwinding process. The next morning he'd beg me not to make him go back.

And of course, the sinusitis returned during the first week of school, and this time it didn't go away. His poor teachers were forced to try and get James to participate while wiping thick green mucus off his face. By December, he had lost all use of his nose, and at night would gasp and pant in his sleep, struggling to get enough air. The months of infections and the rounds of useless antibiotics had destroyed James's adenoids. Only surgery would solve the problem, we were finally told, and interestingly, the surgeon said that James might have had this trouble a lot sooner had I not nursed him so long. Perhaps my son knew instinctively that the nursing was keeping him healthy, and that's why he refused to give it up.

The sinusitis cleared up immediately after an adenoidectomy, but I sent my son into the operating room feeling like an utter failure. After all, what child needs such surgery these days?

With mucus no longer pouring out of his nose, James became slightly less repulsive to his teachers. However, the head of his preschool became so tired of trying to rouse him out of his coma or restrain him in his classroom that she told me he could not come back for the summer session.

She said curtly, "He doesn't fit in here. I've told everybody to stop spelling out words. He's got to learn to talk like *everyone else*. The question I have to ask is, do the other fourteen children deserve some attention from their teacher, or should she spend all her time on *James*? If you're told to put him in special ed, you better *do* it."

Shortly after that, Doug and I attended separate sessions of James's school. On both occasions, he clung to us, sitting huddled in our laps. He seemed terrified, as if his life were in danger. Appalled, I pulled him out of school that very day. The preschool experience was not "socialization" for him. It was not a learning experience; it was torture and abuse.

A Disorder vs. a Delay

Experts in the field of child development make a distinction between a simple delay in development and a disorder in development. A *delay* means that development is progressing normally but at a slower than normal rate. A *disorder*, on the other hand, is more serious, with a more uncertain outcome. The child's development is strange and unpredictable. And as with James, it is also uneven—overdeveloped in some areas (e.g., he knew the alphabet by age two), underdeveloped in others (he had almost no useful language by age three).

Children with disorders are apt to be treated more harshly by therapists than are children who are simply delayed or retarded. For one thing, disordered children are more frustrating to therapists—they don't respond well because their needs are not well understood, and they react to pressure by becoming defensive or by shutting down. This prompts more pressure from the therapist, which leads to an even greater shutdown.

For another thing, disordered children frequently have personalities that are less than winning. Often James seemed like that historic snake on the flag, with "Don't Tread on Me" written in giant unseen letters all around his body. There was no enchanting smile, no cute look of bewilderment, no sweet appeal for help. Disordered children often fail to bring out feelings of protectiveness and mission in a teacher or a parent, particularly if they insult you and your friends by being indifferent or even hostile to gifts and attention; if they dislike Christmas and birthdays; and if, in fact, they rarely appreciate all the headstands you perform to get them to respond to you. They want to be left alone, and after a while, you want to accede to their wishes. In fact, sometimes you can hardly get away fast enough.

This doesn't mean that a disordered child doesn't want or need your help. In fact, such a child is generally desperate inside. Your task as a parent is to try to reach him somehow, to figure out what he really needs, and what can really help him. Without much verbal ability on your child's part and with his well–practiced ability to shut down under stress (what writer Jane Healey calls, "putting the brain on idle"), reaching him can be almost impossible.

A Breakthrough for Us

We got our first real clue as to what James was going through from another parent. She had recently learned of the odd term "hyperlexia," a developmental disorder characterized by an even stranger set of symptoms: intense fascination with letters and numbers; precocious, self–taught reading before age five; inability to learn language through the normal spoken channels; and as a result, severe social problems, introversion, ineptness, etc. This was James!

I was put in touch with the American Hyperlexia Association in Elmhurst, Illinois, and was able to read about this unique condition in children. Then, using my own observations, I was able to understand what James was going through and plan strategies for helping him. Everything he did suddenly made sense, given a little insight into the situation. Essentially, James's brain was not ready to accept and process speech simply by hearing it. Some theorists believe that this occurs because the left side of the brain (which more naturally acquires speech, particularly by hearing it) develops much more slowly in children like him. This hemisphere is also responsible for *processing* language (as opposed to memorizing or mimicking speech), for understanding little words such as pronouns and prepositions, and for generating original speech. Speech can be learned on the right side, but it is often limited to the acquisition of nouns and verbs; heard speech is memorized rather than processed, and little words often cannot be understood at all. (This again sounded like James.)

Fortunately, the left side of the brain develops postnatally, and is stimulated by certain kinds of activities, primarily routine, repetitive, and monotonous. Memorizing numbers or counting one's steps stimulate the left side of the brain. So do monotonous activities such as swinging, riding up and down escalators, counting the light fixtures, and lining up playing cards—those "pathological" activities that James somehow knew he needed. And sitting in front of a pile of lollipops examining each one for flaws and imperfections also stimulates the left brain, since it requires focus and discrimination. In fact, all those monotonous pastimes of his were "left–brain" activities. Instead of trying to suppress them, I was right to follow my instincts and let him engage in them. Indeed, he wasn't stagnating at all but growing in ways that *he* needed!

Those "symptoms" of his disorder were actually like the sneezing, coughing, and runny nose of a cold—they were all part of the healing process. And it was only natural that the therapists would fail to see this and try to suppress those symptoms. After all, American pediatricians to this day advise you to sabotage a fever with Tylenol, thereby making your child's body work harder to fight a disease. Stifling the natural healing process is one of the cornerstones of modern medicine.

But James's brain proved to be even more miraculous. The obsession with the alphabet was another aspect of the healing process. In the absence of the normal auditory channels, his brain pushed him toward learning language using another channel, the visual, which is primarily a right–brain activity and fully functional at birth. He used his eyes to understand the written elements of language, and by four, he had taught himself to read, really read, the way a normal child teaches himself to talk. Don't ask me how he learned to sound out the words in our strange, irregular language. (All that spelling his teachers did helped him visualize a word and hence understand it "visually.")

I found, too, that, as a child who hungered for left–brain stimulation, he actually craved pattern sentences, written tests, grammar drills, spelling tests—all good "left–brain" stuff. I bought him a series of ESL (English as a second language) books, and I became his English tutor. He loved it. And I came to realize that a child like James is much better off than a language–disordered child who doesn't have the ability to read. My little deaf–mute actually had a very special, talented brain. Again, it is understandable that the experts would see hyperlexia as some sort of sickness rather than a cure for an overall problem. Even brain researcher Jane Healey, who is usually quite insightful, advises parents of hyperlexic children not to encourage reading, thereby shutting off the major avenue they have for learning language! Fortunately, most parents of hyperlexics do not need such advice—indeed, there is almost no way to stop their special children from doing what they need.

Auditory Training Helps Solve the Problem

Perhaps the most significant breakthrough occurred when James, at four and a half, received auditory integration training from Sharon Hurst of Carol Stream, Illinois. When I read *The Sound of a Miracle*, about Georgie Stehli's recovery from autism, I was impressed that Georgie's autistic speech sounded very much like James's.

After auditory training, James seemed much more comfortable with everyday living. He no longer lay down on the floor in a crowded, noisy shopping mall or tried to leave a crowded room. He didn't sink into his comatose state so often. He no longer hid when people came over. And his ability to speak—his vocabulary and his pronunciation—improved greatly, since the last half of his AIT was intended to stimulate the left side of his brain. I feel that AIT was the only therapy worth pursuing for him. Predictably, the speech therapists were against it and many continue to be so, even though children like James have been helped by it and have not been helped by those half–hour language sessions in claustrophobic therapy booths. (Note that auditory training lasts only two weeks and costs as little as $1,000–a fraction of what the years of speech therapy cost.)

As James's ability to communicate improved, so did his behavior. Or maybe, as James's left brain became more functional, he no longer needed to engage in so many left–brain–stimulating activities. Now James is much more interested in the world around him, does not engage in so much defensive living, and is enrolled in a Montessori school, where his teachers are satisfied with his behavior. Before AIT, he had never asked a "why" question. Now he asks them incessantly: "Why do living things die?" "Why is that part of the road called the 'right' side when we go to school but the 'left' side when we come home?" "Why does it rain?" "Why does the sun come up?" "Where is God?" Then he blows me away with questions like, "Is time permanent or temporary?" A year before, he didn't use the word "yes."

It has been almost two years since James's auditory training. He is no longer the child described at the beginning of this article. His social aloofness, the last problem to fade away, is utterly gone. In fact, he can get along with just about anyone. With his outstanding reading and computer skills, he plays as an equal with kids much older than he is, and he truly enjoys the intense teamwork and interaction sometimes involved in getting the bad guys of today's computer games. Often I hear him coaching one of his pals on how to jump over a certain obstacle or avoid a certain alien on the screen, and he sounds like an articulate adult instructor.

His bad memories are still there, however, as well as some residual fear of new experiences. I know he recalls sitting in the corner of the preschool room waiting to go home. Coming out of his shell was the hardest task for him because of the negative experiences he had to set aside. Had I not forced him to go to school at four, or tried in vain to socialize him as my critics insisted, perhaps he would have had an easier time at joining the world. Had I continued to treat him like the eighteen–month–old he was inside rather than pushing him to evolve, he might have made his debut more gracefully.

In fact, had the therapists and I not insisted that he respond verbally before his brain was ready to process speech—and thus force him to resort to echoing and memorizing—perhaps he would have had a simple speech delay rather than a disorder.

Jane Healey, who has written extensively on early brain development, warns about the dangers of forcing a child's brain to receive something before it is ready. If a child is forced to learn something (through punishment or therapy) before the appropriate portion of the brain is ready to accept it, another part—whatever is available at the time—will step in and accept the learning. But that area is almost always less specialized, inadequate, or inappropriate for this learning, and so the skill is learned incompletely, defectively, inappropriately. In James's case, in the absence of the appropriate left–brain speech centers, he tried to learn language in a right–brained fashion, which is globally and without much processing (hence the echolalia and inability to generate much original speech).

In other words, nature causes delays but parents, therapists, and the environment often create disorders.

Causes of Left–Brain Delay

Fetuses and newborns are essentially right–brained creatures. (The right hemisphere of the brain, as I noted, takes everything in the way a baby does—globally, without much synthesis.) The left side of the brain does not start functioning much until—interestingly—around eighteen months.

Until that time, experience is apparently a cacophony of unprocessed sensory input. But at eighteen months, the left side of the brain is more able to synthesize and process what the entire brain takes in. Language processing really takes off then, and random words suddenly bloom into complete sentences.

Interestingly, development of the speech centers in the left brain is stimulated by sound, primarily heard speech. (Music stimulates both hemispheres; perhaps that explains why toddlers sometimes better understand instructions that are sung to them.) If a child hears no speech, obviously the speech centers remain underdeveloped. But what if a child like James, or Georgie, is exposed to language but is consistently tuning it out because it is unpleasant? Then the left hemisphere, which badly needs stimulation to get back on the correct developmental track, suffers further delay, perhaps dooming the child to keep acquiring right–brain, disordered speech.

The normal brain is also described as being "lateralized." The hemispheres are separate and unequal in size and they serve different, sometimes separate, sometimes coordinating, functions. But in some children, proper lateralization does not occur. The dyslexic brain, for example, has portions that are the same size on both sides, and hence the two sides apparently compete rather than having separate co–functions. In other children, as I noted above, left brain development is severely delayed, and hence the child learns and processes information (of all kinds—not just language) primarily on the right side, employing right–brained skills. His social skills (apparently the responsibility of the left brain) do not develop. Current research points to stress in utero as the cause, whereby the mother's stress hormones mixed with fetal testosterone alter or retard brain development, particularly on the left side (most of the kids with these disorders are boys).

I was under extreme stress when I was carrying James; many other mothers of developmentally disordered kids were not, however. In my case, I fell into an unexplained suicidal depression which lasted throughout the pregnancy. Although I wanted to be pregnant and longed to be a mother, I felt miserable and spent many hours sobbing, sometimes in the local church. The tiniest problem would send me into hours or days of continuous crying. I feel that some sort of allergic reaction was taking place between my body and the baby I was carrying. (The role of a pregnant mother's allergies in childhood brain disorders is currently being studied.) Some researchers feel that a woman can actually become allergic to the baby she is carrying. That is how I felt at times. The morning I went into labor (four weeks before my due date), I woke up and decided I could not stand another moment of the depression. I wanted to die.

That evening my water broke, and instead of dying, I became a mother.

The depression, unfortunately, lasted for the next three years. In the middle of the night, I still sometimes suffer acute guilt feelings for the incredible psychic burden I must have dumped on my son. One of the things that is underemphasized or scoffed at by experts is the strong psychic bond between a nursing mother and her child. Dr. Williams Sears speaks of an infant and mother synchronizing their sleeping rhythms when sharing a bed, and I feel that a nursing mother and child who are always together start sharing their psyches, too, in what Carl Jung calls *participation mystique*. Therefore, I feel quite strongly that the hideous depression I experienced mirrored what James must have been feeling in some way. Perhaps I made his problems worse, though I like to think that, by taking on some of his depression, I took some of the burden off his own little soul. Fortunately, he never stopped having often a close relationship with Doug and me, whereas truly autistic children retreat equally from their parents as well as the world.

Causes of Antisocial Behavior

One of the most troubling aspects of James's personality was his aloofness and need to get away from children his own age. One doctor explained it as his fear that others would make fun of his inadequate communicating skills, and since children are the least tolerant of deficiencies in others, he would naturally fear them the most.

This seemed partly true, but not the whole story. Certainly two-year-olds, who also have inadequate language, normally don't show the aversion and extreme withdrawal my son showed.

It took a student of brain development to give me some insight into the problem. The right side of the brain, he told me, experiences the world much more directly (and more literally) than the left, which interprets and judges. A right-brained individual like James experiences people without much censorship—it's as if he merges with them when he meets them. To him, they often seem as if they are lunging toward him, and he cannot build "left-brained" barriers between them and himself. As autistic novelist Donna Williams explained, it's as if people were jumping out of the TV set and attacking you.

In this light, it is understandable that a disordered child cannot make eye contact. He is probably seeing more than we can see. And putting him in a roomful of rowdy preschoolers is probably experienced as torture, the bombardment of personalities as if they were bullets. Dumping him in a social situation so that he can "get used to" other children is similar to force-feeding ice cream and cheese to a child with a severe milk allergy so he can get used to them. After all, these foods are tasty for the rest of us—why should the allergic child be any different?

As James's left hemisphere develops, the researcher said, he will be more able to feel separate from other people, and less attacked. Perhaps his inability to learn how to use "I" and "you" correctly stemmed in part from his inability to tell the difference between himself and another person. It is a common problem with babies, particularly between a baby and his mother. It made sense that retarded brain development could make James experience other people the way babies do.

Therefore, once again, James's problems stemmed from too much of something rather than the reverse. He wasn't oblivious to other people but all too aware of them—in ways a preschooler could not handle. He used the only defense he had—shutdown. And I finally had all the information I needed to understand my son.

Parenting Before and After AIT—My Questions and Concerns

Before James received auditory training, he demanded and I gave him a particular kind of parenting. His life was a web of obsessions and phobias, and I found that I had to indulge the obsessions and protect him from his fears all day long. People would be constantly telling me that he was "pushing my buttons" or that I was spoiling him, but I knew that his strange needs were as necessary as food to him—even more so, since he had little interest in food.

Needless to say, I was usually angry at him, though I felt I had no choice but to be a party to his weird world.

Following AIT, a lot of the weird needs started dropping away. Of course, I was absolutely thrilled, but part of the rage that I had repressed from before started surfacing. Do other parents feel any rage about what their child has put them through? Do they ever yell or become abusive *after* AIT, to release the pent–up frustration of having to raise him *before* AIT? [Yes!—Ed.]

When James started becoming normal following AIT, I found that sometimes I couldn't adjust my parenting style accordingly. When he was behaving strangely before AIT, I would often tell bystanders about his developmental problems, his lack of speech, etc. But now James is a loud, intrusive chatterbox who needs to be the center of attention—and I have to stop thinking of him as my shy little deaf–mute. Do other parents have a hard time readjusting their thinking about their child? Do parents and teachers sometimes find themselves trying to put him in his old box—since it is familiar to them—rather than accepting what he's become? Do they ever resent him for becoming a fuller, more complex person rather than the kid you could park in the corner and forget about at times? [Yes to all questions.—Ed.]

Finally, the hardest thing I'm facing is setting limits. Here my son has just "come out of Siberia," as I sometimes describe it, and my tendency still is to indulge the new self—letting him talk nonstop, buy all the normal toys he wants (since he never cared about toys), ask and receive answers to the thousands of "why?" questions he asks (since he'd never asked such questions before AIT), indulge all his needs to do normal kid stuff, buy all the foods he wants, etc. It is hard for me to realize that now this is *not* in his best interests, that he came out of Siberia a year ago and is not going back. Now he needs limits just like any other child, but I don't know how to set them appropriately. I keep pitying my poor son, forgetting that he is not my poor son anymore. Have other parents had that problem? [Yes. Me especially.—Ed.) How do they manage to resolve their feelings on this issue?

How strict are they with their child now? Does he rebel against his "new" mom and dad? Is he angry for what he suffered before AIT? Does he still use the old tactics (tantrums, shutdown, etc.) to get his way? Can they ignore them or harden their hearts? How do they punish or retrain their child? In sum, my emotions have been flipping and flopping ever since AIT, and I haven't really gotten my bearings. I am still angry at James for his horrible toddler years; he is still angry (on some level) for having had to endure them; I am so thrilled that he is over them that I spoil him; he is used to getting his way and resists limits.

Excerpt from a Letter to Annabel Stehli from Joan Matthews:
"Between scheduled activities with kids today, I was able to skim the articles on auditory training [seven articles on auditory integration training which appeared in the May, 1994, issue of *The American Journal of Speech/Language Pathology.*—Ed.] So far, the only real negative stuff I read was not actually critical of the training itself—merely the traditional cry for more scientific data before anything new is tried. I am glad that I don't have that kind of mind—I try anything that I sense is right (and it usually is, for me). I remember a speech therapist shrugging and saying, "Don't consider auditory training. It cured one girl," then my thinking, *It cured one girl!! Maybe it will cure one boy, too, namely my son!*

"I talked to Laurie from Boston today. (You gave her my number.) I always enjoy talking to mothers of special kids, even though I know how difficult everyday life is for them. I try not to sound like a "born–again" preacher for auditory training, but that's usually what I slip into. When I talk to other mothers, though, I think, "My hunch was right. It changed James's whole life—maybe it will change her kid's future, too." Anyway, keep giving people my name, particularly mothers of hyperlexic kids, since they seem to do extraordinarily well following AIT. ■

Chapter 14

Todd

by Marie Robinson

Todd was twenty–eight years old when the December, 1990, issue of the *Reader's Digest* featured the condensed version of Annabel Stehli's *The Sound of a Miracle*. Her description of her daughter Georgiana's bizarre behavior as a young autistic child was amazingly similar to our son's. Although we had been told Todd was schizophrenic, I now realized that he was autistic, and that autism was a treatable disorder. Hope entered our lives at last.

I tried to reach Annabel by phone for several weeks but the line was always busy. I was able to contact Dr. Bernard Rimland in San Diego, head of the Autism Research Institute. He explained that auditory integration training, the treatment that had helped Annabel's daughter, was not yet available in this country but he would send me more information and let us know when it would be available.

Todd had what appeared to be an entirely normal infancy. He was a bright, happy, beautiful baby with large brown eyes and curly brown hair. He had his first ear infection at seven months, but was otherwise remarkably healthy. He walked and talked early and was an active, inquisitive, into–everything toddler. He adored his older brother and tried to do everything his brother did. Looking back, I now realize there were some indications of his impending problems. Even as a very young infant, he did not like to be cradled in my arms but had to be held upright with his head over my shoulder. He was a crib rocker. Certain sounds seemed to bother him. At two–and–a–half, he began to have tantrums which almost anything could trigger, and they were unbelievably intense. I had no idea how to handle them. He began to race up and down, up and down the hall. He never sat still, never watched TV. I would find him in the bathroom, standing on tip–toe in front of the basin, letting the water run over his hands. He would have done this for hours if I had let him. He laughed at inappropriate times. He seemed impervious to pain and stopped making eye contact. We were concerned about his odd behavior but felt that when he started school and was around other children, it would improve. We were in denial and we were wrong.

First grade must have been a horrible experience for Todd, but he never protested, never cried. He bravely got on the school bus every day. He never spoke a word in class the entire year. His teacher told me he stared at the light and covered his ears at the sound of the bell. He repeated the first grade and this time we were told to have him evaluated at the mental health center.

The doctors and psychologists we consulted diagnosed him as retarded or emotionally disturbed. We were told it was our fault—his father was too domineering and I was either overprotective or a "refrigerator mother," cold and unfeeling.

In the mid–sixties there were no special education classes, no support groups, we did all we could on our own. At different times we had him tutored and sent him to private schools and special schools. He remained withdrawn. I became a Cub Scout den mother, hoping he would make friends and learn to be more comfortable with other children. He ignored them. Nothing seemed to help. He isolated himself in his own world and only occasionally interacted with us.

In 1978 we moved to Louisiana, where a highly recommended adolescent psychiatrist told me bluntly that our son was schizophrenic and there was nothing to be done but institutionalize him. The outlook seemed hopeless. Thank goodness we did not listen to him. Instead, we were able to have Todd placed in a class for multiple handicapped children in Baton Rouge. The school was predominately black, in a run down part of the city, but it was wonderful. He had a fantastic teacher, Barbara Tinsley, who managed to win his trust and love. The whole school, teachers and students, had been well prepared for the handicapped kids and treated them like movie stars. Todd ate lunch with the cheerleaders. For the first time in his life he was accepted; school did not mean being taunted and mistreated by the other students. That is when Todd came out of his room and began to try to join the world. His efforts were painful to see, but we had wonderful neighbors and friends who encouraged him. He got his driver's license, and was a good driver because his focus was entirely on his driving. He drove in a very limited area with little traffic and never with the radio on. We did not realize how significant that was.

At twenty–nine, Todd led a lonely, painful life. We had moved back to Virginia and he spent hours pacing and rubbing his hands together in a washing motion or shaking them vigorously. He is 6' 1" tall, but appeared to be shorter due to the fact that his posture was stiff and twisted, with his face averted. His speech was very difficult to follow. He would stop and restart a sentence a dozen times. He wanted desperately to have friends—to be "normal," but it was impossible for him to maintain social relationships. Todd was easily offended and very compulsive about many things. He was aware that he was an adult and resented anyone asking or telling him what to do, particularly his parents. We had to weigh our words very carefully when we spoke to him. He was very difficult to live with. He would often walk out of a room when his father walked in. This hurt my husband very much and there seemed to be no reason for it. My husband adored our son, he would have done anything he possibly could to help Todd. At night, in bed, I would imagine Todd pacing the halls of a nursing home after we died. We saw no future, no hope for him until we heard about auditory integration training (AIT).

In July of 1992, when I found out AIT was available in Lynchburg, Virginia, only four hours from our home, I immediately called and scheduled an appointment. When I was told the treatment was only $1,000.00, I was thrilled—I could put that on Visa—we would have second–mortgaged the house. On July 13th, Todd and I met the two wonderful speech pathologists who would administer AIT, Aditi Silverstein and MaryBeth Coffey. I was on pins and needles while they tested Todd's hearing. We had always been told his hearing was normal, but his audiogram looked like a mountain range with peaks of 10 decibels. Several frequencies were very painful to him, especially in the lower frequencies. Perhaps this was the reason he avoided his father, who has a very deep voice.

Todd was very quiet after his first session of AIT. It was too early to check into our motel room, so after a fast food lunch, I drove out into the countryside. Todd fell asleep, which was very unusual for him, but I thought it might be a reaction to finding out how simple the therapy was since he had been very apprehensive. Four hours later, after his second session, Todd appeared to be stunned. He moved slowly, almost as if he were under water. We had dinner in our room and he fell asleep right afterward. I could not wait to call my husband and tell him that at last we had a reason to hope.

The second day Todd continued to move slowly. He took a nap between sessions. That evening I couldn't take my eyes off his face, he looked so different—so handsome, his features had smoothed out and relaxed. I realize now that he had been under constant stress from his painful hearing. The third day the stiffness had left his posture, although he was still moving somewhat slowly, by the fourth day his speech was no longer fractured, on the fifth day I was standing across the room from him in a sandwich shop and was startled to realize that he looked *normal*. He was standing straighter, with his arms folded naturally, and he was looking around with interest. By this time I was living in a constant state of excited anticipation, I couldn't get enough of looking at my new son. He was so much calmer, with no more of that dreadful inner tension and agitation.

By the end of the first week, we had fallen into a routine: since Todd was still sleeping so much, we would get up about 9:30 A.M., eat a continental breakfast, and go for his therapy. Then we would have lunch—he ate like a lumberjack the entire ten days—change into swimsuits and enjoy the motel pool. Then after a short nap, we would go back for therapy again. He would be tired in the evening, so we would have dinner in the room and watch TV or play games. I was really expecting miracles by now and was a little disappointed when I realized his math skills had not made a quantum leap.

Todd always lowered himself carefully into the water at the motel pool, but on the seventh day, he leaped into the deep end. I came close to crying—I could not remember ever seeing him act so spontaneously and joyfully before.

After the twentieth session, I hugged Aditi and MaryBeth, we said our God blesses, and Todd and I headed home. I couldn't wait for my husband to see our new son. I didn't expect him to say much, I am the emotional, verbal one and he is the rock, but he was pretty excited. The changes were so obvious in Todd's posture, in his speech. He could now set the table. He had never been able to remember the order of the knife, fork and spoon before. He did things on his own initiative without being asked. We would go out to cover the lawnmower because it looked like rain only to find Todd had already covered it. We were able to actually discuss things with him, without being met with defiance. He also began to give me quick hugs and even told me he loved me. If I had to sum it up, I would say he had become more affectionate, reasonable, and aware.

It has been over a year now since Todd had AIT, and he continues to improve. It definitely has not been a smooth, steady progression. Shortly after we returned from Lynchburg, just as I was happily adjusting to our wonderful reasonable son, he entered the dreaded *defiant* stage. I can best describe his behavior as adolescent. Instead of reasonableness, we had, "You can't tell me what to do—I'm an adult!" At that point, he was thirty going on sixteen! We wondered if we had made a big mistake. It was pretty bad for several weeks, and then gradually he improved.

We noticed other changes. His skin had been very oily and his hair almost greasy if he didn't wash it frequently. No more, now his hair tended to be dry. It may be hard to believe, but his body odor definitely changed. Trust me, a mother knows. He definitely was much easier to live with. So many of his obsessions had eased. If I didn't clear the time off the microwave or if I forgot and put his coffee mug in the dishwasher, it no longer triggered an outburst. We no longer had to stop everything and figuratively call out the National Guard if a favorite pair of socks couldn't be located. He would now comment, "It'll turn up." The frequent migraine headaches were no more. He was definitely more sensitive to temperature now; before, hot or cold weather did not seem to affect him. His tactile sensitivity increased. When he had a neurological exam in 1991, he could not distinguish sharp from blunt or identify what number was traced in the palm of his hand. Now that is no problem. He stands tall now and will look you right in the eye.

Todd's case is unique in several ways. He was first treated on a BGC machine. Four-and-a-half months later, he began to resume some of his former behavior: pacing, speech somewhat fractured, trouble sleeping. His audiogram looked awful. By then,

I was an AIT practitioner myself, and I had my own equipment, the AudioKinetron, so I gave him a second round of treatments. I may have over–reacted, but he resumed sleeping and stopped pacing. I did not notice any dramatic new changes.

He has had two other serious regressions. The first was four months after his second round of therapy. He had become withdrawn, his speech was again fracturing and again his audiogram was terrible. His hearing was painful at 2000 Hz. He was also suffering from iritis, a very painful inflammation of the iris of the eye. He did not complain about his eye hurting, and it wasn't until it became horribly red that I sent him to the doctor. As his eye improved, so did his behavior and his audiogram. I did not give him any additional AIT.

Again, last August, his behavior began to deteriorate. Over a period of two weeks, he began to withdraw and have trouble sleeping, and he began pacing again. His speech was almost incoherent. I arrived home one day and found him with his mouth full of cotton. He had had a wisdom tooth pulled. He had made the appointment himself, and had not said a word to me—he had become that independent. But because he hadn't complained about the pain, he'd had to wait almost two weeks for an appointment. Once the tooth was gone, we had our new son back again. I feel whatever mechanism Todd used to block his painful hearing all those years, blocked some of his other sensory input. Now, it seems that whenever he is in pain, this mechanism automatically starts up and he regresses. We have made Todd aware of this, and that his stoic behavior can only hurt him.

We still have a long way to go with Todd but we are so proud of him! He has endured so much and has been so brave. He is a very fine young man, very decent and kind. He is working on his self–confidence. He is very aware that he has many years of experience to make up. He is working on his GED and is confident he can pass the test. He works part–time in my office, filing, typing, and running errands; he now drives in city traffic—with the radio on! I suspect he would like to cut the apron strings if he could find another job. He has actually put in an application for a subsidized apartment. He wants a life of his own.

He does not care to talk about his life before AIT. He has even denied some of his past behavior. He doesn't want to remember, he wants to move on. I firmly believe that if he had had AIT as a child, he would be living a normal, productive life now. I will always grieve for the years he has missed.

Several months ago, we were reminded of something we had missed as parents. Around 8:00 P.M., Todd announced he was going to the store and would be back "soon." It was after midnight when he returned. I had been frantic. The only reason I had not called the police was because I knew what their response would have been when I told them my thirty–year–old son had never stayed out that late before. When he finally showed up, his explanation was appropriate for the situation. He apologized for being so late, saying he had stopped at a friend's house and had had such a good time he hadn't realize how late it had gotten. The entire episode was perfectly normal. Fortunately, we realized this in time to react calmly. After all those abnormal years, "normal" takes some getting used to. Lets hope that this is an adjustment we will have to continue to make.

Most recently, nutritional supplements have played an important part in Todd's continuing progress, particularly "Omega–3 fatty acids." ■

Chapter 15

Mollie

by Patricia Kilbride

I was raised a Catholic. In all honesty, I cannot consider myself a "good" one. There have been many days when I have sinned, and many moments when I have ignored God's call. Still, I am a Catholic, and when I pray, I pray as Catholics do. I pray the Rosary.

Since Mollie was diagnosed, I have fingered my rosary beads often, sometimes in thanksgiving, more often in pleading, and, when things are really bad, in despair. It is then that I pray the Sorrowful Mysteries. I meditate on those five terrible times in the life of Christ when things were really bad for Him. And as I pray, I remember:

The Agony in the Garden. We'd wondered for a long time — Keith and I—just what could be wrong with Mollie, our beautiful but mysterious three–year–old daughter. She was our third child— her sister Alexis was eight and her brother Rory was seven. We considered ourselves to be experienced parents. Then why wasn't she talking? Friends with third children had warned me that our youngest child would probably follow her older sister and brother around the house, constantly imitating all they did and growing up much too quickly. This didn't seem to be happening. In fact, Mollie rarely interacted with Alexis and Rory. My pediatrician told me not to worry—that Mollie seemed bright enough, she was just independent and hard to get to know. That was for sure! But I was her mother, and sometimes she didn't seem to know who I was. Despite our pediatrician's recommendations to the contrary, Keith and I arranged for her to be professionally evaluated.

When the psychiatrist's examination had been completed, Keith and I met him at his office. We listened in anguish and disbelief as he told us, in no uncertain terms, that our cherubic three–year–old would never play or speak or function as other children do. His testing had revealed that her lack of interest in the world around her, her inability to relate to others, her strange staring spells and terrible tantrums added up to two heart-breaking words—autism and retardation. As Keith questioned the doctor about his diagnosis, I felt my world fall apart.

What kind of life was in store for our little girl? And how would our older children be affected by the news that their little sister would never be "normal"? Already they were puzzled by her disinterest in them. They had never treated her with anything but loving kindness, but would everything change now? And my husband—though he'd never said so, I knew he was hurt by Mollie's seeming lack of affection toward him. This was a man who loved his children above all. What did the future hold for all of us?

The Scourging at the Pillar. How could twenty-five pounds of blonde curls and big brown eyes torment us so? There were days when Mollie screamed from morning 'til night. She screamed when she opened her eyes from sleep, and when we carried her down to breakfast. She screamed when we started to pour the breakfast cereal and she screamed when we stopped. She refused to leave the house, and screamed if we insisted that she accompany us anywhere. She kicked the floor, threw dishes, tore off her clothes, ripped magazines. The experts called them tantrums, but these were not the ordinary, garden-variety tantrums parents expect from toddlers. What was causing her such misery? Why couldn't I help her? Every cry tore into my heart, lashing me with my inadequacy as a mother. There were times when I actually wished that death would come to both of us—to end her unhappiness and mine.

Throughout this terrible time, I would not have survived without Keith's loving support. He refused to give in to despair. Each day he'd console me by relating some little thing Mollie had done which to us seemed miraculous. She'd stacked blocks! She'd looked at a puppy! She'd let him hold her for a moment. Keith regarded all these things as signs of improvement. Before we slept each night we'd hold hands and pray hard for her recovery. We would need God's help in the days to come.

The Crowning with Thorns. Mollie's "recommended placement" by the local school authorities was an especially devastating experience. We'd hoped that at last we'd be getting some help for Mollie from the experts. She'd never been to school before, so I dressed her carefully. Little plaid school skirt and blouse, white tights and mary–janes. It was winter and I buttoned her into a pale pink coat with matching hat. Sometimes her beauty dazzled me—rosy cheeks, golden hair, little snub nose—even the psychiatrist's report had noted that she was angelic–looking. As she walked into her first classroom, I watched her proudly. But what I saw in that room made me gasp. The children in this school were all physically and mentally impaired. Some had misshapen heads or bodies. A little boy stared with sightless eyes as drool ran down his chin. Though all of the children were several years older than Mollie, they were diapered. The teacher told me to leave my supply of diapers in Mollie's cubby. She seemed surprised and skeptical when I told her that Mollie was potty–trained.

Was this what Mollie's label meant? Did autism mean she was destined to spend her life among children, and later adults, who could not perform ordinary physical functions? My heart twisted with pity for these unfortunate children, but inside I was screaming, "She doesn't belong here." I was afraid the scream would burst through my lips before I left the classroom but somehow I managed to make it to my car before breaking down. I cried and sobbed, pounding the steering wheel, cursing God and fate. I was powerless to stop what was happening. Mollie and I were being sucked into an abyss. Would we be lost forever?

The Carrying of the Cross. It seemed the "professionals" could not tell us what had caused our daughter's problems. One actually recommended that we not put any effort into finding an answer at all since there was no "cure" for Mollie. Somehow, we had to find a way out. I knew I needed to find my own answer, though. I started working—all the time—sixteen hours a day, seven days a week. I dedicated all my time to Mollie. Soon after she had been diagnosed, I'd given up my part–time legal practice. Housework and cooking now were also "incidentals." I made a conscious decision that our two older children would have to be put on the back burner. It was awful to think that they would not be getting the attention they needed. After all, they were my little ones too— only seven and eight. But it was just for a year, I promised myself. I'd keep it up for just one year!

During this time, I learned everything I could about autism. I became knowledgeable about nutrition, including food allergies and candida albicans. I investigated all kinds of therapy—music therapy, speech therapy, occupational therapy, and holding therapy. All kinds of programs: the Higashi School, the Options Program, The Institute for the Development of Human Potential —you name it, I learned about it. I corresponded with as many people as I could, phoning people in Switzerland, England, even Japan. I found despair in some places, but hope in others. I kept swimming upward, pulling Mollie along, wanting always to break through into the light.

It was about this time that I read the story of Georgie—a little autistic girl who had recovered from autism through auditory training. I wrote immediately to her mother—the author of Georgie's story—whose name is Annabel Stehli. To my eternal gratitude, Annabel wrote back immediately. Although Mollie would not receive auditory training until two years later, Annabel's letter was a sort of touchstone for me. Here was actual evidence that a mother and child had emerged victorious over autism—this nonfatal, but nonetheless deadly, disease.

There were many sympathetic and knowledgeable souls who helped me in my search for answers. Dr. Bernard Rimland, an expert on autism and himself the father of an autistic son, provided me with volumes of material for research and study. Jane Rudick, whose little boy had recovered from an autistic–like condition through surgery, inspired me with her relentless search for a cure for her child and other children like him. And throughout the country, indeed throughout the world, were mothers like me. They'd become proficient at biochemistry, psychology, even brain surgery—all for the sake of a little lost child. They willingly shared their experiences with me.

Sometimes I felt that these moms were an "underground railroad" for autistic children. They were disregarding medical opinion, ignoring the advice of school authorities, flouting the dictums of the Autism Society. They were teachers, lawyers, housewives, surgeons; they were Jewish, Christian, Muslim. Perhaps once they had been timid or afraid, but all of them had faced their most terrible fear—the loss of a child to autism. They had nothing to lose and they had so much in common. They just could not bear to see their child's light go out—unnoticed, unappreciated, unknown—never having been able to participate or to contribute. Never having been able to love.

Surprisingly enough, I received very little help from our local chapter of the Autism Society. It was a large organization, with many members, but it had what I termed an attitude problem— "although autism could be treated, it could never be cured," and "the experts haven't a thing for us—so nothing is to be had" seemed to be the general way of thinking. There were support groups for me to join, but I wasn't joining. I knew I'd be encouraged to accept Mollie's condition as irreversible and to go on with my life. I simply couldn't do that.

The Society sneered at what they considered "radical" approaches to the treatment of autism. Megavitamin therapy and cerebral allergies were never given the dignity of discussion in their newsletter. Since we'd seen good progress with Mollie after she'd begun taking the B6 and magnesium that Dr. Rimland had suggested, I couldn't understand their position. Auditory training also was given short shrift. I was present on one occasion when a representative of the Autism Society verbally attacked Dr. Stephen Edelson as he lectured on this subject. He was accused of giving people false hopes in order to reap financial benefit. I could understand a certain reluctance to open up to possible disappointment, but I couldn't countenance this blanket refusal to investigate new findings.

Throughout this time I became good friends, best friends really, with the mother of an autistic little boy. She shared my determination to make our children better. We gathered information together, learning the truth of the old saying "two heads are better than one." Without Alicea's support, I might have had to slow down and that would have been intolerable at this point. When things got awful, I could cry on her shoulder and she would understand.

And, things were getting awful. Mollie still had almost no receptive language. She could repeat some words—this is called "echolalic" speech—but she could not speak spontaneously. Her tantrums were getting worse—and this struck terror in my heart. Though she was small, she was strong. Soon I would not be able to control her. At eight or nine, she would be too big for me to handle. In the future loomed institutionalization. I knew too, that autistic children sometimes became self-injurious. It was not uncommon for an autistic child to strike her head against the floor until she was bleeding. Some bit their own bodies, drawing blood and causing infections. Some scratched themselves, leaving long disfiguring scars. Was this a testament to the rage and frustration they felt at not being able to speak? I did not know, but the thought of it chilled me to my bones. Somehow these temper tantrums of Mollie's had to come under control. She could not live with us otherwise, and I could not bear to think of her living away from us.

Alicea and I had been investigating various educational approaches when she suggested that we contact Ivar Lovaas at UCLA. Dr. Lovaas had conducted an experiment with autistic children roughly sixteen years earlier. The children in the experimental group received forty hours a week of intensive one-on-one behavior modification. The children in the control group received only ten hours a week of behavior modification. A second control group was made up of children who received no behavior modification at all.

The children in all three groups were young: two-and-a-half to three-and-a-half years of age. They were alike in most other respects, including diagnosis. At the end of the treatment, however, the children in the different groups achieved considerably different outcomes. The children in the two control groups fared about the same—almost all were assigned to learning-disabled or educable/mentally retarded classrooms. The children in the experimental group, however, did better than the researchers ever could have predicted. Forty-seven percent of these children finished ordinary first grade and passed into second grade unnoticed by their teachers! They were, in fact, indistinguishable from their normal peers. They had, in fact, recovered from autism! Could this be possible?

Although Alicea and I had read "miracle" stories about individual children who had recovered, we'd never before heard of a group of children in a scientifically documented experiment who'd managed to become "normal." This seemed to be the breakthrough we'd been hoping and praying for. Alicea immediately contacted UCLA, who arranged for a young Ph.D. candidate in psychology, Jackie Wynn, to come to our homes to get our programs underway.

In the month before Jackie's arrival, Alicea and I began the time–consuming process of interviewing and hiring the people who would eventually become "behavior modification" therapists under Jackie's tutelage. We contacted every nearby college and university psychology department explaining our needs. We were looking for people who were totally reliable, unbelievably committed, supremely enthusiastic and, most of all, who believed in miracles. The response was astonishing. Alicea and I easily scheduled the required forty hours per week, then lined up some wonderful young volunteers who viewed this as a valuable learning experience. On the date that Jackie arrived, she found twelve eager young therapists—ready to go to battle for Mollie and for Alicea's little son, Michael.

We decided to open up our first day of Jackie's training to the public. We felt that there might be other parents out there who wanted to become familiar with the Lovaas program. A nearby nursery school provided us with space and sent two of their teachers to observe. Alicea and I were a little nervous. Autistic children do not usually respond well to crowds and Mollie and Michael were going to receive their first therapy session in front of a large group. I held onto my husband's hand and tried to relax.

Mollie's session followed a lecture given by Jackie to the group. Jackie smiled at her when she was led into the room. As usual, Mollie showed no response—staring straight ahead. Jackie produced two wood blocks. She placed one in front of herself and set one in front of Mollie. "Do this," she commanded, and hit the table hard with the block. When Mollie did not touch the block, Jackie said, "No," in a matter–of–fact tone. "Do this," she repeated as she banged her block down again. This time she prompted Mollie by putting her little hand over the block and making the required motion for her. "Good!" I'd brought one of Mollie's favorite treats and we quickly popped a little piece into her mouth. Mollie smiled with pleasure.

This was the essence of behavior modification—the "discrete trial." Mollie would be given a command. If she responded, she would be rewarded. If she failed to respond, she wouldn't get the treat. The food rewards would be paired with social rewards, like hugging, kissing, and praising. Over time, we hoped that the social rewards would become rewarding in themselves.

Critics contend that this method is dehumanizing, even "robotic." I couldn't disagree with them more. We were teaching Mollie to become more human, less robotic. This was a way for her to learn, where special education and ordinary training had failed.

Over the next few days, Jackie undertook the tremendous job of "programming" Mollie's education—which would take place in our home over the next several years. She broke simple tasks down: "Look at me," "Come here," and "Do this." She made them into "drills" which would be repeated by the therapists many times daily. She taught us how to record the progress made in these drills in a data collection log. In this manner, we could see what worked best for Mollie.

It was a wonderful four days, and during that time, Keith and I saw a noticeable difference in Mollie. She seemed more "tuned in," more responsive. Her eye contact was improving. Although we were exhausted, we were very hopeful that this process would work for our little girl.

We were especially buoyed up by the optimism we saw in our young therapists. These students were just so wonderful— filled with hope and determination. It was thrilling to watch them learn to interact with Mollie. Without them, we knew we could not have attempted this fantastic but labor-intensive program.

When Jackie left our home, she went on to set up a program for Alicea's son, Michael. Then she was off to the West Coast to work and plan for other children. We were on our own—but we were on our way!

Death on the Cross. It's been a long haul since then. Our family's lifestyle is very different now. Our home is filled with therapists seven days a week, six to eight hours each day. As Rory wrote in a school composition, "If you would come to my house you would see lots of cars and lots of people. That's because my little sister does a special program called Lovaas." Hiring, managing, training, and overseeing the group of talented, wonderful young therapists who work with Mollie consumes most of my life. Now that Mollie's program has expanded, I've needed to learn how to program her drills myself with Jackie's assistance and guidance. In many ways, the old me is gone. I am a different person now. Family and friends have to come second. It is as if Mollie and I are swimming across a river. When we began to swim, I did not know that the river would be this wide. But now, there is no turning back.

It has been twenty–two months since we began our Lovaas program and Mollie has changed immeasurably. She speaks in sentences now, has a vocabulary of at least fifteen hundred words, plays with toys, and is interested in other children. This September, she started "normal" kindergarten, accompanied by one of our therapists. It is our hope that by January we can "fade" the therapist so that Mollie will be attending school on her own among ordinary children. She still has outbursts of temper—but they are much, much less frequent, shorter and more controllable. Because Mollie can speak we know *why* she is tantrumming. This is a great help to me *and* to Mollie. A few months ago, Mollie finally received "auditory training" and this, too, seems to have lessened her temper tantrums.

Do I expect Mollie to recover completely? According to her UCLA Progress Report, Mollie has made "optimal progress" and if she continues to do so we can expect a gratifying outcome. Just last week I took Mollie to her first dancing lesson. I'd never thought, back when things were really bad, that I'd see Mollie in tap shoes and tights. But there she was, smiling with pleasure at the other tiny students in her class—learning heel–toe and shuffle–down, just like any other little girl. A miracle, really—as every child is a miracle. But this was our Mollie and it felt just wonderful.

At the end of the rosary, we Catholics pray that we will obtain the promises of Christ—that after suffering and dying we will be born again in the spirit of God. In Mollie, every day there is a new birth. As she learns to discover the world, I am discovering myself. We have suffered and we have died and we are looking ahead to a new beginning. ∎

Chapter 16

Brian

by Janet Currence

B rian's story with us began when he was two days old. We received a call that evening that the adoption agency had located a baby boy for us. It was ironic, because I was in the hospital at the time, having a tubal ligation. For a couple who wanted children as badly as we did, this was a devastating time. In the previous year, we had lost a child to toxemia and the doctors had considered the situation so serious that it would be dangerous to try a second pregnancy. When I had awakened from surgery, I had prayed intensely to the Lord. He had reminded me of His promise that He would not allow us to go through more than He would help us to bear. We had waited to have the surgery until after we knew we had been accepted by the adoption agency as prospective adoptive parents.

The surgery for me was much more extensive than a normal tubal ligation. An ovarian cyst was discovered during the surgery and I awoke with a long and very painful incision. When I told the nursing staff that I had a baby, they thought I had really lost it. They were on their way to call my doctor when I began making phone calls to our families and friends.

One of the nurses listened in to the calls and realized that I was serious. We did have a baby. For the rest of that night (I couldn't sleep for obvious reasons) the nurses smuggled me baby care and baby name books from the hospital nursery. During the remainder of my stay in the hospital, most of the hospital staff (including administrators) came to congratulate us.

Five days later, Brian was in our arms. There were hints at the time that he was not developing quite normally. He was in the hospital for seven days—not the normal two or three. When we arrived at the hospital to take him home, the nurses told us that he was "very aggressive and demanding and knew what he liked and disliked." They thought that he was extremely bright for his age, which in a way was true. He also spit up easily. We were told not to give him more than an ounce or two at a time and not to jostle him very much afterward.

We soon learned that Brian was a very sensitive little guy. When we rocked him, he would scream. We needed to wrap him tightly in a blanket and lay him down in his bed so he could quiet himself and go to sleep. My husband and I needed to take extra clothes everywhere for Brian—and for both of us. It was not unusual for him to spit up most of what he was fed. I was frustrated because I was never sure if he was getting enough to grow properly. His progress as measured on early growth charts was normal, but it seemed as if I was always feeding him.

Brian's early years were a lesson in patience for everyone around him. He was much more demanding than he should have been for his age. He played with little cars for hours on end and did not like to be redirected to another activity. I could read to him if he was sitting on the bed with me or if he was on the floor in front of me, but not if I was holding him on my lap. Attempts at nursery school, normal church programs, gymnastics, Cub Scouts, and other social interactions brought mixed results. On some occasions Brian reacted quite normally. On others, he seemed to be in his own world and it was hard to break through to him. When we visited relatives, especially if there were many people present, he seemed out of control and could not be quieted or disciplined. Needless to say, this led to suspicion in many minds of our family, friends, and others that our parenting skills needed some help. We were desperately trying to help Brian grow normally and we were being burdened by guilt by other people, many of whom were very important in our lives.

Early school years were a disaster. Brian simply did not fit into a structured classroom environment. He could recite all the rules to us and explain why the rules were there, but he couldn't follow through and obey them himself. His speech was quite normal in pronunciation, but the content of the speech was immature and he was unable to relate stories back to us in sequence or to make up stories himself. His imagination has developed to this day in a very limited way. Everything has had to be very concrete.

After almost four years in three different traditional schools, we realized that we were fighting a losing battle. Brian was just not going to do well in that environment. The West Virginia State Legislature had just passed a homeschooling law and we brought Brian home. I had worked at a facility for the mentally impaired in Wisconsin and had earned graduate hours in special education before I was married, so I was confident that I could get better results with him at home. We had sought help from the local mental health facility and the local school system. They could not understand what was wrong, so the conclusion again was that it had to be our parenting skills.

We are entering our seventh year of homeschooling with excellent results. His standardized test scores have been very impressive. During this time, we have sought help for Brian in the areas that were outside our expertise. He was eleven years old before we had any official diagnosis. His first one was ADHD with possible learning disabilities. After a trial on medication, the learning disabilities label was confirmed. Shortly after this, we learned that he has what is known as sensory integration dysfunction. One of the therapists at the Cincinnati Occupational Therapy Institute told us that Brian's life is "as if he is in a rush–hour traffic jam at all times." Occupational therapy was begun for the sensory difficulties. His motor planning and visual–motor skills were far behind what they should have been. Later, a psychiatrist suggested possible fetal alcohol and/or cocaine as the cause of his problems. He also diagnosed anxiety and oppositional defiant disorder.

We were noticing other things about Brian. Instead of broadening his life experiences and letting him develop normally, the modifications we were making in our life—style to accommodate him were isolating our whole family. By now Brian had a little sister who was adopted as an infant when he was nine years old. She needed to be raised normally. We began analyzing what was happening. The TV was hard to hear because Brian kept turning the sound down. Long before, I had stopped driving in heavy traffic to keep Brian from becoming anxious. I was arriving at appointments early to let Brian calm down before he had to see the doctors, therapists, etc. We had begun going to restaurants only during off hours and had to avoid certain restaurants because

Brian would not go in. Trips to malls were disastrous unless the mall was almost empty. When a resource teacher gave Brian his annual homeschooling test at the local middle school, he reacted very strongly to the school bells and to the rush of the students in the hallways changing classes and going to the cafeteria.

In the middle of all of this, my mother called me and told me to turn on the television to the 700 Club. Annabel Stehli and her daughter were relating their story. I sat in amazement and chills were going through me. Their story was so similar to ours in so many ways. I immediately set out on a quest to obtain the hearing therapy for Brian. There was no doubt in my mind that it would help him. As I had turned to God after my surgery in earlier years, I was now turning to Him for another specific request. "Please help us get this for Brian."

Early in 1992, I received a mailing from Dr. Bernard Rimland listing David Smith, an audiologist in Huntington, West Virginia, as a trained technician in the Bérard method. I was stunned. His office was only thirty minutes from our home. I called immediately and was sent a packet of information. This included a checklist of sounds that might be a problem. When I filled it out, I found that I had checked almost everything on the page and had added other problem areas at the bottom of the page. Treatment was scheduled in November.

We did not know what to expect, so on the first day of treatment my husband, Alan, took the day off from work and took Brian to Mr. Smith's office. Because Brian is so high functioning and so verbal, he was able to guide Mr. Smith to appropriate decibel levels. On the second day of treatment and every day after that, Brian went into the treatment room alone. He was highly motivated and wanted it to work. Each day, I stayed in the waiting room and did school work with our daughter, Rebecca. When Brian came out of the room, we would head for the nearest food establishment. Later in the two–week period, I simply packed extra food to have in the car. He was ravenous. This might not seem unusual, except that Brian was fourteen and weighed about 82 pounds at the time. He had had problems gaining weight since we entered him in school when he was five. Certain tastes and textures were obnoxious to him and when he started school, the added stress had compounded the problem. At Brian's last doctor's appointment he weighed 95 pounds. On some days he now eats an entire box of cereal along with his regular meals. (As I was writing this paragraph, I had to stop and find an alternative breakfast for our daughter. Brian had eaten the last of the cereal she wanted this morning. I bought it two days ago.)

We have seen evidence of many changes both during and after the AIT. Please keep in mind that at the time of this writing it has been only nine months since the completion of the treatment. We continue to see changes as time progresses.

After the first day of treatment, many observations were noted. Brian had a slight headache. He was extremely hungry and said so. When we went to the restaurant, he ate four pieces of pizza instead of his usual one or two. He was more talkative and his thoughts seemed better connected. He seemed happier and verbalized that the treatments were "not so bad." He seemed more compliant, as if he really wanted to please us. This was new, because usually he seemed to be more flat emotionally. Brian seemed to be smiling more. We went to a friend's house. She noted that he stood in one place while I was speaking with her instead of moving all over the room. In the evening at home we were able to turn the volume of the TV up a little and he didn't seem to notice. He came up and hugged me spontaneously, telling me that he loved me for trying to help him. I think he instinctively knew that the AIT was going to help him. We noticed that he finished his thoughts and sentences verbally more easily and that his usual stuttering was decreasing. Before going to bed—a little earlier than usual because he was sleepy—when Brian noticed that the back door was unlocked, he locked it. Normally, we would have had to do it.

On the way to treatment on the second day, I noticed that Brian was watching what was going on around us. That should not seem unusual, except that before this, being in traffic seemed to be an exercise in endurance for him. Normally he would watch the cars around us as if he were afraid that they would hit us. This time he was noticing people on the sidewalks and talking about what they were doing. I know he won't like my relating this, but he mentioned how nice the girls looked when we passed the Marshall University Campus. Brian was not known for expressing his personal feelings.

After the second day of treatment he was again ravenous. He again had a slight headache and said that his ears "felt funny" when we asked him if he noticed anything. He seemed much calmer and his constant hyperactive movements were much less intense. He was less reactive to the sounds around him. His vocal demands seemed less urgent and he seemed to be more patient. His auditory processing seemed to be better and he was following directions more easily. He seemed to be a little more "touchy" or "grouchy," but we interpreted that to be positive, almost as if he was learning to respond more appropriately to what was happening around him. At home he went off by himself more and was less intrusive to us. I remember going to see if everything was alright, only to find him reading a book. He turned the TV volume up himself and we were all able to hear it appropriately.

On the way to AIT on the third day, I turned the radio volume up a little to see if Brian would react. He didn't. In fact, he was so busy looking at a car magazine that he had brought with him that it seemed as if the traffic wasn't even there! And when we were getting out of the car at Mr. Smith's office, he kissed his sister, Rebecca, on the cheek—instead of bossing her.

The third day of treatment was when we noticed the largest number of changes. His headache was worse that day and the right side of his face hurt. At home that morning he reported that there was something wrong with the furnace motor. Alan, my husband, checked it and there was nothing wrong. We discovered that the fluctuation in sound occurred only when Brian tilted his head to the right. When his head was upright, it went away. When we went for his morning treatment, Mr. Smith checked his ears and gave him an extra hearing test. He determined that nothing unusual was happening physically.

On the third day of treatment, we went to the Autism Training Center at Marshall University. They had offered the use of their facilities for families waiting between AIT sessions. Brian was very friendly with the staff. He was much more willing than usual to talk with people outside of our family. While there he did some artwork. Art has always been a creative outlet for him. On this day, he was coloring a "pencil–by–number" picture. His coloring was faster and neater than usual, and he was staying inside the lines. He was smiling more, because he was also noticing the improvements. This activity had been his idea—I had not prompted him to bring it from home. That evening at home he tried drawing on plain paper and his work was more detailed and recognizable than anything he had done before.

Brian seemed much happier now—and so did his sister. She said to me, "Brian's better." There was definitely more interaction occurring between the two of them. Brian seemed calmer and was able to remain with an activity for a longer period of time. This pleased her.

After the morning session that day, it had been raining. When I started to drive away from the office, my shoe squeaked loudly on the brake pedal. I instinctively looked over to see Brian's reaction. He didn't even notice!

After the afternoon session that day, we went to the restaurant. Usually, Brian was in a hurry to eat so that he could get out of the restaurant and away from its noises. On this day he asked me if we were in a hurry. When I told him that we weren't, he ate slowly and really seemed to enjoy his food.

At the Autism Training Center on the third day of treatment, we watched a film about how the brain and computers work similarly. Later, I asked Brian what the difference was between a computer and a brain. Among the answers he gave me was the word "conscience." We had often wondered if his conscience was developing because of his high level of impulsivity. I asked Brian if he knew what "conscience" meant. He said, "It's the voice in your head that tells you not to do something." He also said, "I used to tell it to shut up before I got my medicine." That happened almost three years previous to the therapy and he was just now verbalizing this to us.

During this time the frequency of negative behaviors decreased. He was simply too engrossed in his new experiences to have time to be bored or to misbehave. I believe that he was also able to make a better connection between his conscience and his actions. I noticed that I didn't have to repeat myself as much when giving him directions.

That evening Alan and I were whispering together in our room about the day's occurrences when Brian complained that he couldn't hear what we were saying. He had always been able to hear everything, no matter how quietly we spoke. (We hadn't fully known this until now.)

Later that same evening, Brian went to his closet and pulled out clothes for the next day—clothes that he had not worn for a while.

We have always had a problem getting him to wear a variety of clothes. It was easier to wear the same thing all the time. And now he was planning for the next day. (!!??!!)

On the morning of the fourth day we noticed that it was easier to awaken Brian. He has always slept very deeply and has been extremely hard to awaken. On this day, Brian seemed more agitated and fidgety. He was still experiencing headaches right after the sessions and complained on this day that he "can't hear as well." He was very worried that he might lose too much of his hearing. The quantity of food he was eating was still well above that before treatment, but was lessening and evening out. He didn't seem as enthusiastic as he had earlier in the week. When we entered a small elevator to get to the Autism Training Center, he panicked and said he would never ride in it again. He didn't want to go to the Autism Training Center the next day (we went to the mall instead). While he seemed subdued, he was still calmer and seemingly more reflective about what was going on.

The weekend between the two weeks of treatment went pretty well. He slept a lot and continued to eat increased amounts of food. He seemed able to direct his own behavior better. He was less reactive to sound and definitely was not running to the window as often to see what was going on outside. He seemed more argumentative and less compliant. His short term memory was worse, as if he was distracted by what was happening inside of him. We wondered if he had expected more from treatment than he was experiencing. He kept asking us to speak more loudly and complained that he couldn't hear as well as before.

Alan took Brian to therapy on Monday of the second week. Before they left, Brian came out of the room with a summer shirt on. When his dad told him to change, he stomped off to his room, slamming his bedroom door. I packed away all of his summer clothes after they left. Alan reported that Brian did pretty well all day, but was rather quiet and sulky. He felt that Brian was trying harder to be part of the family instead of just existing in the same space. When they came home, I asked Brian how his ears were doing. He again reported a slight headache and said his ears "hurt a little."

Brian had a tennis lesson on the sixth day of treatment. The instructor felt that he was less focused and didn't do as well. In the car, he fell asleep and slept all the way home. On the second

Tuesday of treatment, I noticed that Brian seemed to be having increased trouble in dealing with people. He was less patient than he had been the first week. He seemed more agitated. When we went into a fast food restaurant for lunch, he retreated to the car, saying that it was "too noisy."

By Wednesday of the second week, Brian became much harder to deal with. He was a "kid with an attitude." He seemed to be more aware of his own behavior and didn't quite seem to know how to deal with it. We thought we would have to explore proper ways of expressing frustration. What we did not know was that he had stopped taking part or all of his medication. I found pills in waste baskets, under the kitchen stove, and in other locations around the house. Did he think the AIT was going to completely cure him? Now we were alarmed. I talked with him and explained that no one could predict exactly how much the treatments would help him and that he would still probably have to take his medication. I think he understood what I was telling him. His behavior again settled down.

On the ninth day of treatment, Brian awoke easily and was not as combative as we got ready to go to Huntington. His dad had taken him to treatment on Wednesday and they had taken a long walk at a local park. Brian always seems calmer after intense exercise. We were not at this point receiving any complaints of headaches or ear problems. When the neighborhood children were playing outside or our cats inside were meowing, he didn't seem to notice them. He was reading for more extended periods of time without jumping up to find out what was going on outside. His reactions to noises were reduced to a more normal level.

When we went to the Autism Training Center that day, Brian climbed under a table in their library and "cocooned." This was a term that I had learned from the staff of the Cincinnati Occupational Therapy Institute. They had explained that this is a way that children with sensory problems self–medicate. They "pull themselves back together" when they feel overwhelmed. The staff of the Autism Training Center were alarmed, but when they encouraged him to come out and help them find a book they were looking for, he came out readily. I felt that he probably was so relaxed in that environment that he wasn't afraid to do what he needed to do to make himself feel better. I had often found him in unusual places at home.

On the last day of therapy, most of the changes we were seeing were still evident. He was calmer and happier. And he was upset that this would be his last day of treatment. He had told me that he had never been treated so well before. When I started to tell David Smith this at the last session, Brian broke in and told him himself. Brian's past experiences with people had mostly been with people who did not understand him or his special needs. During this two–week period, both at the Huntington Hearing Center and at the Autism Training Center, he had found people he could relate with and trust! And the auditory integration treatments were working!

Since treatment began, Brian has written several poems. This was the first creative writing that he had done without it being a part of his school assignments. His feelings were evident in the writing. He hasn't written any poetry recently, but has continued to make many beautiful abstract pictures.

Brian has used large print books and Recordings for the Blind because of his learning disabilities for several years. After AIT I had to call them and ask them to send books that were harder to read. He was immediately bored with the ones they had been sending. Now he reads Agatha Christie novels and other books at that level. He can sit for long periods of time enjoying reading because outside sounds are no longer interfering.

Brian's psychiatrist has seen him twice since AIT. At the last appointment he felt that Brian is obviously much better than he was. When I expressed my concerns about Brian's increased anger, the doctor felt that this was a positive sign. He thinks Brian is learning to work out his frustrations instead of keeping them bottled up inside of himself. We just have to help him learn how to do so appropriately.

Our optometrist is now seeing Brian for vision therapy. When she first saw him—before AIT—we felt that he would have to have the therapy alone. Now, he is having it with two other boys and so far is doing quite well. She has made the statement that he is not the same kid that I first brought to her office.

We are not as isolated as a family now. I no longer plan our days around traffic patterns or busy times in the mall or restaurants. When we go to the mall, Brian can actually look at merchandise and decide what he likes. He is not constantly reacting to the sounds and the people around him. Because of this, our family have become regular visitors to the local children's museum on Saturdays for its hands–on science demonstrations and planetarium presentations. The staff there are actually happy to see him. We also go to the library more often and stay longer each time. Homeschooling activities and field trips are now more enjoyable. While he did not skate, he did not mind being at the skating rink while his sister skated. We intend to continue exposing him to increased outside activities as he can handle them.

Brian's tennis lessons are now more enjoyable and more successful. His pro is very impressed with his increased ability to concentrate and his improvement in physical ability. There is now a possibility that he will eventually be able to play an actual game.

The relationship between Brian and his sister, Rebecca, is more normal. He enjoys playing with her on her own level. And he is not as bossy or aggressive toward her. He is fifteen and she is six. Yet, when they play together, there doesn't seem to be much difference in interests or activities. He seems to be progressing in many ways just as she is. Could it be that he now has the freedom to mature and he is modeling her behavior? His potential may just be beginning to be tapped.

Teaching him has become more challenging. He is going through the material more quickly and seems to understand it better. We are still finding abstract skills difficult to master, but he is retaining facts better.

Brian is definitely more content with his life. He doesn't seem as anxious and uses his energies more constructively. He is trying new foods, since tastes and textures are not so much of a problem. He has gained about thirteen pounds in the nine months since AIT. He is more affectionate toward us and often initiates hugs.

Others have noticed that Brian is functioning better. Our families and friends are impressed with the changes. They are much more willing to be around him—and he enjoys being with them.

To update (April, 1994), Brian has now received vision therapy and the results have been significant. Vision therapy occurred over a period of several months and the improvements were more gradual than those with AIT. Brian has always had trouble copying things correctly from one page to another. This is especially troublesome in math. After he had had about five months of weekly sessions with the optometrist, I noticed that his math scores had risen dramatically. When I checked his back assignments, I found that the wrong answers that he was making were rarely because of copying errors.

Another evidence of improvement came two weeks ago when a Sensory Integration Praxis Test was repeated. The original test was given approximately three years ago. This test showed a significant deficit when Brian tried to copy forms from one page to another. While all the results of the SIPT are not back, the tester commented that she had never had a person do so well in copying the complicated forms that were represented on the test. We are waiting for the results of the rest of the test to see if there are any other major changes.

During the past few months, Brian has again been changing. He is now sixteen. He is taller and his body is developing very quickly. We are noticing increased behavior problems at this time. We are noticing some increased sensitivities to sound and other stimuli. We are presently attributing this to his age and development. After his development stabilizes, we will probably repeat AIT, since there seems to be evidence in other cases that repeating the process for some persons does yield additional improvement. His psychiatrist is also going to attempt a medication change in the near future. All parents have to deal with problems and changes during this time. We will just have to take one day at a time and see what develops. ■

Chapter 17

Danny

by Patty Dobbs

It is a glorious September afternoon. My son Danny, who just turned seven, is outside playing with his friends. From where I sit at my writing desk, I can see them through the window, tumbling over each other like puppies. Surrounded by journals, letters, and photograph albums, I am trying to see the past with perspective. Sometimes my memory reflects the truth like a mirror, but more often my perception shatters the past into jagged pieces. It seems too painful a task to fit them all together.

I will begin on New Year's Day, 1986. After the previous night's party, my husband and I are sipping champagne together in the bathtub. We had a beautiful daughter named Jennie, a cozy townhouse, and each other. But we wanted more. That morning we conceived Danny. Had we been too careless with our good fortune? Having a second baby was our New Year's Resolution, so this was no accident. A New Year's Day conception seemed fitting, and I was sure I was pregnant again. I was so sure I was pregnant that I had the test done professionally; no at–home kit for me. But the negative test result was confirmed by the nurse in the stiff white uniform with an equally stiff smile.

I obey nearly every instinct I have now, and question nearly every professional. But back then, I believed chemicals didn't lie and professionals didn't make mistakes. Having recently weaned Jennie, my periods were still sporadic, and I figured I was just a little late. Besides, there was always next month. So I made myself a cup of coffee, and then another. We went to a party that night and I indulged freely. I was at the end of a two year stint of nursing and on the brink of another pregnancy, and I felt entitled to kick up my heels. Who was I hurting but myself?

I will never forget the blue ring that formed in the at–home kit I finally bought. My elation was tempered with anxiety from the moment my pregnancy became a fact. I remember the dream I had that night: Ron and Jennie and I were at the beach, and there was a tiny baby inside a paper bag. I accidentally leaned on the shadowy paper sack, crushing its contents, and woke up when I began to realize the horror of what I'd done. But this was just a bad dream, after all, and to this day I am not sure what, if anything, went wrong during those early days of pregnancy. Though I have spent years blaming myself, there may have been genetic factors or environmental causes that leave me innocent. What is certain is my feeling that from early in the pregnancy, Danny was already listening to a different drummer.

Then we were kicked out of our Eden. Our sins were not to be forgiven, but punished by confusion and doubt. Ron's career path led us to the East Coast and I dutifully followed, accompanied by a lovely toddler, a swelling belly, and a strange premonition.

I delivered Danny after a long and difficult labor. He was a large baby, over ten pounds, with an unusually large head. My two painkilling shots were my first conscious failing as Danny's mother. But he cried immediately, and nursed right from the start. As we left the hospital, carrying my robust son and holding Jennie's tiny hand, one of the nurses said, "There's a picture." Without a camera, I decided to take a mental snapshot, and vowed I'd never forget that perfect moment. It was to be one of the last perfect moments I would know.

From the time Danny was a few weeks old, he would scream from morning to night. My pediatrician told me there was nothing wrong with my son, and that I could leave him to cry for up to an hour. That was the last time I asked him for parenting advice, and I chalked Danny's screams up to colic.

I took comfort in crossing off the days to his magic three month birthday. All the magazine articles assured me he would then blossom into the contented baby I deserved. When his three month birthday passed and his screaming didn't, I stepped up efforts to soothe him. Car rides usually did the trick, but they were expensive and often inconvenient. The baby carrier sometimes helped, and Ron and I took turns "packing him." But many days passed when Danny's screaming only stopped when he was sleeping or nursing. He seemed hypersensitive to sound. Even pleasant noises like Jennie's sparkling chatter would make him stiffen and turn away.

I have videotapes of Danny as a baby, and many years later Ron and I would watch them and gasp in astonishment. Videotapes, unlike a mother's memories and perceptions, do not lie. Danny's face was slack and nearly expressionless, and his blue eyes were dull. At five months, his cooing seemed stilted, as though it was a physical effort for him. We handled him like a time bomb, and smiled at him gingerly, afraid of upsetting our cranky little boy.

When he was a toddler, television became a haven for him when the world pressed in too close. Although we always tried to limit his watching, he soon became obsessed with it. He was always very particular about what he watched, and we went into debt buying Disney movies and vocabulary/spelling tapes. He would hold them, line them up, watch them repeatedly, and even take them to bed with him.

When we would take a stroll around the neighborhood, he would inevitably stop by the drain in the street and drop pebbles down, one after another, for hours. In the back yard he would line up rocks on the steps, and later make intricate patterns. He would come to me then, and take my hand to show me his creation with obvious pride. Sometimes I was impressed with the beauty of the design, but the care he took with his arrangements often made me uneasy.

Danny began to throw unbelievably long and frequent tantrums. It nearly drove me crazy trying to understand his instability and volatile nature. Was it food allergies, bad parenting, or my overactive imagination? Looking back, this was the worst time, trying to explain something I was also trying to deny. To add to my pain and confusion were the reactions of others. Danny was not growing up in a vacuum: he was surrounded by relatives, friends, and total strangers in the grocery store. They all had opinions about what, if anything, was wrong. In a terrible Christmas Day fight, my in-laws informed us that we were not giving Danny enough discipline. My parents, far away in Arizona, continued to deny that anything was wrong, and wondered if I was doing Danny a disservice by focusing on his differences. My best friends, Annie and Steve, were understanding, and admitted their bewilderment matched mine. Others were sure Danny's problems reflected some character flaw in me, or in my innocent son.

When Danny turned two, we began to be worried about much more than other people's opinions. He was still not speaking very much, just random, functional words ("milk," "cookie," etc.) interspersed with peculiar jargon and snatches of dialogue from television or books. He had developed the odd mannerism of peering sideways at any parallel object (chair rails, power lines, etc.). He also had other strange movements such as twirling his finger in the air and clapping his hands, especially when under stress. He hated the outdoors, and when forced into the backyard, he would either trace the boundaries with a finger, or sit in a corner of the yard with his back leaning against the house. Although we found this unsettling, we didn't admit how concerned we were. This was partly due to our pediatrician's repeated assurances that he was fine, and mostly because of our paralyzing fear that something was terribly wrong with Danny. We kept hoping he would outgrow his difficulties, and were encouraged by the fact that he knew all his colors, letters, and numbers to twenty. In fact, he could even count backwards, ending this progression with "Naugi." This confused me until I happened to see a bit on Sesame Street where someone about to jump out of a plane counted backwards and then said, "Geronimo." This struck me as an important clue to the puzzle that was Danny; he could easily learn to count backwards, but could not remember how to say "Geronimo."

At two-and-a-half, we could no longer deny what was happening. We took Danny to a developmentalist whose tests indicated he was functioning, at best, at an eighteen–month level. He was diagnosed as having Atypical Pervasive Developmental Disorder (PDD), and we finally had a label to attach to our mysterious child. In the middle of this heartbreaking diagnosis, I began to cry. Without missing a beat, the developmentalist swung his eyes to meet my husband's dry gaze. He said he could not rule out retardation, and he suspected a genetic condition, perhaps Fragile–X. He told us to investigate special education, keeping in mind that, although special education might help with behavior problems, the disability would be lifelong. Lifelong. I thought about that word on the quiet ride home; I repeated it inside my head like a mantra. Before this day, any problem in my life had always been temporary: difficult college courses, money crunches,

Danny's supposed colic. My future had always seemed a pure and shining beacon to follow when I weathered storms. But now that future had been ripped from me and replaced by this single image: a full grown Danny, shuffling behind me in the same grocery store in which he used to throw tantrums, only now the same people who used to stare would avert their eyes. Lifelong. It felt like being sentenced to life in prison with no hope for parole, and I couldn't even take comfort in my own innocence. Perhaps this is what I deserved. Every sin I had ever committed, every impure thought and unkind act, was pulled out and exposed in harsh, unforgiving light. Underneath the lid of depression, these thoughts would stew for years, until the very air around me would reek with guilt.

In a panic, I launched myself into frantic activity, and spent the next six months testing Danny for various conditions. The first step was to give Danny a CAT scan, to rule out brain abnormalities or tumors. The news was good: Danny's brain was normal and his ventricles were not enlarged. Although there was some extra fluid at the base of his skull, it was within the normal range. There was no tumor. I remember scooping up my sedated son and stepping out into a lovely spring morning. We were alive and would remain so. There would be other problems, but they would no longer be so black and white. Instead, they would exist in the grey netherworld that lies between life and death.

The next step was to rule out Fragile–X, a common cause of autism in children with large head circumferences, and the second leading cause of retardation. After a traumatic blood drawing with Danny restrained in a type of straight jacket, I spent the next six weeks in painful suspense. A lapsed Catholic, I remained lapsed, but I spent a lot of time making deals with a God I didn't believe existed. I desperately wanted to believe; I longed to cleanse my soul with ten Hail Marys. I wanted to feel the smooth rosary beads as they slid between my fingers, and to see the statue of Jesus, with his palms held open to me. But I had found organized religion empty. As a child I had stopped believing when I happened upon a picture of some chubby babies lounging in purgatory. My religious instruction teacher told me these were babies who had died without being baptized. Because of their parents' neglect, they were destined to spend eternity hovering somewhere between heaven and hell.

The Fragile–X test came back negative. Although we were relieved, I became driven to find out what was wrong. By this time Danny was almost three, and I began to pore over books in the library. It was there that I made the connection between Danny and autism. The echolalia, the difficulties with transitions, the poor eye contact; it was all there. My developmentalist had attempted to obscure the autism connection by referring to his disability as PDD. When I called to question him about autism, he asked me who had "used that word"? Who let the ugly cat out of the bag?

I was sure my life had ended, but other people I loved were moving on. My younger sister, Nancy, was getting married, and she wanted me to be her Matron of Honor. She lived in Arizona, along with my parents and brother, and since we lived so far away, we saw them infrequently. This would be the first time we had seen my family since Danny's diagnosis.

I was very apprehensive. Despite the hours we spent on the telephone discussing Danny and his development, my parents had clung to the belief that we were overplaying his differences, and that Danny would come around in time. Their belief in him and their unlimited optimism were a source of comfort to me, and it made me nervous to introduce reality into our discussions. Danny was now approaching three, and if anything, he was growing stranger as he outgrew his baby charms.

We flew out for the wedding and found ourselves in the bright Arizona sun with no place to hide me or my abnormal son. Danny was not even at his abnormal best; he either remained glued to the television watching his favorite tape obsessively (I cannot watch *Sleeping Beauty* to this day without feeling sick), or he threw horrendous tantrums. Ron and Danny would retreat to a back room when things got too difficult, while Jennie and I attended luncheons, parties, and finally, the wedding itself. My brother's adorable little boy, just Danny's age, was the ring bearer. Simply looking at him filled my eyes with tears. It was like seeing a vision of what Danny could have been. My sister Nancy was also a bittersweet sight in her yards of white lace, with her biggest problem how to keep her hat on straight.

The morning before we left, my mother gently admitted that there was something wrong with Danny, and my last defense against denial crumbled away. The night we returned home, I grieved for my perfect little boy, and it was like experiencing a real death. Because of something I had done, the perfect Danny would never exist. Instead we would have this strange little boy who sometimes screamed for hours and then fell asleep with his puffy face on a wet pillow.

The Irish have a saying: When a door closes, a window opens. Our window opened just a few days after we returned from Arizona. I was writing words with chalk for Jennie to read, and I was amazed to discover that Danny could read nearly all of them. Most of them seemed to be sight words. For instance, he read "light" as "eight." But he also sounded out unknown words. (One night he pointed to the CBS logo and said, "Sibs.") I could tell he comprehended at least some of the words he said; the way he said "Mommy" was a dead giveaway.

I noticed that Danny could read every word he could say, and that reading a word seemed to be the way he incorporated it into his spoken vocabulary. He seemed to be able to read as easily as other kids his age could speak. But our developmentalist was not impressed. He said many of "these kids" could read and that it was called hyperlexia. He said it was simple, mindless decoding (he was wrong). A book I found on the subject called it "barking at print." Although I knew it was true that some kids with developmental delays could learn to read more easily than they could learn to speak, I disagreed, at least in Danny's case, that it was meaningless (I was right). I just didn't know what it meant.

I returned to the library. By this time I had exhausted the books on autism, but I found new and exciting information in the scientific articles. One day I stumbled across an article titled, "Hyperlexia, A Marker for Improvement in Developmentally Delayed Children." The article stated that developmentally delayed children who learned to read at an early age, even without full comprehension, overall had a better than average outcome. This was all the validation I needed to continue my work with Danny's reading.

I began to read to Danny for hours each day. Before long, he was reading the books to me and comprehending simple story lines. Reading together was a way of joining our minds, the way most typical babies and moms do so naturally.

The vast majority of the time I did not know what Danny's attention was focused on. Many times it seemed to be focused inward. This hampered my ability to teach him language, but when we read together we were of one mind, focused on the same page. I could ask him questions that he could choose to answer or not. The important thing was that we were in the same ball park. Even if he got no more out of reading than this, it was well worth the time.

I began to observe Danny closely. For whatever reason, he was not paying attention to what most three-year-olds were concentrating on. He was focusing on shapes and letters and images on the video screen, while his tiny peers seemed programmed to respond to faces, gestures, and social interactions. As time passed, it became more and more obvious how these differences were reflected. He could count to 100 and spell simple words before he was three, but he could not wave "hello" to my next-door neighbor.

Danny was not merely interested in letters and numbers, he became obsessed and fixated on them. I developed a respect and grudging admiration for his fixations, although they often made our lives difficult. I was relieved to see him learning, even if it was in such unconventional ways. I was a bit in awe of his intense drive and concentration and was unwilling to stand in the way. Sometimes it was a matter of not being up to derailing a train and redirecting it dozens of times a day, but more often it was simple instinct that made me work with his fixations rather than against them.

And so, when Danny began his first fixation with letters, we soon had hundreds of little plastic letters around the house, and dozens of books. He would spend his days reading and spelling words on his magnetic board. Most of his first words reflected his passion for video tapes.

When Danny was three, we would often come around the corner to see the words "FBI WARNING" spelled out in colorful plastic letters on the refrigerator. But with a bit of effort, I was also able to teach him to spell "My name is Danny" and "I am a boy." From the fertile raw material of letters he learned to read, write, and spell. This opened up incredible avenues of communication and ways of learning about the world.

After Danny turned three, he began to make extraordinary progress. He would often borrow phrases learned from his books, videotapes, or cassettes and apply them appropriately to his own experiences. We were walking in the woods when I decided to turn around because of impending rain. "I think I better go home now," he said as he dashed to the car. This sentence structure was far beyond what he was capable of at the time, and only someone familiar with Bambi would notice he was imitating Thumper. Later that week he was drinking a cup of milk when he said, "Danny drinking milk. Danny is happy." This phrase had been lifted from a book we had just read, with his own name cleverly replacing the main character's. This confirmed to us that he knew his own name, although nearly a year would pass before he could correctly respond to "What is your name?" His spontaneous speech was extremely limited, and the vast majority of what he said was echolalic, relating to nothing in particular.

About this time, I conceived again, an act incredible, foolhardy or brave, depending on your point of view. It remained a mystery as to why Danny had been born with a disability, or even whether the disability was genetic. But as I grew, I began to trust my instincts about what was good for him. I just knew that another baby would be good for all of us, and nine months later, Christopher was born. He was extraordinarily calm from the moment he was laid in my arms. He walked at eight months and talked up a storm at fifteen months. Like Jennie, he surrounded Danny with love and normalcy. When Danny's attention wandered, Jenny and Chris would bring him back, often turning his face with their little fingers to make eye contact. They were natural born therapists.

We then turned to our town to investigate special education. They offered Danny a place in a large group of segregated children, most, if not all, with communication problems equal to or worse than his. I felt strongly that he needed peer role models to teach him the social skills he so clearly lacked, but I knew of no program at the time that seemed right for him. I was not yet aware of his legal right to an appropriate education, and very unclear about what appropriate education would consist of. So I continued to teach him at home, concentrating on reading, writing, "playing" with Jennie and her friends, and taking endless walks around the neighborhood.

It was tempting, sometimes, to hide Danny, and sometimes we did. But more often we forgot he was different. Life did go on, even for us. Groceries were shopped for, shoes were put on, children were cuddled to sleep. Danny's bright chatter, even when it made no sense, was a familiar refrain. Often he was a dissonant chord, but sometimes he was as sweet and pure as the notes of a flute. My home was basically no different from many other lucky places where children are loved and cherished. I was rarely embarrassed by his odd speech and mannerisms.

It became interesting to see how others would respond to him. Some people would wait patiently for Danny to reply to casual questions, while others would huddle to gossip about my strange little son the moment we passed. He began to seem like litmus paper, revealing people's character. This included me: when I understood him the best, I was at my finest level of human awareness. By helping him, I also helped myself. Because of his impatience, I had to develop the patience of a saint. Because of his intolerance, I had to be tolerant and understanding. Because he needed it, I had to forgive him, over and over again. For someone as quick to anger and as fond of holding grudges as I was, this was quite an accomplishment.

Time passed and Danny's development continued to be uneven and disturbing. He was over four years old now, and I began to feel that time was slipping away, and with it, my chance to help him. Videos, books, and cuddling could only take him so far; he needed to build forts, ride a bike, and roam with the neighborhood gang. When he was four-and-a-half and still very far from these goals, we decided to take him to Yale Child Study Center to get a definitive evaluation and some advice on education.

We were very pleased with the results. Dr. Sparrow, an expert on precocious reading, spent hours with Danny, and her thorough report and test results enabled us to understand Danny better. We discovered that his intelligence was at least average, and very likely higher, and that he was comprehending much of what he read. Dr. Sparrow attended a PPT to advocate for Danny, and I'm sure her presence influenced our town to send him to the Stephen August Early Intervention Center. This was a wonderful school for children with language delays, with small classes, soft-spoken teachers, and a rich and inviting environment.

One of the best features of the Intervention Center was its Parent Participation Program, where parents were encouraged to attend classes with the child. When the children were off to therapy, the mothers would meet in a type of support group.

It was in this group that I met Monica. She had a child with autism named Timmy, who was born just a week before Danny. Monica and I had a lot in common besides our sons. She was as driven as I was to help her son reach his potential. We both wore jeans with holes in the knees and no make–up. We spent hours on the phone doing research, or talking to each other about what we had discovered. She chain–smoked and I drank gallons of coffee. We were instant friends because we never judged each other, or ever had to explain how bad a day could get.

But Monica was different from me in some ways. She was infinitely more patient with her son, and never considered having Timmy as a tragedy. She taught me to value Danny for who he was, and not to measure the distance he was from normal. She also kept me humble, for as the years passed, Danny made much better progress than Timmy, even though they were receiving the same therapy and similar brands of mothering. This showed me that biology plays a large role in any breakthrough.

Over the course of the next few years we tried to find the cutting edge of research on autism, and to live there. This proved exhausting and expensive. We tried orthomolecular medicine, behavioral optometry, sensory integration, music therapy and behavior modification. I tried to approach each new treatment scientifically, but this was difficult. Life is full of random occurrences that skew results. We didn't have the luxury of trying one treatment program at a time; anything we could afford that held promise we would try.

Twice we put Danny on megadoses of a wide range of vitamins (orthomolecular medicine), and both times we stopped when he began to rub his mouth and make sputtering noises. (One possible side effect from too much vitamin B6 is a possible loss of sensation through nerve damage. I did not know if this was what was happening, but both times Danny stopped touching his mouth when we discontinued the vitamins, and both times we noticed no loss of functioning upon discontinuation.)

We researched behavioral optometry, but found it difficult to grasp. We knew there was something peculiar about Danny's vision, but we also knew his vision was a great strength for him. For a short while, he wore "prism" lenses, designed to change his vision, but I was not comfortable with my understanding of the process. I did not want to tamper with his sight, since he relied so heavily on his vision to learn about the world.

On Dr. Sparrow's advice, Danny began to see a psychiatrist once a week, initially to see if any medication might help him. Dr. McWilliam didn't feel drugs were an answer for us, but we continued to see him for years, and found his advice and emotional support for Danny to be invaluable.

When Danny turned five, he spent three mornings a week at Stephen August Early Intervention Center, and five afternoons in a developmental kindergarten. His kindergarten teacher believed in his unlimited potential, and he made wonderful social progress there. He was even invited to some birthday parties (something any mother knows is a measure of acceptance). He loved his little classmates and would fantasize at bedtime about playing with them, but his communication problems and limited play skills held him back. Only the most highly structured activities, with a familiar theme and realistic props, allowed him to "play" with them.

Swirling the social activity around him, his teacher would point out relevant social information: "Danny, Jessica is cooking dinner now. Would you like to have some spaghetti with her? Jessica, tell Danny to sit down so you can serve him some spaghetti." This illustrates what I feel is an important point in educating children with autism: exposure to normal children is not enough. Initially, social and play skills must be taught, both by a knowledgeable adult and imaginative children. For a long time I would put words directly into Danny's mouth, and tell other children exactly what to say to him to get him to respond.

One winter day when Danny was five, he lost a precious page he had cut from a magazine, an advertisement for the recently released movie, *Home Alone*. It was his autism that made him love that page, full of intricate details and featuring a glossy picture of Macauley Culkin looking surprised. (I would say the press also became fixated on this photo. Danny is not so unusual after all.) When he lost the page, he came to me in tears, hoping I could find it. Usually Danny could not comprehend that I was truly unable to find something, and he would cry anxiously and urge me to keep looking. He would beg incessantly, until we nearly wished he had not learned to talk at all. But on this memorable day, I was able to convince him that I did not have the power to find the page. He went to his room to cry for a few minutes, and when he came out his lovely blue eyes were glistening with tears. "Do you even know I'm disappointed?" he asked me earnestly. At this my own eyes filled. Danny was not only able to label his emotion, he went one step beyond to wonder if I recognized his grief. And I did recognize it. I even felt it. My son and I were sitting together on the couch communicating about our feelings. Something so simple, and so incredibly complex.

Danny's writing and reading comprehension continued to improve. One of the first "books" Danny wrote, complete with illustrations and copyright information (written echolalia), featured a character named Patte. The title of the book was *Really Good* and it began: "Deep in the day there was a rainbow. Patte watched the rainbow. When the rainbow got away the sun came up. They went in the house."

Another early book features a boy who goes to a grocery store named "Patte's" to buy milk. Since I had nursed him into toddlerhood and was currently nursing his little brother, I felt this demonstrated his ability to think symbolically.

Around this time he began to tell me his dreams. Interestingly, he would sometimes blend plot lines from his books with the threads of his own imagination to weave his dreams.

Danny wrote many books over the course of the next couple of years, and they gradually grew more complex. He wanted them to look as professional as possible, and he would often get frustrated when his product did not match his vision. I never did do any kind of facilitating with Danny, other than getting him the materials he needed to complete his project.

We were so pleased with Danny's progress in writing that we bought him a computer, which he soon mastered. In fact, he had an affinity for the computer, and spent many happy hours playing computer games and writing. Once he decided to go exploring and he began altering the system files. It took Ron all afternoon to repair the damage. Ron alternately swore under his breath and laughed out loud while he worked, for he kept admiring Danny's logic as he traced the paths he had taken. There was an integrity to Danny's thoughts, and an intelligence behind his cloud of autism.

It was through the written medium that Danny's awareness of the larger social world began to deepen. Once, in the middle of reading a book to me, he suddenly stopped and asked, "Hey, wait a minute Mom, who wrote words anyway? Did Daddy write them?" I explained the concept of an author, and pointed out his name on the cover. Danny got very excited, grabbed another book, and asked what an illustrator was. I felt like Annie Sullivan finally reaching Helen Keller through her connection between the word and the concept of water.

Danny began to ask questions about who made the logos he was so fond of, and why. From this vantage point, he was easily able to understand the concept of companies, advertising, and marketing.

Once when I was giving Danny a bath, he grew pensive and asked, quite out of the blue, "Who made Danny? Was it the Danny company?" This startled me, not only for its insight, but because his sly smile told me he was joking. In a moment he said, "Did God make Danny?"

"Yes, He did," I said, perhaps for the first time in my life certain this was so. I began to realize that this child I had grown to love so deeply could not possibly have been a mistake.

About this time, my best friend Annie told me about an article she had read in *Reader's Digest* about auditory training, a simple ten-day procedure that supposedly helped in an autistic girl's recovery. I read the article, and later the book, *The Sound of a Miracle*, by Annabel Stehli, with a healthy dose of skepticism, as I had already been around the block with fruitless "cures." I was no longer searching so much for a cure. Rather, I was investigating ways of making Danny's life easier for him. The promise auditory training held for me was to reduce his sound sensitivity, which obviously caused him so much pain. All Danny's fears were sound related (sirens, hair dryers, overhead fans, etc.) and these fears seemed to grow worse with every passing day. But auditory training cost about $1,000 and we were dead broke from years of buying things that might help educate Danny. Children with autism are expensive, both emotionally and financially.

In desperation one Saturday afternoon, I called Annabel at her home, and was warmly received and pulled into "the network": a group of mothers of autistic children Annabel hooks up to help one another. Later it was she who arranged a scholarship for Danny so that he could receive the training with Dr. Binet in Montreal. For this I will be forever in her debt.

Five days after training had begun, I absentmindedly flipped on the overhead fan in our hotel bathroom, and then instinctively cringed at the pained cry I was expecting. It never came. Danny remained absorbed in his book; Ron and I looked at each other and decided to tempt fate. "Danny, come here," we called, and with his full attention we again turned on the fan. He looked apprehensive, then confused, and then he smiled. "My ears don't hurt!" he announced, and the joy we felt was incredible. We had found a way to help our son.

We would have been happy with the training even if this was the extent of its effect on Danny. But Dr. Binet and Annabel seemed convinced that other changes would follow and that improvements would continue for six months to a year. This is exactly what has happened with Danny. Slowly, in fits and starts, Danny has normalized his development. For us, this did not happen in any single miraculous moment, but over the course of a sometimes painful year. Any kind of growth is painful, and Danny would become frustrated by the gulf between what he wanted to do and what he was able to do. For instance, he now wanted to play with other kids on the block, but they held back, afraid of his past differences. Danny wouldn't seem to know what to do with a playmate when he finally got one in his living room. The little visitor would look at me searchingly while Danny abandoned him to watch television or make elaborate books or advertisements for his favorite movies. At this point, Danny's fixations ruled him more than social convention, and this put a big damper on his social life.

About this time Danny wrote a book called *Anytime* that I believe summed up his feelings about friends:

> "Danny Was A Great Sport. He Could Run So Fast
> That He Will Never Stop Running. He Never Got
> tired Of Running. He Had A Red Bike, A green
> Licensce Plate on His Bike, And A Black Handle.
> He Had The Word CHALLENGER On His Bike
> Too. He Liked To Show Off. "Thanks!" Said The
> Boys. "AnyTime," Said Danny. And The Next Day,
> I Showed Off Again. The Boys Didn't Watch. So He
> Didn't Show Off. I Got In Michael's Way "Get Out

> Of My Way, Dan!" He Whispered. "I'm Not Playing
> With You Or Your Lives!" Danny Shouted. Poor
> Danny Went Home. He Walked His Bike On The
> Sidewalk Just In Case Of Cars. "So?" Asked My
> Mom. How Was It Going?" Great, Except I Had An
> Accedent Michael Whisped To Get Out Of His Way."
> "And?" Said Mom. "And Then I Walked Up The
> Sidewalk And Went Home," Answered Danny. He
> laid On The Couch, Looking At The Ceiling."

Here is another piece of untitled writing that shows how
Danny tried to make sense of his social experiences. He wrote this
one day when he came home upset after playing with the kids on
the block:

> "On Daniel's Day with Danny's Friend's Time, He
> Set Off To Bike To His Friends. There Was A Lisnese
> Plate On The Back Of His Bike. It Said "Awesome
> Dude!" His Friends Saw It. their Guess Was It Was
> Awesome. They Climbed Up To The Middle Of The
> Road. They Played Hide & Seek. They Hid In The
> Very End Of The Forest. Danny Could Not Find
> Then, But He Had Another Friend That Liked
> BasketBall. He played BasketBall. They Threw Their
> Balls In The Air. When Daniel Came Back To His
> Friends. They Said There Was A Jaguar Suckin'
> Blood Down. Daniel Had A Plan. His Plan Was He
> Would Go Home And He Friends Would Call Him
> Back. And It Was A Jaguar All Right . . . "

A careful reading of this story reveals he had been both
ditched and teased by his supposed friends. It was extremely
difficult for me to let Danny out the front door after reading this,
but I could not keep him isolated, even if it meant keeping him
safe. It is a normal rite of passage to be teased and ditched, and I
found it preferable to being ignored. Gradually he began to make
friends and the kids seemed to forget about his past differences
and to accept him as just another kid on the block.

Danny began to watch situation comedies intently. I believe
he was struggling to understand humor, which was difficult for

him because of his poor sense of cause and effect. (Sean Barrow also mentions watching sitcoms in his book, *There's a Boy in Here.*) Danny also began to beg me to tape him with the video camera doing a variety of things: pretending to be Bob Saget, doing gymnastics, putting on plays, etc. These video productions gradually became more elaborate, complete with rolling credits, movie trailers, and scripts. One day the entire neighborhood got involved in one of his productions, and to this day the kids still beg me to let them watch it over again.

Gradually I began to see Danny as a little boy with a different way of learning about and relating to the world, rather than a child with a disability who was somehow inferior to "normal" children. I came to accept him for who he was, and tried to surround him with people who shared my vision.

Last summer we acquired a social dog from Canine Companions for Independence, a beautiful golden retriever named Madison. Madison jumps for joy every time Danny comes home from school, and Danny will say, every time, "See? He loves me." Stroking Madison at the end of a long stressful day is a powerful tranquilizer for him.

Danny recently started first grade, and in most ways he is an ordinary first grader. He loves playing his Nintendo, going to his gymnastics class, riding his bike, and wrestling with his friends. He is happier today than ever in his life, and sometimes when I put him to bed, he asks me, " Will tomorrow be as fun as today?" He is still rough around the edges socially, and misses subtle social cues. He also speaks haltingly, as though he is still learning a foreign language. Sometimes when you listen to him, it is obvious he learned language in a vastly different way from his little friends. Once, at the end of a long, happy day playing, Danny said to his friend, "We had fun today, indeed we did." In the future, I am hoping Danny's immersion in literature will make him a good writer.

He is left with other positive traits from the unusual developmental path he took: he is an extraordinarily brave, determined, and sweet boy. He reads and comprehends written language several grade levels above his peers. He is no longer plagued by unusual fears, fixations, or movements, and the only remnants of his autism seem to be his tendency to be over-emotional, to speak too loudly and behave too impulsively.

Interestingly, I would now say he fits the profile of an attention deficit disorder child, and wonder if this condition is on the autistic spectrum as it stretches to normalcy.

In retrospect, it is hard to say what helped Danny most in his struggle to adapt to the world. Learning to read and write was crucial because it gave him alternate ways to learn about the world and express himself. Although we never had a need to facilitate Danny's written communication, I feel he is a good example of why it is important to try to get the child (or adult) with autism to express himself with the written word. Many people with autism count their vision as a great strength, and many can learn to read more easily than they can learn to speak. The trick seems to be tying the words they read with the meaning so they can comprehend. We did this with Danny by pairing the written word with pictures and occasional props.

Auditory training helped normalize Danny's auditory pathways and to integrate his senses. This improved his pragmatic language, for it allowed him to pay attention and learn from other people's conversations and social banter. Psychotherapy bolstered Danny's self–esteem and helped to improve his communication skills. Music therapy, speech therapy, and occupational therapy have all been important, and we have been fortunate to have worked with some very talented and kind therapists. It is sometimes difficult for parents and professionals to develop a good working relationship, but it is vital for the child with autism to have consistency between school and home. If parent and professional do not communicate as equals, the child will pay the price.

I resisted the concept of behaviorism, believing myself to be a humanist, until I realized I was already using behavior modification techniques instinctively with Danny. He seemed to require firm limits, clear guidance, and consistent discipline to make sense of his chaotic world. However, the idea of using behavior modification on children without love and respect flowing in both directions concerns me. I view autism as a severe learning disability which requires early and intense intervention in order for the child to reach his full potential. Although I kept Danny at home until he was four, I wish I had been able to enroll him in an excellent and appropriate program at age two. This wasn't available for Danny, but hopefully it will be available, free of charge, for all children with autism someday. A society is judged on how well it takes care of its most vulnerable members.

My friend Monica died last week, just days after Danny and Timmy both turned seven. She died of lung cancer, and up until the last time I spoke with her, she was more concerned with her children than herself. I am still grieving over the loss of my friend, and trying to make sense of her experiences, and mine. I don't believe I see the hand of God in Danny's good development, but I did feel His presence as I struggled to help my son. Monica struggled as hard as I did, and along the way we laughed and cried and loved our little boys together. For now, this is all the meaning I can find in our similar experiences and different outcomes. There are things I still don't understand about life and death and the mysterious condition of autism.

I recently had a new baby, a lovely little girl named Kelsey. The day I brought her home from the hospital we all sat together in the living room: Ron, Jennie, Danny, Christopher, Kelsey, Madison, and I. "Wow," Danny whispered in awe, looking around, "What a family!" Without a camera, I took another mental snapshot. It was not a perfect moment, but it was a happy one. I no longer believe in perfection. If there is a miracle here, it is the simple power of love. If there is a triumph, it is of the human spirit to transcend the weakness of the human body. If there is a message for other parents of children with autism, it is that you are not alone.

The September sun is fading, and I can no longer see Danny through my window. Any minute now he will burst through the front door, calling for his dinner and my undivided attention. I take a moment to watch as a flock of geese fly south in a tight black wedge. Usually that is all I would see, but today I notice a straggler flying outside the formation. Without the wind current to help him, he must try harder to keep up with the flock. I silently wish him well. ∎

Chapter 18

Janet

by her Grandmother,
Audrey Crandall–Champagne

Her dad called her "Bumpy" because she just lay there like a bump on a log. No reaching out, no babbling, no cooing. Passive, unresponsive, was Janet deaf?

At six months, Bumpy attended a family wedding. I carried her around, a limp rag doll, totally unaware of her surroundings. Another young couple brought their "normal" six–month–old who bounced engagingly in her mother's lap, smiled, squealed with delight, reached out. The comparison with Bumpy was startling and agonizing.

Guests would ask how old was Janet. When I answered, "Six months," there were frowns of disbelief.

Perhaps Janet might have cerebral palsy with involvement in her arms. I had taught children at the Crotched Mountain Rehabilitation Center many years before and could see some similarities. She was flaccid, unresponsive, her thumb tucked under her fingers. She did not wave her arms about or study her fingers as three– or four–month–old babies do. She seemed snug in her tiny cocoon.

Janet's parents realized she was developing far differently from her older sister, Lauren. At three, Lauren was a flower girl at the same wedding, clutching her carnations, following directions, observing. The differences with Bumpy could not be overlooked.

So Anne began the tireless trek from pediatrician to specialists, to psychologists. The evaluation was succinct, powerful: "Indications of Infantile Autism."

To me, the diagnosis was accurate but deadly. The only autistic children I had encountered were severely retarded with erratic behavior, head–banging, and no communication whatsoever. This could not be the outlook for my granddaughter! I could observe the developmental pattern of her behavior, read the results of the Vineland Social Maturity Scale, and could not deny the findings. But my heart and mind were devastated.

Again, I remembered the college lectures: intelligence grows when it is nurtured. Early stimulation is necessary. Mental growth before age four has prolonged effects on later development. If you treat a child as though he or she is retarded, your low expectations will affect the child's development adversely.

As a college professor with a Ph.D. in elementary education, I might know the theory, discuss the research, but the reality was totally different. Her parents needed encouragement and emotional support, not research results. If I was devastated, how must they feel? The day–to–day care of Janet and Lauren could be overwhelming.

The Early Intervention Program recommended speech/ language therapy and a developmental therapist, occupational therapy, and physical therapy combined. At a beginning session, one–year–old Janet sat propped in a playtable as the speech therapist tried to stimulate her response to a rolling ball, a toy car, stacking three blocks—nothing. Over and over the therapist tried, over and over, no response. One more try, she picked up Janet, hugged her and caressed her, saying, "Good girl, Janet. We love Janet." Nothing. More hugs and soft, warm words. "Err, err," Janet cooed. The wall had been breached! The thrill of that first communication was dramatic.

I would rock Janet, two–and–a–half, singing, "Twinkle, twinkle little star," over and over. Music and rocking comforted her when she was upset, but did she comprehend any words? She copied the melody in humming tones and imitated a few song words here and there, " . . . ita tar."

She still did not respond to her name or simple directions, yet she looked so normal. The honey–blonde hair waved naturally into curls, the enormous brown eyes with dark thick lashes searched your face. The pixie–like body danced and whirled like Tinkerbell responding to a distant music. The barrier may have been breached, but would every single word have to be taught? The enormity of the task ahead!

She loved to dig in the dirt around a colorful houseplant. Telling her "no" was like whistling in the wind. She continued to dig. Anne would say, "no, no, no," and physically remove her from the plant. Many attempts later, Bumpy approached the flower pot, pointed at it, and said, "No, no, no," and didn't dig. Perhaps she could understand words coupled with actions. I watched for clues.

She could walk, climb stairs, feed herself with huge fingerfuls, slurp a drink, but did not play with toys. Perhaps, I could arouse her curiosity? I took a jumbo musical top from the toy basket, pumped it hard many times, then watched it spin its bright colors. No response. Many more attempts were made. Nothing. Discouraged, I replaced the top. The following day I heard a banging in the living room. Bumpy had taken the top from the basket and was trying to make it twirl. I casually helped her push the handle. No interest. Several days later, I heard the top again and found Lauren demonstrating and Bumpy watching. More clues were being given. Direct teaching might not work, but seeds of actions might begin to sprout later.

At breakfast, Lauren and I were chatting. I was baby–sitting a few days while Mom and Dad had a special trip.

"My sister's funny."

"Do you know about Janet? . . . Uh," I searched for the right word.

"Yup, she's got autism."

"Do you know what that means?"

"Yup, she can't talk." At four years of age, Lauren had matter–of–factly summarized it all.

"But you know you can play with her just the same."

And play they did. They were puppies rolling on the rug, monkeys climbing on the jungle gym, whirl–a–gigs twirling around the bars and swing set. Janet never seemed dizzy and was totally fearless in climbing ever higher.

It was recommended that Janet attend a day care for developmentally delayed toddlers. Anne and I observed from across the room as the teachers did finger–painting with chocolate pudding (sensory awareness), demonstrated a push–pull toy (eye–hand coordination), did picture identification games (language development). Lunch was training with spoon, bowl, and applesauce: (1) dig, (2) push, (3) lift, and (4) mouth. Repetition was the modus operandi.

Bumpy was in the all–day program and Anne was distraught when the speech therapist recommended a change in program for the second year. "Janet will model the behaviors of severely retarded children if she stays another year. It was a good beginning program, but not a long–term solution."

I kept looking for clues and improvements with Janet. But progress was infinitesimally small. At four or five, no toilet training was working. She would not sit on the potty. The brown odoriferous oatmeal that oozed out frequently, but never regularly, did not bother Janet whatsoever. In fact, she might smear it around a bit. Anne was dealing with five years of Pampers and how many more years to come?

We went to a restaurant for dinner. Janet ate huge fistfuls of spaghetti with sauce smeared ear–to–ear and an equally large portion dropped on the carpet. We left a generous tip and hurriedly exited. Could we ever go out like a normal family?

At three, Bumpy could open the back door by herself and whirl out to the swing and the yard, fenced in, of course. Anne was not aware she could do this when Lauren screeched, "Look what Bumpy's doing!" Lauren dragged her little sister away. She knew you should not eat those mushrooms growing in the lawn. They were poison! Bumpy was happily munching away as Anne snatched her up, trying to make her spit out the mushy white mass. A call to poison control told Anne what to do. Lauren and Anne's quick actions had averted a tragedy.

Another fun activity for Bumpy was "potty swimming." You pull up the toilet seat, lean over, and paddle, splash, swish and swirl the water in the toilet bowl. Anne had to attach clip locks to the toilet seats to prevent further excursions. All kitchen cabinets had child–safe locks, of course.

Another family party took place with a dozen children all talking at once. Janet, at five, pulled away, strongly biting her own finger. I held her close and spoke slowly in a lower pitch. Janet turned up her heartbreaker eyes and kissed my cheek. Too much noise obviously upset her, but a lower pitched, softer tone seemed to get through. Another clue?

We went to Funspot, where there were special rides for young children. Animal–shaped dodge–em cars, three seater merry–go–round, flying airplane. Colors, music, lights, noise, Janet pulled away, lay flat on the entrance mat, and licked the face of the clown that was woven on the mat. The clue was strong. "Don't overpower me with too much input." The pattern of the clown's face is more important.

Bumpy was a climber. The dining room light fixture glistened and gleamed, inviting her to explore. On top of the table, she went scrutinizing, tongue–licking, patting the flower–shaped crystal shades. "No, no, no," had no affect when Bumpy compulsively had to inspect the chandelier. Anne's moving the furniture to block access to the dining room was the only solution.

At the beach, the waves rolled toward the tall sand dunes. High tide approached and the rumbling roar increased. Janet, who had been patting the sand happily, suddenly began to sob and sob. She could not be comforted, so we left the beach. Another clue?

After many years of speech and language therapy, she was initiating only a few words, "up" and "cookie." At a museum, the family had to wait in line to buy tickets. Farther down the line another dad was entertaining his young children by swinging them back and forth like a pendulum, then high in the air. Janet broke loose from her dad, dashed down the line, and tugged on the other dad, saying, "Up, up, high." He obliged kindly. She had, at last, initiated language appropriately.

When I first read of auditory integration training, I remembered the clues Janet had been giving me. Could she understand more than she could express? Her attention span was so fleeting, could she pay attention long enough for learning to occur? How could she possibly take a valid audiometric exam? She still didn't respond to her name. How could she follow the directions of the test? I read more and it seemed to offer a glimmer. If Bumpy's world was buzzing confusion, how could she comprehend what she heard? Anne was now president of the Maine Autism Society and knew of the Bérard–trained therapist who would be in the area soon. With much trepidation and apprehension, Janet was signed up.

Anne drove the fifty miles daily and wondered if it might hurt more than help Janet. Her dad drove the next week for the training sessions. The therapist admitted she did not obtain a valid audiogram, but having administered many tests, she had found certain frequencies were similar among children and she adjusted the AudioKinetron accordingly. Janet seemed upset by the session, but not seriously upset. There was no immediate change as dramatic as Georgiana, in The Sound of a Miracle, but Janet was six–and–a–half and Georgiana had been five years older and on the brink of adolescence. Let's wait and see. Change may come slowly.

Janet was now in regular grade two, after attending special preschool for language–delayed children, regular kindergarten, and grade one. Personally, I felt this placement must be for social purposes only. How could she participate?

Janet was using the Cannon Communicator with a teacher/ facilitator, a controversial program with negative research results unless the facilitator and child saw the same picture. I tried to analyze that picture–labeling was a separate skill, and differed from a child generating language which was important to him/ her. Then occurred the adverse television program proclaiming the fallacy of F.C., but slower to emerge was the evidence that some children could type responses that the facilitator did not know. Was the child or the facilitator doing the typing?

Janet became very upset. Anne did not know what she wanted as she whirled about in a dilemma. Anne grabbed the Cannon and Janet typed out JIF. Peanut butter.

Anne asked Janet what she wanted for breakfast, toast or cereal? Janet twirled about very upset. The message on the communicator looked like neither toast nor cereal. She wanted to say something else. Dad worked with her. "What's troubling you?"

"R B R D A."

"What's R B R D A?"

"Plnt tree."

"When is it?"

"Tomoro."

"Anne, you should read what she types. She doesn't give a hoot about cereal or toast right now, she wants to plant a tree! It's Arbor Day." He had learned to follow Janet's lead.

When Janet was promoted to regular grade two utilizing *inclusion* principles, I was more than skeptical. How would she survive a regular classroom? Would she receive the special services she needed? But the stories came in. The teacher had missed Janet, who was still a wanderer about the classroom. The teacher looked all about the classroom. Where had Janet gone? The hall, the bathroom, outdoors? She was about to begin a directed reading activity using the *Weekly Reader* with the children seated on the floor in a semicircle. There was Janet sitting with the others, her *Weekly Reader* opened just like the other children, waiting for the lesson to begin.

But how could you know Janet was reading? Flashcards? Picture–word matching? When I had taught children with physical handicaps, they at least had the yes–no response.

We could base all instructing on that yes–no response. But Janet did not understand that. I had not observed Janet in a classroom since preschool, but I could note changes in her day-to-day activities, particularly since there might be a three- or four-month interval between visits. I waited at the Orlando Airport for the family to arrive. Holding on to Dad's hand was seven-and-a-half-year-old Janet, dressed in a matching jumper like grown-up, ten-year-old Lauren.

We went to dinner at a family–style restaurant where Janet ate her favorite macaroni and cheese with a spoon, drank from a glass with one hand. Nothing on the floor! I remembered the earlier disaster at a restaurant. She greeted grampa's golden retriever, "Bosun, prettity, prettity, Bosun," as she gently patted his head.

Dad strapped on her helmet and she climbed on the special seat he constructed for her to ride in front of him on the adult bike. "Ride, whee–ee," and off they went. Janet was initiating purposeful speech.

She read phrases from "Hop the Pop" and "Is Your Mama a Lama?" over and over with Mom and Dad. A dozen books have been worn out. Is it sight reading or rote memorization? Janet seems to learn visually, rather than auditorially, but she loves rhyming words.

Is this a contradiction? We know the left side of the brain controls the right hand and this is the side for most verbal skills, but could Janet be learning language through music and songs via the right side of the brain? Just as a physically disabled or brain–damaged child may have difficulty with reading by inverting letters, was—saw, on—no, and not perceive and associate as normal learners, could Janet be unable to perceive and associate sounds? There were more questions than answers.

It seemed important to visit with Janet's teachers and learn of her current progress a year after the AIT program. Had Janet's schoolwork improved? Anne had shared with me bits of news, "Janet was in a spelling bee, Janet was in the school musical play with her aide beside her, but she hadn't liked the mask she was supposed to wear, Janet received a real report card."

I needed specific views from the speech/language therapist, occupational therapist, resource and classroom teachers and Janet's special aides. Fortunately, they had worked with Janet for several years and could offer an excellent perspective (only the classroom teacher could not join us). They remembered Janet, the wanderer.

This town practiced *inclusion*, so often read about in theory, but often a mishmash in actuality. Janet's aide offered an important insight: "Janet listens now. For so long we thought nothing was getting through, not even her name. Now, she pays attention and responds to her name. She follows direction in art and music class. There's been a change in her behavior, too. She's calm and interested in other children. This year she has friends."

Speech/Language Therapist: "A boy in the class was having a bad day. I asked Janet if she wanted to say something to him. Janet typed, "Get Happy Joe." We use FC with Janet and sometimes I think it's my language, not Janet's. Then she initiates something I don't know about."

Occupational Therapist: "Janet has dyspraxia and cannot initiate, coordinate, and sequence some motor activities. Once she is guided to begin an activity, she can follow through. She's just learned to use scissors independently. In art class, the children were assembling large butterflies and had stickers to paste on the wings. Janet had no use for stickers. She cut fringe around the edges of the wings, adding another dimension to her butterfly."

Aide: "When Janet gets upset in class, she says squish, squish. So I apply deep pressure. I asked where she had learned about deep pressure. "From Di, the O.T.," she said. She went on, "Janet does better on the playground with children this year. While standing in line for the slide, she will gently touch the next child on the arm so he or she will move ahead. No pushing or shoving, just a gentle touch."

"Resource Teacher: "Janet loves spelling bees and is often chosen among the first ones. She uses the Cannon Communicator to do the math program also. This year she took the Addison Wesley Math Test for Grade Two and the Gates Reading Test for Grade Two. We don't have the scores yet, but it's significant that she was able to follow directions and take the test. Last year she couldn't. We could honestly give her a real report card based on what she did in class."

Speech/Language Therapist: "What is emerging, Janet has a sense of humor. She will do something silly, then type, "Janet funny, ha ha." Of course, she has bad days as well, but we share that among the team. One day Janet took off down the hall in a wagon. She had had enough.

Aide: "We still work on toilet training. She sits on the potty regularly to urinate, but no success with BM's." Here was true inclusion. The whole team cared and shared techniques, gained insights, and changed Pampers if necessary. This was an exceptional team. However, the team had no specific knowledge of the AIT program and no record of it was in Janet's file. Some follow-through is certainly called for.

It's Janet's eighth birthday with swimming, boating, and a picnic supper on the deck. Janet is all dried off and has on her new clothes when we hear several splashes, gurgles, and swishes. Janet is swimming with her clothes on. Anne tells her to come out immediately and she does.

Which services have helped her more? Was it early language therapy? The AudioKinetron? The Communicator? Or perhaps the sincere and able teachers, aides, therapist, and above all, a caring, attentive family? We didn't wait for all the research to come in; we tried to follow Janet's clues. Her footprints in the sand have led; we follow.

No, Janet does not have normal eight-year-old language, but what she initiates is appropriate and shows concepts far beyond our awareness.

Perhaps it is the weaving together of all these—family, services, technology, and education. Someday, Janet may verbalize, "I want the book that God reads," but the beginnings are here.

Bumpy is no more, Janet begins to shine through.

Last June (1994) a video tape was made in school, following Janet all day, and from it you can really see how well she understands direction. She is eight, and is in normal grade three, working at grade level, with a full-time aide. (Her parents have just been transferred to Seattle, and the video was made in order to show her new school that she does type and that she understands what's going on.) She has some fine motor problems. She can take off her socks and clothes, but can't put them on. She types independently occasionally, but usually needs to be supported at the wrist. There is no doubt, however, that Janet is doing the typing. For example, when someone asked Janet where her grandmother lived, her facilitator thought she lived in New Hampshire. When Janet typed Florida, her facilitator was surprised, but Janet was right: her grandmother lives in Florida in the winter.

AIT has made it possible for Janet to hear and understand. Although she hasn't had dramatic breakthroughs with expressive language and is still verbally slow, she listens carefully and absorbs information in a normal way. She is able to participate in school activities, behaving appropriately, and she has one good friend with whom she plays nicely. Her school is accepting of her. ■

Chapter 19

Richard

by Angela Ditrio,
as told to Janet Cagliostro

Puzzles have always fascinated Richard, and I often reflect on the pieces of the puzzle in Richard's life: their shapes and sizes, mixing and matching. What doesn't fit here but might fit there. The number of pieces, and the challenge of putting them together to form a unified picture.

When he was born, Rick and I were thrilled. God had granted us a second miracle—another beautiful son who added joy to our lives as only beloved children can do. I took video pictures of Richard at ten months, in his walker, mesmerized by the camera and waving at Daddy. Rick filmed the boys together in a little red wagon with me pulling the wagon and them waving "bye bye" to the camera. We filmed Richard as we watched him walk at fifteen months, and were elated to hear those first words: "Mama, Dada!" I quickly reached for the video camera when his brother, turning the music on, began to dance with Richard while they clapped their hands to the tune of "La Bamba." At bedtime I read them stories, we said our prayers, and I softly hummed a lullaby as my babies unwound from a fun–filled day and prepared for yet another glorious day. (We still keep to this routine.) Our family life was truly content and filled with love.

Our lives were regular then. But after Richard recovered from a bout of childhood illnesses beginning when he was fifteen months old, roseola, bronchitis and an ear infection, one after the other, I noticed that he just was not the same. It seemed like a gradual change at the time, and yet how drastically it had all happened—within a span of pediatrician visits—in as little as three months. Suddenly I was constantly comparing Richard's language development to his brother's. Since Anthony had been premature, delayed milestones had been anticipated, but Richard had been a full–term baby and was still slower. When Anthony was a toddler, he would respond when spoken to. Richard responded only when we physically approached him.

I questioned the pediatrician about a possible hearing loss at his eighteen–month well visit. I explained that he didn't respond to us as well as he had before his recent illnesses, that he seemed to hear us only when he wanted to. The pediatrician wasn't concerned; in fact he reassured us. He suggested we wait until Richard was two before we tested him for a hearing impairment.

At least, I consoled myself, Richard was still affectionate, and continued to hug and kiss us and return the same affection that he had always allowed us to shower on him. I felt truly blessed that Richard had not lost this basic method of communicating, and that we could still cuddle and snuggle in ways that only parents can understand. Through our touch at least, Richard always knew how much we loved him.

Our twenty–four–month well checkup was a turning point in our lives. Although I anxiously anticipated the pediatrician's response to Richard's development, I had made up my mind that we would begin auditory testing regardless of his opinion. To my relief, the doctor immediately scheduled an evaluation. The results indicated that Richard heard within normal limits, could hear our voices, but chose not to respond to "tones." We were told it was nothing to worry about. However, results of speech and language testing indicated a severe expressive/receptive language and articulation delay.

Immediately, we enrolled him in private speech therapy and felt assured that his problem was temporary and would easily be corrected. After six months of speech therapy, the therapist suggested that Richard be enrolled in a language–based program starting in the fall.

We found an appropriate school and interviewed the program coordinator, the speech and language evaluator, and the social worker. We were thrilled when Richard was accepted, believing that the social interaction would help him learn to communicate effectively. It was recommended that we take him for a neurological evaluation.

The neurologist's tests revealed something called expressive/receptive aphasia. When I questioned the meaning of this new, foreign term, he shocked me by saying that it meant that

Richard was educable, that he "might" be able to talk, and that he might be slightly retarded. In my mind I screamed, "Are you speaking about *our* son?" And then I thought, "Why is he being so vague?" Why was he speaking in such broad, general terms when our child had only a mild, correctable speech problem? Of course he was educable—after all, he played with toys and puzzles, and he was good at it. Of course he will be able to speak. What was this man talking about? He was discussing our son in such a callous, impersonal manner, offering nothing but his terrifying diagnosis; no suggestions, no help, no "where do we go from here." Feeling insulted and betrayed, I stood up to leave. I gathered Richard in my arms and said, "You will be all right."

I don't remember driving home that day. I phoned my husband at work, and he met me at home immediately. Devastated, we cried together in the kitchen, clinging to each other for a long while, as if the strength of our love for each other and for our children could somehow eradicate the heavy cross we were about to carry. Time and again we looked at each other in disbelief. We questioned how this could be, and why *our* son? We never expected this diagnosis. We thought Richard's problem was temporary and was correctable. Although a part of me still thought the neurologist had been talking about another child, the reality of the situation began to settle in, and I knew we must act quickly—but how? What were we to do now? Who were we to turn to?

Somehow, we followed every suggestion offered to us. One by one, as they presented themselves, we evaluated the pieces of our puzzle to see if they fit. Even sign language was suggested to accelerate Richard's communicative ability. He underwent an EEG, blood tests, chromosome testing, Fragile–X testing and thyroid testing. We tried to have an MRI (Magnetic Resonance Imaging), but he could not tolerate the procedure. All the tests came back normal.

When we called the neurologist back several months later to let him know Richard's status, he informed us that he had found a mistake in the laboratory tests—one which he had failed to pick up. Apparently the Fragile–X test was inconclusive. He sent us to a genetic specialist who suggested that Richard be tested again. The second time around, three tests were done simultaneously, and all three test results were normal. Unbeknownst to us, the genetic specialist was conducting a study and had suggested retesting yet again. I informed the genetic specialist that I was aware of his study and that I would not allow my son to be tested again so that he could become a statistic or case study. It was obvious to us that he did not have Richard's best interests at heart. We needed concrete advice that could help us help our son.

We were advised that intensive speech therapy in a structured program would help him communicate more effectively, and when a summer program was suggested, we were sure it would be helpful. At the meeting of the Committee for Preschool Education, however, the chairperson, for no apparent reason, was against the summer program idea. Instead, he suggested that Richard be reevaluated by a medical team consisting of a physician, psychologist, pediatric developmentalist, educational therapist, audiologist, and a speech and language therapist. The team confirmed to the chairperson that Richard would benefit from the summer program! Richard was placed in a twelve–month program which began with the summer program.

The psychologist on the team diagnosed Richard as having pervasive development disorder unspecified (higher functioning), and that he functioned at a higher level than 75% of the children with this disorder. He explained Richard's way of learning to us. He likened the brain to television channels, and said that while some people watch the news on several different channels and are able to grasp and assimilate all the information, children with Pervasive Development Disorder have only one or two channels open. Together Rick and I sighed in relief that at last we were given a diagnosis and an understanding of Richard's development.

The summer program accommodated Richard's needs just as we had thought it would, and the following fall, he adjusted beautifully to school. One of the team members, Mary Bernard, a skilled educational therapist, took an interest in him, offering to work with him once a week on his imaginative/creative play skills. She continued to work with him, and he made great strides. She helped us, as well, by introducing us to monthly parent meetings which have eased our transition into Richard's world. She passed away in April, 1994, and we will always remember her for the extraordinary amount of time, energy and support she gave to families in need of her services.

The second year of school for Richard was not as successful as the first. Perhaps the difference in the academic curriculum and a less structured program affected him. Whatever the case, he had become aware of his own feelings and those of others, and cried when I would leave the classroom. Ironically, I smiled with pride when I saw that my son was affected by my absence. Since he had always been oblivious, I took this show of emotion as a sign of progress.

During the year, the speech therapist at the school expanded on Richard's already existing computer literacy. Earlier, we had introduced him to the computer keyboard as a means of play. The speech therapist introduced us to software that allowed Richard to develop his language and to experience a sense of achievement when he received feedback from the computer in response to his touch. Instead of Leggo or Play-doh, the computer became Richard's creative toy.

In the middle of the school year, we decided on another neurological consultation for a second opinion. The neurologist confirmed the original diagnosis and assured us that Richard was in a good program. Occupational therapy was suggested and all the specialists agreed it would be beneficial. Occupational therapy has proved to be important for decreasing Richard's tactile sensitivity and hyperactivity, and increasing his body awareness. It has helped him behave more appropriately, with less interest in tuning out. Techniques such as joint compression, massage, and "brushing," although they seemed odd to us at first, have been useful.

Richard progressed during the school year on target for his diagnosis; however, I still felt the need to investigate more possibilities. Several social workers at Richard's school suggested I read *The Sound of a Miracle*, and one of them offered me her copy. The book underlined the need to question and keep questioning until we received answers. I telephoned Annabel Stehli, who gave me the names of several parents who had experienced auditory training with their children whom she thought I should contact. My conversations with them convinced me that we had found yet another piece of the puzzle, a significant one. Richard's educational therapist was also supportive of our decision to consider auditory training. At this point, Richard was four-and-a–half, and could only say words of one or two syllables if they were pointed out, such as car, pretzel, or apple. He did not initiate speech.

Annabel provided us with a list of practitioners who provide this service in the United States and Canada, and we decided to travel to North Haven, Connecticut, for the ten days of training. It was a great comfort to have my parents accompany us and stay with us until Anthony and Rick could come for the weekend. Their presence and constant love and support eased our tension and fortified our will to go through with the auditory training.

We had reserved space in a nearby hotel where families undergoing auditory training were given an extremely warm reception. They offered discounted rates not only for our rooms, but for the use of the pool, an amenity which proved to be important. We arrived the night before the first session and anxiously awaited the next morning.

The office of the auditory training practitioner was in a new building, with a waiting room filled with information, books, pamphlets and a loose leaf binder containing the story of a teenager's positive experience with AIT. A children's corner with various attractions kept Richard's attention while we waited. We had prepared Richard at home by having him listen to music through earphones for half an hour at a time, and I had filled out all the paperwork, but still I was apprehensive as I sat there wondering what was going to happen.

The audiologist and the AIT practitioner were very pleasant, and put me at ease as they reviewed the training process. Sally, the practitioner, explained that during the sessions, distractions such as toys, books, and stuffed animals would not be allowed in the room, but juice boxes, Cheerios, and/or raisins were permitted if they were necessary to calm the child (one mother used french fries!). I was reassured that Richard would be able to cooperate, and my fears gave way to excitement and anticipation.

When the initial audiogram was attempted, Richard couldn't stand wearing the headphones. I wondered if we had come this far for it all to end here at this juncture. He had been able to tolerate the earphones at home for the required thirty–minute period, and I wondered why he had a problem with them now. Sally assured me that we could still go ahead with the auditory training, that he would benefit from AIT even without an audiogram.

We were guided into another room and earphones were placed on my ears first so that I could experience the type of music which Richard would be listening to. These headphones were large, padded, soft, and much more comfortable than the ones used for the audiogram. Richard was able to tolerate them with no problem and completed the first thirty minutes without any fuss.

During the three–hour break, we had lunch, explored the local shops, visited the park, lit candles in the local church, walked, talked, and went back to the hotel where we could watch TV or go swimming. After the second session, we discovered a nearby mall, an ice cream shop, all the fast food restaurants, and a bagel shop. What a treat! No cooking for ten days!

In the soundproof room where the training was conducted, there was a table, a chair, and a set of earphones. Sally also supplied a swing supported by the frame of the door to accommodate young children if they were unable to sit at the table. This was a wonderful help at times for Richard, and the swinging motion soothed him. We were happy to see that at times he held on to the earphones, making sure they didn't fall off. I repeatedly told him that the music in the earphones would help him, and I know he understood. After several days of training, when we returned to the hotel he placed the paper coverings meant for the tops of the glasses over his ears, pretending they were headphones—indicating, I'm sure, that he liked the music and knew it was helping him.

As we went through the next ten days, Richard's moods varied. Sometimes he cried or fussed, and woke up crying in the middle of the night. After the training sessions were over for the day, often we couldn't go shopping because he couldn't tolerate the noise in the stores and the mall. Sometimes we had to return to the hotel because he was simply exhausted and needed to lie down. As we watched, listened, and loved him through the whole difficult process, these reactions were confusing to us. How could he wake up in the middle of the night absolutely distraught, banging his little fists on the sides of his head and screaming as if he were in pain, if this training was a positive piece in the puzzle? Richard had always been a sound sleeper and had never awakened in the middle of the night in such a state. All I could do was cry in sympathy as I held and rocked him to prevent him from hurting himself. I sang to him and talked softly to him, all the while reassuring him that I was trying to understand his pain and that hopefully it would end soon. After three or four bad nights, Sally said that this was a side affect of AIT, although not a typical one, as most children's sleeping habits improved with auditory training. The days and nights wore on.

Each day I kept a journal. I watched him carefully, knowing that any changes, negative or positive, would mean that the training was working. During the evening of the third day, we were amazed when he put his stuffed Pooh Bear on the bed and said, "Look at my baby." When my parents left that evening, he said, "Bye bye." Later on he wrote the number of my parents' address, #1426, while doodling on paper. He clearly realized his grandparents had left! On the fourth day, when he saw the swimming pool in the hotel, he said, "Bathing suit. Swim. Water." He also said, "My baby," and "My house," for reasons I did not understand. On the fifth day, he said "1426"—was he trying to tell us he missed his grandparents?

On the sixth day, Rick and Anthony were with us for the weekend. Richard was sitting on the floor playing with Rosary beads when Rick asked me if I thought Richard was hungry. I said I could offer bologna, cheese, or pizza. Richard came to me, looked at me, and repeated, "Bologna, cheese, or pizza," the longest phrase he had ever said. On the seventh day, while waiting in the office for his session to begin, Richard played with four colorful balls and repeatedly stated each color, "Orange, purple, green, and purple." Throughout the eighth day he said, "Baby cry," and "It's a happy." On the ninth day, he again said repeatedly, "It's happy," or "It's a happy," and he also spelled "H —O—M—E" and said the word. I reassured him that on the following day we would be going home.

Before the last day's session, when Richard realized that there were only three of the four colorful balls he was used to playing with, he yelled, "Four balls," twice. I proceeded to find the fourth ball for him. At the end of the day, when we returned to the hotel, he said, "155." It was the number of our hotel room. Toward the latter part of the ten–day process, he had begun sleeping through the night once again, and we were relieved to see him drift off after the last day's sessions.

Although we left Connecticut with a feeling of hope, the next two weeks were almost a living hell. Richard returned to school right away, beginning his third year of schooling. He was enrolled in a new school, in a local TEACCH program (Treatment and Education of Autistic and Children with Communication Handicaps, developed at University of North Carolina Medical School in Chapel Hill). His teacher and I communicated daily to chart his progress and behavior. Though it was the beginning of the school year, and she had only known Richard for two weeks prior to the training, she observed his frustration in trying to communicate. She reported that if Richard felt that anyone did not understand him, he would proceed to pinch or bite! We were distraught at this new behavior; however, as quickly as it happened, it stopped, and he appeared to be more in control of his feelings and better able to cope with those around him.

Over the next three months, the negative behavior lessened, occurring only occasionally, and then escalated. He began to have tantrums where he would again beat his little fists against the sides of his head, throw himself onto the floor, awaken at night in a screaming frenzy, and lose control in school. His teacher recorded his negative behavior as the result of frustration because of his inability to communicate, and it was heightened at times because of the attention he received. It appeared that Richard was better off if he were not approached during these episodes, and the behavior was allowed to run its course.

Sally suggested we consult a behavioral optometrist. Minimal prism glasses were recommended, and we were told he would either adapt to them easily and immediately or refuse to wear them altogether. Richard not only wore the glasses, but he didn't want to take them off even at bedtime! They helped him throw and catch a ball, something every little boy loves to do, but they didn't help his behavior.

My maternal intuition started to work on overtime, my gut feeling being that something other than the auditory training must be causing his increasingly terrible behavior, something which we were on the verge of finding out. I began to think it was something physical, affecting him from the inside—perhaps his chemical makeup, or something in his immediate surroundings. Was he allergic to something he was eating or drinking, or something in the air?

When I consulted a nutritionist/M.D. on the telephone, he said that Richard's nutrition should be in order before testing for allergies. The results of a urine test indicated toxic levels of chlorine which caused his cells to be catabolic. In addition, he had vitamin deficiencies and a low level of calcium. Had we stumbled on another piece of the puzzle? I was used to hearing about lead in the water, but what about chlorine? Since Richard was tactile defensive and hearing sensitive, it made sense that his chemical makeup would make him sensitive to environmental hazards.

We had the chlorine in our water tested three times to be sure, and each time high levels were found. We installed a filtration system to filter out not just the chlorine but any other impurities as well. The nutritionist suggested that Richard drink distilled water and that we use filtered tap water for cooking only.

Within five days, Richard's behavior had improved dramatically. Although we had also made changes in Richard's nutrition, we believe the improvement was a direct result of the lack of chlorine in his system. We were still waiting for a delivery of homeopathic vitamins, and had limited his intake of sugar, processed foods, foods with dyes, additives or preservatives, beef, pork, salt, and chocolate. Richard's urine was tested again, within eight weeks, and to the nutritionist's amazement, the level of chlorine was normal and the levels of nutrients were almost normal.

Family members, friends, and Richard's teachers and therapists began to comment on the radical change in Richard's progress and behavior. He was more focused, his receptive skills increased dramatically, his speech was clearer, his general disposition was calm and peaceful, and the only negative that emerged was that he could no longer tolerate his prism glasses and stopped playing catch. I started to see traits in him that I hadn't seen since he was fifteen months old. I asked Sally about it, wondering how he could retrace his lost steps to complete his developmental stages when he was now almost six years old. He appeared to be catching up.

In retrospect, we do believe that early intervention was essential, and that it would have been dangerous to assume that his developmental delays just would have worked themselves out. When Richard was eighteen months old and I first communicated my concerns to his pediatrician, he should have been evaluated immediately instead of wasting six or seven months waiting to see, if time would tell.

Last week, almost a year after auditory training, I took Richard to the park and could clearly see the evidence of it in the changes in his behavior. Instead of running around or just sitting in the sand watching the grains slip through his fingers, he took notice of things. Each time a car drove by, he looked up at it. When the wind blew, he looked at the leaves rustling in the trees. If someone walked by, he raised his head and glanced at the passerby. We even made an imaginary cake in the sand with sticks as candles, sang "Happy Birthday," and knocked over the candles as if we were blowing them out. He repeated what I did and laughed.

Today was a good day. His teacher communicated to me through our notebook dialogue that he had a calm, happy, verbal day at school. When he got off the school bus, he gave me a kiss (at my request), said hello to his brother, and had his afternoon snack. Today, he decided not to play with his brother, as he did yesterday when he laughed and giggled while playing in the tent or with the race car set; instead, he chose to sit at his computer and play software games. This was his challenge for the day. We may not know how many times he guessed the right answer or how many times he missed, but I know that he is occupying himself in a worthwhile endeavor and that he is making choices and thinking on his own. When I announced that dinner was ready, I approached him to turn off the power on the computer, and he complied with understanding and ease. We asked God to bless our food, to which Richard promptly responded "Amen!" At the dinner table he even asked for water and more broccoli and carrots, and I, also, complied with understanding and ease. As a family, we interacted at the dinner table as it was meant to be.

The pieces of the puzzle which we lack are forthcoming because Saint Theresa never fails to send a rose in answer to my prayers. Faithfully, I pray to her and ask her to heal Richard. This past Sunday she placed a bouquet of yellow roses at Blessed Mary's Altar. My family and I sat in front of the Altar during Mass, and when we genuflected to leave the Chapel, Saint Theresa's roses seemed to jump into sight.

"Saint Theresa, Little Flower,
Please pick for me from your heavenly garden
a rose,
and send it to me with a message of love
and ask God to grant me the favor
I thee implore,
and tell Him I will love Him each day
more and more."

* * *

To update (December, 1994), we have consulted our homeopathic doctor and have found that Richard has several food allergies: bananas, cantaloupe, carrots, cheese (severe), eggs, cow's milk, peanuts, radishes, rye, sugar cane, tangerines, wheat, and yeast. He has more yeast in his system than before, and is taking acidophilus, as well as multivitamins with higher doses of B6 and magnesium. A papaya enzyme helps his digestion. He will be seven at the end of this month, and is doing first grade level math, reading, and writing. Last year, although I had to push for it, he was mainstreamed for play time for forty–five minutes to an hour with great success. Richard again will be mainstreamed for some subjects in January. Although he is behind in his social skills, his memory is outstanding, and his academic work is on grade level.

The following describes how we obtained insurance coverage: It started in November of 1992, and we didn't obtain coverage for a year. I submitted an insurance claim for auditory training, as I would for any necessary treatment or medical need. Feeling pretty confident in our coverage, I double–checked with my insurance company to see if there was any "pre–information" they would need in order to process the claim smoothly. I was told that after the treatment I should include the following with the claim: the bill, an explanation of what auditory training is, a prescription from a physician (I was told a pediatrician was able to do this), and a statement from me, the parent, as to why I was of the "opinion" that my son needed this procedure done.

After Richard completed the auditory training, I followed the instructions, and figured that in six to eight weeks I would get a check for the usual 80% of the total. Instead, I received 80% of the $150.00 for the audiogram. Thinking there might have been an oversight on the part of the department which processes the claims/forms, I called the insurance company to find out what happened. I was advised to send in a *resubmission* of the bill, prescription, explanation of the service, and another parent letter.

Six weeks later, I received an explanation of benefits— "The provider of this service does not meet the definition of a physician contained in the plan. Therefore, this charge is not covered." Just to re–cap, I was told prior to auditory training that I only needed a physician's prescription—not that a physician had to perform the service.

At this point I was going to forget it. Richard was showing signs of having benefited from the training, and I felt it had been worth going through it even without reimbursement. But after speaking with the auditory trainer and learning that some people had succeeded in obtaining coverage (including Annabel Stehli, who got 80% from Blue Cross, Blue Shield in 1977 for Georgie's auditory training), I decided to call again and find out how to get the claim processed or at least find a more reasonable explanation as to why the insurance company couldn't reconsider coverage.

After the phone call, I was more determined than ever to get my point across and get the coverage I felt I was owed. This is what was stated:

1. That there was no licensed/certified person who did the training. (This is not true because the audiologist is licensed and certified.)

2. That the insurance company thought it was some kind of speech therapy, even though in my letter I explained it was for hearing and audiological processing.

3. That a "degree" was needed (this was never mentioned originally, and I am still baffled by what type of degree).

4. That although this particular provider was not covered, the service itself could be covered.

At this point, I was advised to send in an *appeal* in writing to the Technical Quality Control Unit of the insurance company with a statement clarifying the issues. After several weeks of not hearing from them, I called and was told they were still negotiating. After several more weeks, when I called I was informed that the insurance company had made a mistake in the first place by sending coverage for the "hearing test." Then I was told I needed to submit the following in writing:

1. New documentation
2. A report from an audiologist
3. The degree of the problems
4. A letter of prognosis from a psychologist which would also state the condition of Richard before, during, and after auditory training.

I couldn't see any reason for any of the above, so I asked to speak to a person with more authority to review appeals. I was told that they do not speak to anyone over the telephone, and that everything has to be done in writing. With frustration in my voice, I asked to make an appointment with someone who reads the appeals and to review and explain my son's condition, how he was before the training, and how marvelously he is progressing as a result of it. I said I was willing to travel for three hours to the insurance company. When they refused to make an appointment, I made it clear that I was not going to stop asking questions until I got some answers that seemed satisfactory to me. I wanted to know who "they" were, and having learned that, I was ready to travel out to the insurance company without an appointment. "They" were retired physicians who review claims or appeals. At this point, I posed a question to the person on the telephone: "Do these doctors know what auditory training is? Do they know what PDD. (pervasive development disorder)/autism is?" I said I didn't think so, and I offered to explain it to someone who might understand something about the whole situation. By the grace of God, I talked to a woman whose niece is autistic and who knew what the procedure was and the possible benefits/results. After we spoke at length about Richard's progress during the past year, she promised to look into the situation. Four weeks after speaking with her, I received a letter from the insurance company stating, "We have completed our review of your son's claim file regarding treatment rendered by . . . " Based on the circumstances involved with this claim, we will make an administrative exception and allow the $800.00 in charges previously denied for services rendered from September 22, 1992 to October 2, 1992. The benefits available for these charges will be mailed under separate cover. We trust this explanation is helpful to you in understanding our position. Should you have any questions concerning this matter, please contact our office."

One week later, a check came in the mail.

I have learned a lot from being nicely persistent, and I feel I didn't ask for or expect anything unreasonable. Richard has made a lot of progress as a result of my persistence, in school, in life, and in his very existence. I will not give up on any possibility, especially when I know he will benefit from it. ∎

Chapter 20

BL

by Anita Goode

I found out I was pregnant when I went to the doctor with the flu. What a surprise! During the rest of the pregnancy I felt great and everything was normal until the last month when I gained twenty to thirty pounds of fluid. BL was breach and he had not turned by my due date. Two days later, I went into the hospital to have a C–section.

BL had to be respirated and his body temperature was low. During our hospital stay, he was kept in an isolator in the nursery except for feedings. Other than that, he was a beautiful, healthy 8 lb. 7 oz., 22 3/4" infant who never looked like a newborn.

As BL did not breastfeed well, I had to supplement with formula. After four months of terrible gas problems, I switched to soybean–based formula, and within four days he was doing fine.

Generally, no major health problems surfaced during his early years. He had his share of ear and sinus infections that were cleared up with antibiotics, but still tended to carry fluid in his inner ear. Strangely enough, each year, within one week of his birthday, BL has been sick with various symptoms.

The year BL turned three was the worst. We were out of town and he developed a fever of 105. My sister and I rushed him to the hospital emergency room, and found his throat and ears were extremely infected. Strep was suspected. After taking an antibiotic for three days, his whole body was swollen and covered with red splotches of various shapes and sizes. His feet, ears, and hands turned completely red. The pediatrician suspected an allergic reaction to the medication, but testing did not verify this and the final diagnosis was of a viral and bacterial infection manifesting through the skin. (When he was seven, against my pediatrician's wishes we finally had BL's tonsils and adenoids out. He stopped having ear and sinus infections, and his eating and sleeping habits also improved.)

Although he never crawled, BL appeared to develop on schedule until approximately sixteen to seventeen months. At that time, there was a complete change in my happy, wonderful child. I had a difficult time explaining the change, but the best I could do was to say that nothing made him happy and he had no desire to try anything.

From that time until he was three, I lived from day to day and just tried doggedly to do my best. The general comment was, "He is so cute, but what is wrong with him?" My family was supportive, but critical of how I handled him.

He seemed different to me, but very intelligent and loving. There were many things he could not do: feed himself, go to the bathroom, chew food properly, dress himself, play independently or with other children, respond to basic questions (name, age, etc.), verbally express his wants and needs. There were some things that he could do beyond his years—at eighteen months he mastered the use of the VCR and TV controls, and by the time he was two-and-a-half, he could identify every upper and lowercase letter of the alphabet, spell basic words when given objects (dog, cat, hat, etc.), count to 20, and quote sections of videos or books from memory.

At our three-year-old checkup, the pediatrician tried to get BL to respond to basic questions, but it was as if he was not speaking. At that time the doctor asked, "Are you sure this child can hear?" Although I had been trying to tell him for a year and a half that something was wrong, he had always given me a pat answer. "All children develop at different rates, and he will be all right," he said, in an effort to reassure me.

When we took BL for an audiogram, he wouldn't cooperate and it was a disaster. We had to resort to sedation and electronic methods to determine if sound waves were traveling from BL's ears to his brain. Everything appeared to be normal.

Next was a developmental evaluation. After testing, the psychologist said he had never seen a child so skewed in his abilities—from eighteen months to seven years. He would not give a diagnosis, but suggested more testing by a neurologist, and speech therapy as soon as possible.

When BL was three, everything seemed like a struggle. We began language therapy, two days a week for thirty minutes, and he had to be restrained in the chair. First, basic things were worked on: eye contact, paying attention, reducing echolalic speech patterns, expanding language usage while decreasing nonverbal behavior (nervous breakdown fits and screeching), increasing receptive language skills, and initiating communication. (After five years of speech, BL did get most of a summer off in 1993, but started back in August.)

As soon as we could get an appointment, we visited the neurologist. After observation, he suggested an EEG to see if the brain was functioning properly. The EEG appeared to be normal. BL received a diagnosis of Attention Deficit Disorder with hyperactivity, autistic tendencies or autistic–like characteristics. At that time, PDD and Asperger's Syndrome were not given as diagnoses. No one wanted to give BL an "autistic" diagnosis because he was not severe enough to be classified as "infantile."

We continued with language therapy and I tried to read anything I could get my hands on that might be related to BL's problems. When he was three, a "Mother's Day Out" program was willing to take him two days a week, which gave me a break and also gave him more peer exposure. This attempt at inclusion in a typical setting was not as successful as we had hoped. Generally, he was still different, and did his own thing. All the teachers loved him. He was not disruptive and was very loveable, but just did not "fit in" and could not even begin to do the things the other children did.

We found a program called Reaching Rainbows (it no longer exists), and it was just what BL needed, a small group setting (six or less) with two or three teachers—almost one–on–one. He attended Reaching Rainbows from age three–and–a–half to five. He progressed so much, I could go on for pages. This program got him to the point where I could leave him alone in Sunday School class and he could successfully handle a small regular classroom setting.

When he was four, occupational therapy was suggested. BL was treated (one hour per week for almost three years) in various areas: tactile defensiveness, gross motor skills, fine motor skills, upper extremity muscle strength, postural control, oral motor function for feeding, self–help skills, visual perceptual skills, bilateral coordination, and wrist and shoulder stability.

As I stated earlier, BL made great progress during his time at Reaching Rainbows, but after he started occupational therapy, his progress was much more noticeable and profound, probably because it helped him get in touch with his body, along with desensitizing him to external stimuli.

The combination of speech/language therapy, Reaching Rainbows, occupational therapy, and work at home produced a five–year–old who was as close to "typical" as could be expected, a "clinical miracle" to many professionals.

At five, an educational decision had to be made. The class at Reaching Rainbows was dissolving due to the ages of the children. BL was going to be the only one left. His teacher did not want him to be included with the other children because their level of functioning was lower than BL's, and she was afraid he would imitate them. We had worked too hard for him to be allowed to regress.

I contacted the city school system for an evaluation and placement. At the "M–team" meeting, I was told that they really did not have a place for BL, but they would do the best they could. When the placement suggested was a program designed for mentally and physically impaired students, his teacher and I started looking at the private schools where he could have the most typical situation possible along with personnel that could understand his problems.

The only option was a private Catholic school. This school was started for children with a learning disability of any kind. Even though BL was five, I wanted to hold him back a year and place him in their kindergarten program for four–year–olds. After evaluating him, the school placed him in 5K because he knew too much and would be bored in 4K.

BL stayed in 5K for two years with the same teacher. He had two wonderful years academically and the time needed to mature socially and emotionally. He had to be isolated to remain on task when doing his work, and showed signs of stress from time to time, but the teacher recognized this and did not force him unless it was necessary. During his second year he became the leader in many class activities, especially computers, which built up his self–esteem.

After the second year of 5K, BL moved into nongraded first grade. He did so well academically that after Christmas the teacher suggested he be placed in the regular first grade. This took some doing. He had to be shown that he could do the work. From February through May, he remained in the regular first grade. His academic work was basically excellent, but at times he did not understand instructions and would not make very good grades. He is a perfectionist and very hard on himself, and if he missed more than one answer, he felt he had not done a good job. His critical attitude made it difficult for him to find the desire to try because he thought he would fail.

In the summer of 1993, BL was in a regular day care situation and seemed to handle it well. At times, he did have trouble understanding why some children were not as nice to him as he wanted them to be (name calling, making fun of him, etc.). He played machine pitch baseball and made a real contribution to his team. He had some sportsmanship problems, but eventually learned to accept defeat in an appropriate manner.

In July of '93 (he was seven), BL received auditory training. This was the last therapy that we were aware of that could help him. He has not shown any regressive behaviors and does seem to be more independent. He is still sensitive to sounds, but not quite as acutely.

This year, BL is able to be in the regular second grade and doing fine. His organizational skills are not the best—he frequently forgets assignments and notebooks for his homework. He says, "Second grade is hard, but I love my teacher." He is not as positive as in the past, but his grades are excellent.

During the years of evaluations, BL has gone from mentally retarded to borderline genius, and when we went for another psychological evaluation recently, his IQ had risen another few points.

I cannot stop now; it is an ongoing process. He still has trouble with abstract concepts, social interactions, instructions, attending, organization, empathy, and verbally expressing himself, but the main thing is that, basically, he functions on a "typical" level, within the normal range.

Is he a "clinical miracle" or is this what can happen when these children get what they need when they need it? I feel BL is a success story, but many other children can be also. ■

Chapter 21

Niki

by Victoria L. Baczewski

My first pregnancy ended in a miscarriage at eight weeks. My second pregnancy produced Darek, and eleven months later, Nikolas arrived. This last pregnancy began within two months of stopping birth control pills/hormonal therapy for polycystic ovaries. To further complicate matters, part of the first trimester was spent in Poland, where the fallout from Chernobyl is considered a factor in birth defects. I had not known this at the time of my visit.

Upon my return from that country to Germany, where my husband, Darius, was stationed, the first scare in the pregnancy occurred when my son came running to me as I was sitting on the couch. His head collided with my stomach, resulting in cramping and spotting, and I had to go to the hospital. An examination by the doctors there suggested that all was well. The pregnancy continued and all was "well" until the last trimester.

Around the end of the eighth month, Darek came down with an ear infection, his temperature soaring to 105 degrees. We rushed him to the emergency room where we waited all night to be seen. By the time he was examined and released, I had been awake for over twenty-four hours. After that night, every time I picked up Darek, I went into labor. So, the last month was spent going in and out of labor. Still, we managed to make it to the due date plus three days.

The checkup the day before I delivered Niki revealed that I was four centimeters dilated and 95% effaced. The doctor decided to stretch my cervix. This threw me into contractions for the rest of the day. The next day I was weepy in the morning, and by 1 P.M., exhaustion had set in. I conned Darek into taking a nap, and at 3:15, the onset of labor awakened me. It went fast. I reached the hospital at 4:30 in transition, and by 5:50, I was ready to push. But something was wrong. Every time I pushed, Niki's heart rate dropped to an extremely low rate: the umbilical cord was wrapped under his left arm and up around his neck. The doctor ordered me to breathe through alternate contractions to allow Niki's heart rate to come back to normal. This was supposed to prevent him from being compromised due to a lack of oxygen. At 6:15 P.M., Niki came into the world. The date was April 11, 1989.

As with all children at that time, Niki was given the Apgar test. This is a test of a newborn's physical condition based on his responses to different stimuli. He scored a 3/7 out of a possible 10/10 and was considered flopsy.

I can still see the scene in my mind as the nurses did the Apgar. Darius and I knew something was wrong for they whisked Niki to a corner of the room and called a NICU (newborn intensive care unit) doctor to the scene. Watching as they flicked his heel with their fingers, our sense of alarm grew as he failed to respond. The tears began to flow down my husband's face. My heart began to sink as the longing to hold my child was denied. My son was taken to NICU without my even getting a chance to look at him, hold him, count his fingers and toes. Being a stubborn mom, I started to nag the nurses to let me up—to let me go to my son. As soon as I was allowed, I went to him (even before checking into the maternity ward). I found my son crying and hooked up to an IV. Yet he was a full–term 8 1/2 pound baby—the largest in the NICU. It didn't seem real.

My intention as a mother was to breastfeed. I had enjoyed the cuddling with Darek and felt it was the best way to go. However, the pediatrician felt it would be better to have Niki bottlefed while he was in the NICU. So, I pumped my breasts to get the colostrum and milk flowing and fed him with a bottle.

He did not feed well for me or the NICU nurses. The nurses were worried about how little he would drink. It seemed that no sooner would he begin than he would go to sleep. I tried harder to give him really good feedings whenever I was there, but all he would do was root for the breast. So we gave the task to Darius, who had the best success.

Niki came down with jaundice due to ABO incompatibility. He was treated with bilirubin lights, and his blood was tested again and again to check his bilirubin levels. After two days, his levels dropped enough for him to join me in my room. I was allowed to begin breastfeeding my child, and after the fourth day, we were released and went home.

The troubles really began then. Breastfeeding Niki was a disaster. He'd fall asleep every few minutes, making feeding a two–hour task. This would have been okay if there had not been a Darek who needed attention. As it was, I'd end up trying to squeeze in time with Darek between feedings, in the one hour we usually had before Niki would start to cry again and I'd be chained to the couch for another two hours, feeding and burping Niki.

By the end of his second week of life, Niki was screaming from feeding to feeding, with the worst crying right when Dad came home. All of my efforts to calm him failed. Walking up and down the hall did not work. The swing which Darek had loved did not work. Baby baths did not work. Rocking did not work. Walks in strollers, slings, my arms did not work. Pretty soon the family who lived upstairs would tell me in a combination of German, Italian, and English that they constantly heard my son crying. To top it off, Niki's crying set off Darek's crying.

I began to think I was a terrible flop as a mother. One child was okay, but two were beyond my ability. Panic became my companion for a time and help seemed impossible to find. Asking my mother, I found she never had that problem. Begging our pediatrician, I got jokes. Speaking to mothers in the checkout line of the commissary, I finally got something to try.

I put Niki on formula and fennel tea (an herbal tea used for colic by the Germans and okayed by our pediatrician). It helped for the most part during the day. Instead of the constant crying, we were down to a two–hour spell per day when Darius came home from work, and an occasional two–hour period in the early morning (starting between 4 and 5 A.M.). I never could figure out why it was always these times of the day.

When Darius came home at night, it was usually a busy time for me. It marked the arrival of an adult for me to talk with. I would also be running at top speed trying to get meals together for the family. At this stage of the children's lives, it meant three different meals—Niki's meal, Darek's meal, and the adult meal. Perhaps it was just too chaotic.

The very early morning was the most difficult time. Maybe something would startle Niki or scare him out of his sleep, and he was too tired to cope. It was at this time of the day that Darius would be preparing for work. I would finally get Niki settled and Darek would get up. I spent most of that time in a state of sleep deprivation. It was not long before my ability to cope began to wane. Something was not quite right.

Feeling ignored by the pediatrician—Niki was thriving, gaining weight, and checking out fine—I went to a psychologist. Knowing we were not meshing well as a family, I felt there must be something we needed to change. So, we began working on parenting skills. From there, it was individual work with a counselor. We were following the "fix the mother and everything falls into place" theory of life at that point. From there, it was marriage counseling with my husband. Yes, you have it—it was the "fix the marriage and everything else falls into place" theory. Guess what: it did not.

As all of this was going on, I was deepening my involvement with my church and seeking a more mature relationship with the Lord. Understanding His will in my life and making Him the center of it became my top priority. Daily prayer and trying to listen for a response was the one constant in my life. Soon I became more at peace with the chaos I was experiencing in my life. The Lord entered in and allowed me to really feel His presence in my life. I feel certain that this was His gift to me in preparation for this life we now lead. Knowing that we are all held firmly in His hands gives me the peace and courage I need to find solutions for the difficulties my family faces.

In the meantime, Darius would look at Niki and ask me if he could hear. He was concerned because at times we could not get Niki's attention. He seemed deaf. However, I was sure he could hear. He would come running into the room from his hiding place whenever his favorite music video tapes were playing. Also, I had run the bell test recommended for parents with any doubts about their child's hearing. Niki would appropriately turn and look at the bell when it was rung. This confirmed my belief that he could hear.

Thankfully, the child psychologist was still on board. We were running behavior scales every six months on both children. By the third one on Niki, at the grand age of twenty–three months, we discovered a seeming regression because his speech did not keep pace with his earlier development. It did not even get past the starting point.

The psychologist asked to see Niki. During the session, he began to point out things to me that I had noticed but had not felt were significant. Niki did not approach me as a human being. I was there to fulfill needs, i.e. help with things like opening boxes, reaching toys he could not reach, etc. What I had thought was relationship–building was rather just a self–stimulating behavior. Niki would come and climb on my leg to play horsey. I genuinely thought there was more going on because Niki would smile even though he looked right through me.

Other problems we had were head banging, spinning, and tantrums. All children have tantrums. Niki's were shorter than his brother's so I saw no problem there. The spinning was rather strange, especially when he'd get out of control with it. I had a response for that. I'd stop him and try to get him interested in something else. The surest thing was "Disney's SingAlong Songs." He really enjoyed watching these tapes on TV.

The other problem—head banging—was always something that occurred after I had placed a limit on him and he had gone to his room in a fit. I'd stop him from doing something, he'd go to his room in a fit, then he'd walk out and very deliberately—or so it seemed to me—walk over to the wall and bang his head. It seemed so controlled. Yet it had to hurt and pain is usually a great behavior modifier. He'd stop when he made the connection between the head banging and the pain. I tried to help by telling him that he was bound to get a headache and could choose to stop. He didn't.

The final clue to the puzzle was that I was beginning to see Niki as my lost child. As Niki was growing from eighteen months to two years old, the Gulf Crisis was happening. My husband was on call a lot and worked long hours. We lived quietly in an apartment in a farming area. There were mainly three of us in the house—myself, Darek, and Niki. Yet I was always looking for Niki.

I would do an activity with the children, get them busy doing an independent task, and while they did their "projects," I would do a household chore like washing the dishes, preparing a meal, or doing general housecleaning. These lasted no more than fifteen to twenty minutes, enough time for the children to be ready for something new.

I would go back to them, and Niki would already be gone. I started to hear the refrain again and again, "Darek, where's Niki?"

It was becoming clear, especially with the lack of speech development, that Niki needed to be tested for his hearing and for these behaviors. What was going on? Why did Niki like to hide? Were we doing something wrong? I felt as if I was losing my child, and for the first time, I heard the word autism.

We began with the hearing. If Niki was deaf, then naturally speech could not develop. The testing was a nightmare. It began quietly enough, but it became one huge battle once the tones began coming into the booth. He wanted to escape so badly that I had to fight to keep him on my lap. Yet he appeared to hear.

We went on to the other tests. These we did twice because my husband was reassigned stateside. First, we were tested in Germany and came out with the diagnosis of PDD—pervasive developmental disorder. This was explained to me as a less severe form of autism. On the spectrum of normal to severe autism, Niki was seen as being high-functioning and closer to normal, yet still autistic. That diagnosis was made when Niki was twenty-seven months old. Some additional clues were noted—Niki toe-walked, flicked his fingers, and repeated ba, ba, ba over and over. At that time, he was evaluated at eighteen months for expressive and receptive speech.

In the process of all the testing, at my husband's request I increased my efforts with Niki. I began to hold him on my lap even though he'd fight. I spent more time with him on the floor and with his toys. Anything he needed, I would name again and again. I looked for those things he enjoyed and tried to reach him. I was scared for him and us.

We moved, and it took me eight months to get him a new evaluation, diagnosis, and help. No one would take the evaluation from Germany and begin the treatment which I had been told so often was "critical" and "the sooner the better." Once again, we began with hearing.

The hearing test took place in a children's hospital. It was geared more towards gaining the child's cooperation than the previous test had been. Thankfully, Niki stayed with it throughout the testing, turning his head to the tones and watching the lights light up over the speaker. He even anticipated the lights going on, and when they would not, he got upset.

Whenever the examiner would speak into the speaker, Niki would not respond. He'd been showing us he could hear whenever the tones were played, and yet, when the spoken word came through the speakers, Niki once again appeared to be deaf. Even so, the test results indicated normal hearing sensitivity, adequate for normal speech and language development, which told us we needed to continue our search for answers. We began with a neurodevelopmental exam early on a crisp winter morning in February.

The neurodevelopmental evaluation showed that Niki was significantly delayed in communication. He functioned in all other areas of development at a level close to his normal age, but in communication, he was way behind. Of significance to me was one particular test administered by the doctor. It showed most clearly that Niki hated and was hurt by sound. Niki enjoyed all things visual. To get his attention, my communication with him had had to become highly animated, something of which I was aware.

We played some visual games, Niki's favorite being spinning the circle out of the shape puzzle. Then the doctor tested Niki further by putting him on the table in front of and facing me. He asked me to sit on my hands, and to tell Niki what we were doing for lunch. We were going to McDonald's—something he enjoyed.

I did as the doctor asked and was stunned by Niki's response. Niki threw both hands up in front of his face, lay down on the table, and screamed for all he was worth. He avoided, and needed to avoid, verbal communication. I did not know it then but my speech hurt Niki because his hearing was hyper–sensitive. Even my softest, gentlest tones hurt him.

That afternoon, after our trip to McDonald's, we ran the psychological evaluations. The Childhood Autism Rating Scale (CARS) gave us mild/moderate autism with a score of 30. In other testing, Niki again showed significant delays in his ability to communicate. This lowered all the other intelligence scores. When all the evaluations and observed behaviors were put together, Niki was seen in the borderline range of nonautistic to mildly/moderately autistic. All I knew was that the word *autism* had come up for the third time.

The results of the psychological testing suggested one more area to evaluate. This would be accomplished by a speech pathologist. She would be able to tell me if my child was or was not autistic. The tests showed that Niki was less receptive to language than he had been eight months earlier, a result that I suspect indicated that Niki was learning to effectively shut down his auditory system in order to cope with his world. Yet, he was trying harder to communicate and had made some progress in that area. The final diagnosis was severe communication disorder secondary to an auditory processing deficit.

The recommendation was early intervention through a structured preschool program geared to the communicatively disordered child. This was begun in the public school system. The autistic behavior program refused him admission because he was too high–functioning. This may have been due to the work I had begun with him. The holding was—in autistic circles—holding therapy. I had also read some books on autism and the therapies used. Concerned about early intervention, I began to use what I had read about. I did not want Niki to lose out because of our move.

As recommended, I gained control of the spinning. I used the game "ring around the rosy." This had the effect of building in a natural break to the spinning, with "all fall down." I sang to him because he seemed to respond to songs better than spoken words. I would follow him around during the day for fifteen to twenty minutes at a time and talk about everything he was doing. If he tried to leave in frustration, I made him stay by holding him. When he fought me, I'd wrap arms and legs around him and pray silently. I'd hold him through the whole fit until he calmed down. I had him anointed by our priest and prayed over by my friends and relatives.

We did crawl races because Niki had never really crawled and the theory in some neurological circles was that it was needed for the proper development of the brain. We played in sand. We played in water. We played matching games. We played on the computer. We played with play–dough. We climbed, swung, slid down slides. We named and described everything in the smallest words possible. We repeated things over and over and over again, hoping something would stick or sink in. We did puzzles, making sure they were always difficult enough to be challenging for him.

I would turn and hold the puzzles so he could not turn them back. Niki liked things just so, and they had to stay in a particular pattern for him to remain calm. He noticed the slightest difference. So I challenged him by upsetting his environment and holding him through the fit. This was one way in which we worked and played, trying to build a loving, friendly, and safe environment for our family.

The dust was beginning to settle when "Uncle Sam" had other ideas and we moved again. Before leaving, though, a friend gave me a book that changed our lives for the better. The book was *The Sound of a Miracle* by Annabel Stehli. In it I found our story, and saw Niki in Annabel's description of Georgie. As a result, I came to understand that Niki was perhaps hearing–sensitive and, in all likelihood, vision–sensitive as well. I wrote to Annabel. She called me and steered me to a local practitioner of auditory integration therapy (AIT). I also got in touch with Dr. Rimland of the Autism Research Institute in California.

Dr. Rimland sent me a diagnostic checklist to determine if Niki was indeed autistic. His score on the checklist put him in the category of classical early infantile autism or Kanner's syndrome—a rare category according to Dr. Rimland.

The next step was to see Marie—our AIT practitioner. She observed Niki, then checked his ears. A nurse and the mother of an autistic child of her own, she could tell by Niki's behavior that he was hearing–sensitive. In addition, his face was ashen, which seems to be typical for hearing–sensitive children. She agreed to do the training.

We began at a volume level of 20, when the threshold for average hearing is between 25 and 30. Niki screamed in intense pain so Marie dropped the volume level to 13. Niki continued to scream throughout the entire thirty (was that all?) –minute session. In a state of intense pain and panic, he cried, "mommy," "boo–boo," and "stop." I do not know of anything more painful to me than the pain I saw that day in my child's eyes. We held him and tried to comfort him while keeping the headphones in place. Somehow we made it through, and Niki seemed to feel a little better.

The second session began with a little resistance, but Niki settled down pretty quickly once the music began. I had been warned that around the seventh session, he might become aggressive and cranky, that this was a normal part of the procedure. I thought, 'Okay, I can live with that as long as Niki is being helped.' We finished Day three—sessions five and six. We went home and rested for the next day.

That night Niki had an accident and messed in his pants. As he is potty–trained, this was an unusual occurrence. As I cleaned him up, I noticed a strong tinny metallic odor. I also noticed that the feces were sticky and grainy, like small, fine particles of sand. They were greenish in color. I did not think much of it as I drove to Marie's that morning, but all day I noticed that smell. It was in his urine and his sweat. Finally, I asked Marie if she noticed it or knew of anything that would cause it. At that point we had no concrete ideas.

As the day progressed and Niki became moody, aggressive and defiant, I initially thought it was typical of this stage of the training. But as the odor continued, I began to re–evaluate these events. The moodiness, aggression, and defiance were not typical Niki traits. It occurred to me that perhaps Niki's body was throwing off something. When a person comes out of anesthesia and the body eliminates it, the urine, feces, and sweat are affected in a similar manner to Niki's on that fourth day. Also, it is typical of withdrawal to become aggressive, cranky, and defiant. In addition, Niki was able to take a substantial increase in volume without pain on the fifth day. This seemed to substantiate the theory that Niki's body threw off something on the fourth day.

Marie began to check with other mothers to see if they recalled a similar occurrence with their children. They all responded affirmatively. It was also at the same time that the aggressive behavior started. Again, this suggests that the cause of the behavior was some sort of withdrawal as opposed to a random occurrence for no particular reason.

I do not know what Niki's body eliminated that day. But, I am convinced that it caused the hearing sensitivity which contributed to his "autism." Since this same string of events happened with the others who received treatment, perhaps whatever is being thrown off is a chemical or biological substance within the body that is out of balance and causing our children to be autistic. If the problem is a biochemical one, then we can discover it. If we can discover it, then we can alleviate the suffering of our children—suffering that need not—and should not—continue.

A final note. Through the grace of God and the people he has sent my way, Niki is receiving a lot of help and our hopes for him continue to grow. In the two months since his training, he has made slow but steady progress. He is doing better in school, improving significantly since the beginning of the year. As with all language development, it takes time. He is socializing more at home. He hugs one of our friends, remembering his name and calling him by it. Even more exciting to me is the fact that recently, my son snuggled with me for the first time—one of those comfortable, trusting, all–relaxed snuggles on Mommy's lap. The behavior scale measuring the number and severity of his autistic behaviors moved from a 99 before AIT to a 33 after AIT.

In addition, my son is now pointing out things to me. I'm beginning to like the sound of "Mommy 'wook,' a doggie." Just now, as I've sat here writing this story, my son has sat with me looking at photographs. He calls himself "Giki," and calls his brother, his father, and me by name. He calls his dog "doggie." His vocabulary is growing every day. His ability to follow directions without me walking him through them is expanding day by day. I am very happy with his improvement here at home. Hopefully, the school will also see these tremendous improvements over the course of the next year. ■

Chapter 22

Andrew

by Annette F. Elliott

"The thrill of victory and the agony of defeat." Parents of autistic children truly know the meaning of these simple words. Although I wouldn't wish autism on anyone, and life has been a roller coaster since the discovery of my son's disability, the defeats have taught me to view things differently. I have learned the importance of communication and how difficult it is if that ability is lacking. And when I experience such seemingly simple things as my autistic child looking at me or saying "Momma" for the first time, all the defeats are washed away, and I relish that victory and hold it close to my heart for a long time.

Andrew, our second child, was born in January, 1989, while we were stationed at Fort Meade, Maryland. He was precious and beautiful, with dark hair and the longest eyelashes I had ever seen. His first year of life was quite uneventful, highlighted by a trip to Disney World which he reacted to with gleaming smiles. As parents, Victor and I noticed few differences between the development of our first son, Elijah, and Andrew. Elijah was a bit more vocal, but we thought Andrew was simply quiet, like his father. He began to use words when he was a year old. He had a great first birthday party, and enjoyed smearing cake all over his face. We felt we were very fortunate parents with two wonderful, healthy boys. Victor and I dreamed of our boys' future—riding bikes together, playing baseball, graduating from high school, going to college, and becoming two successful adults.

When Victor was transferred to Fort Carson, Colorado, and we moved, all our dreams seemed to mesh and fade into a nightmare. Andrew was now sixteen months old and had lost all the communication he'd acquired. A doctor noticed his coldness and distancing, and after many heartbreaking tests and questions, the diagnosis had come—AUTISM. As Victor and I sat in the speech therapist's and psychiatrist's office, all we knew at that moment was to ask, "Okay, what do we do now to make our son well? What medicine will make him act like a normal child? (Where's the quick fix?)" Needless to say, neither of them had the right answer. They didn't want to be the ones to tell us and we didn't want to hear that things would never be the same again, and that life with and for Andrew would always be a constant struggle. I had so many unanswered questions. How could I make him look at me? How could my beautiful baby be so without compassion and love? Why? Why? WHY?

My husband and I had a lot to accept. We both began with tears. I sat on the steps in my house and cried the hardest I had cried in a long time. During maneuvers, he drove to a quiet spot in the jeep and cried. After feeling sorry for ourselves and for Andrew and for having all our hopes and dreams shattered, it was time to collect ourselves and move on. It was painful to try to explain his behavior to family, friends, and even strangers, but I've now learned that Andrew, Elijah, Victor, and I are the only ones who have to deal with Andrew's actions. Other people just don't understand.

Andrew began speech therapy, and I began educating myself on the subject of autism. The only thing I knew about it was from "Rain Man," and Dustin Hoffman having the ability to count all of those toothpicks on the floor. Although I went first to the library and collected all I could find, unfortunately the Post Library was not very up-to-date or well-stocked on the subject. I read all that was available, and was disappointed to find that most books still blamed the disease on refrigerator mothers.

We were visiting family in Pennsylvania when I first discovered information on auditory training. When my sister asked me if I'd had Andrew's hearing tested, I told her the technician had said it was probably "better" than most children's. My sister then showed me an article in the *Reader's Digest* about an autistic girl named Georgie who had had her hearing altered and was now a functioning adult. In all my research, I had never run across such a theory. I think the Lord was giving me a ray of light at this point, since shortly after that, I saw Georgie and her mother, Annabel Stehli, on the *Sally Jessy Raphael* show. As I sat and watched, it was once again a time to cry, but this time with joy over these strangers who had struggled for the willpower to overcome so much in life.

Victor and I contacted the Georgiana Organization for information. Victor talked directly with Mr. Stehli and you could feel the electricity and hope in the room just because of that phone call. Not only hope for our Andrew, but hope for each mother, father, and child who now had a chance. Even if it was only a minute chance for a small difference in their lives, even if Georgie's was the only miracle, it was enough to move me.

We waited anxiously for the information to arrive. Fortunately, the Organization was very efficient, and a few days later, the mailman delivered it. Neither Victor nor I wanted to build our expectations up too high (we both secretly did), or let each other know how much we were hoping for a miracle. Each could sense the excitement in the other, and I ripped that envelope open with more speed than I had used in years. My frustrations with Andrew had reached a very high peak by now. He was biting and screaming about everything, and nothing seemed to reach him. My cheeks had bite marks, as well as my entire body. He was often very fast and unstoppable. Maybe inside this envelope there would be an answer, maybe we could get back that child who had once had cake smeared all over his smiling face. The envelope gave us a glimmer of hope for Andrew, who no longer could stand any mess on his face or on any other part of his body, and who no longer smiled.

The reading material explained auditory training and gave a list of practitioners. None of them were nearby, so the burden of traveling was added to our decision. We contacted about seven of the trainers by phone and waited once again for information packets to arrive. Once we received them, my husband and I compiled a list of questions to ask each professional. Some of our concerns were Andrew's young age, three-and-a-half, side effects, who is a good candidate, where were they seeing the most dramatic improvements, and how they administered the training. We were also concerned about how they could give such a young autistic child a hearing test. All the practitioners seemed to think it was feasible.

We were in the process of slowly discovering that Andrew had hyperacute senses. He ate only bland things—dry waffles, french fries, dry toast, chicken nuggets, nothing with much texture, smell or taste. This made it frustrating and difficult to feed him a balanced diet. We saw a nutritionist who said that as long as he maintained his weight and didn't have a big discrepancy between his height and weight on the growth chart, he would be fine. He was unable to sit at the dinner table with us because just the smell, look, and idea of food would send him into a rage. When we would go out to eat, he would sit backwards in his chair in order to cope with all the sensory input.

As for his hearing, the lawn mower always sent him running inside. Hair dryers and vacuum cleaners also disturbed him. Our friends had a dog that would sing, and Andrew would scream at the top of his lungs at the sound of it. So we were sure that certain frequencies in his hearing bothered him.

His sight was also quite hyper. Bright sunlight affected him to the point where he seemed to prefer playing outside in the early morning, or late in the day, or when it was cloudy. He refused to wear a hat or sunglasses because of the way they felt on him. Often he would roll things across his face and eyes to get the true colors and shape of an object. These are just a few examples of the many things that bothered him, and of how terribly mixed–up his senses were.

Since he seemed to have hyper hearing, and since we found that there were no long–term side effects from the auditory training, we made a decision that since it couldn't hurt him, maybe it would give him a chance. The waiting lists were becoming longer and longer, and being the anxious people we were, we had worked fast to decide where to go, and had narrowed it down to two places. Knowing that both practitioners were equally qualified, available, and willing to give straight–forward, honest answers, our decision came down to location. We decided to travel to Washington D.C. since it was close to Pennsylvania, where Elijah could stay with his grandparents. Victor would stay in Colorado to work, and Andrew and I would spend eleven straight days in a hotel in Washington. Both children would miss some school, but at this point the auditory training became our number one priority.

We contacted the speech/language pathologist in Washington, and after many interactions on the telephone, we made an appointment for Andrew. We had to send a deposit, fill out paperwork, and send a photo of our little boy. The practitioner seemed very willing to work with someone as young as Andrew. The receptionist was helpful about hotels in the area, and as we made our reservations we felt that everything was actually coming together.

Several weeks before we were to start the training, I began working with Andrew and the head phones. At first it was a nightmare. He would scream and scream. Eventually, with a little persistence, he would listen to a Disney cassette for about 15–20 minutes at a time. Now if only he would do this during the training. We also video–taped some of his behaviors to compare before and after.

Anytime we thought of a question, or just wanted to be reassured about the process, we would contact our practitioner and she was always willing to help us. Andrew's grandparents even made a two–hour trip to her office in Washington, and everyone there was helpful and put them at ease, which in turn helped us.

When the day finally came, and all the preparations had been made, I knew if my nerves held up I'd be okay. I'd look at Andrew and fill with emotion. Was I doing the right thing?

When I boarded the plane in Denver and said good–bye to Victor, I had many mixed emotions and felt a great deal of stress. And yet I was hopeful. "Please God, just make those simple things in life a bit easier. Please give me one more victory. Please give our precious Andrew a chance at life."

The plane ride was long and disastrous. Although I'd brought a toddler seat along, the airline wouldn't let me use it. Andrew insisted on kicking the seat in front of him. I had to hold his legs with such force that he just screamed and could not comprehend a thing I was telling him. I felt queasy from my nerves and emotions. My oldest son wanted to get up and down and visit the rest room. We were delayed at both airports. Just your basic little irritants, and not a good beginning to eleven hard days, but we finally arrived.

We were met at the airport, and Elijah was taken to his grandparents' house while Andrew and I visited for a few days with other family and friends. Andrew had advanced into more bizarre autistic behaviors since our last visit almost a year ago, making it difficult for my family to understand him. Often I would try to explain things to them, but either they just didn't want to accept the fact that Andrew would always be a "different" child or they just didn't want to hear the reasons why. I think they all thought he would eventually get over these behaviors and magically become a "real" boy. Since they didn't have to face the day–to–day difficulties, nobody seemed to understand exactly what we were trying to do for Andrew. All they saw was the screaming, the biting, and the lack of social interaction and communication. I wanted them to see a lovely child who just could not get out of his shell, who was locked inside himself. This was one of the most frustrating aspects of having an autistic child. I would get the same "looks" from family members as I got from total strangers, and I thought my family should at least have made more of an effort to understand than that. Maybe I expected too much from them, but having a child like Andrew makes you expect more from people who are capable of giving, especially your family. Of course, they wished us luck and thought Andrew would come back magically cured, an instant overnight answer. Looking back, I know they tried to be supportive, and meant well, but I think I was too involved in the thought of the days ahead to see it.

When we went to Washington, my mother spent the first few days with us. I left the rest of my family behind, saying good–bye to Elijah as I left him with his grandparents, the first time I would be leaving him for so long. Luckily, I knew he was in good hands, and they would come to Washington to see us. My mother had lent us her car, which we were to use while we were in Washington, and the trip to the city was a two–hour horror ride. We stopped at a rest stop and Andrew refused to go to the bathroom, and screamed as we put him back into the car. Then he proceded to drench himself and the toddler seat. We got to D.C. and ended up on the wrong road because of all the one–ways and changing of street names. Finally, we found the hotel, went in to register, wet pants and all, and carried eleven days'–worth of clothing, toys, and food up to the room. Although this was supposed to be a high–class hotel, our room turned out to be not so luxurious. The heater vent was smack up against the toilet—good thing it was hot outside or we would have burnt ourselves trying to go to the bathroom. So much for the room! At least it had a refrigerator.

After getting settled, we took a walk and found the office where Andrew would be getting the auditory training. Tomorrow would be our orientation day. We would meet the practitioner and settle any unfinished business. I couldn't believe it, we were finally here, and our adventure was beginning. I was like a child getting ready to go into the fun house at an amusement park, wondering what lay ahead.

After a restless night's sleep, Andrew, my mother, and I walked the two blocks to the office for our first day. When we met with the practitioner, she gave us consent forms to sign and a form saying that after the training we would never put headphones on Andrew again. We were informed that a different qualified practitioner in the office would be doing the training, and were given a schedule. We were then sent to George Washington University for Andrew's hearing test.

We walked several blocks in the heat, trying to find our way in an unfamiliar city. When we arrived, they took us into a room for the hearing test and tried putting headphones on Andrew. They tried to get him to raise a toy when he heard a sound. This task was incomprehensible to Andrew. After a few tries and ten minutes later, it became clear that a hearing test was not feasible. This was a big disappointment, since many of the practitioners had assured us that there were ways to perform a hearing evaluation, even on a three–year–old autistic child. Needless to say, we were charged for our ten–minute visit, when I could have told them there was no way they could have gotten any results with that method. It would have been better if the hearing test had been given in the practitioner's office, and if I had known enough to ask about the method that would be used to obtain the results.

Disappointed, we walked back to the practitioner's office and had our first half–hour training. Andrew found a toy he was intrigued by in the waiting room, and once they were ready for him, there was no way of redirecting him. He screamed, flung his body, and tried to bite, as three of us struggled to put him in a restraining chair. He persisted for the entire half hour. One person held the headphones, one held his head still, and I held his hands, wondering the whole time if we had made the right decision. Andrew just screamed and screamed. It was one of the longest half hours. When it was finally over, we ran out of that office and went for something to eat.

Later that afternoon, we were doing the same thing. Andrew screamed for another straight half–hour. He was struggling and yelling, "Help me! Help me! Somebody help me!" At this point I determined that if tomorrow was this stressful for both of us, we were packing up and going home. I was not going to subject my child to this agony again. After another exhausting half–hour, we were mentally drained and eager to return to our hotel. Andrew was physically exhausted. My mother was exhausted, too, and disappointed in herself for not knowing what to say to make things better. Andrew was so tired he went to sleep at 5:00 P.M. and slept straight through until 6:00 o'clock the next morning.

On the second day of training, we walked to the office reluctantly. Luckily, the receptionist had thought ahead and put the toy away that had caught my son's attention the day before. We decided not to strap him into the chair. Andrew was less resistant, and we made it through the first half–hour simply by holding the headphones on and letting him lie in a bean bag chair. When the music would reach a frequency that disturbed him, although he would jump up, scream, or try to take off the headphones, he was able to be persuaded to keep them on. All the practice we had done with the headphones before we left paid off.

I had filled out a questionnaire that was the first in a series to be filled out each night during the auditory training process. It had behavioral areas to evaluate about eating, sleeping, biting, activity, and communication. I gave it to the speech–language practitioner, and she offered to spend some time with Andrew, evaluating him and giving me some suggestions for aftercare. I thought she was trying to be helpful, but then she threw in the plug about how it only cost just this much money. Here I was already stressed out from the financial burden it was putting on our entire family, and she was trying to solicit funds. All I could think of was that this was what Washington D.C. was about— Money, money, money!

The afternoon session went a bit more smoothly, so things were becoming easier as Andrew's resistance decreased. The receptionist was helpful and comforting. She suggested that Andrew go right into the room and then be allowed to play afterwards, she helped with forms to try to get insurance coverage, and she gladly made me copies of the evaluation forms each evening.

My husband flew into D.C. to join us for a few days. He just couldn't stay away, this was too important to everyone. He was relieved to hear that the second day had gone more smoothly. We went out of town to a playground and lake area, and he could see that Andrew had already begun to do things he'd never done before. He actually came to get me to play with him on the playground equipment. He noticed the ducks and fed them.

Our third day was even easier. Of course we had that initial power struggle, but nothing like before. Andrew was beginning to relax in his bean bag chair, and in fact, it was sometimes difficult to keep him awake. He was beginning to understand potty training a little better, and was starting to go to the bathroom by himself. He expressed his desire to go into a bookstore we passed on our walk to and from the training. I was surprised he even noticed it. He was still biting, but less and less. Was this all wishful thinking or was I really seeing small simple changes in Andrew?

Thursday, September 3rd is a day I will hold in my heart forever. It was Andrew's fourth complete day of training. We had decided to take my mother home to Pennsylvania and visit Elijah at Victor's parents'. Andrew sat in the car and enjoyed the ride, but this time when I would say, "Andrew look at the cows!" he would respond and look directly at the cows. I said, "Look at the train!" and he turned and looked at the train. What a miracle! He was responding to a command and was doing it with honesty. It was great to see Andrew so at ease with the world and himself.

When we arrived at his grandparents', Andrew was glad to see his brother. He even walked up to him and acknowledged him. Lots of firsts on this day. When Victor's mother called Andrew's name, he actually stopped in his tracks, turned around, and looked at her. Tears filled her eyes as that contact was made and we all knew at that moment that we had made the right decision in having auditory training done.

After dinner, the entire family went outside. With great sincerity and "real" laughter, Andrew began throwing the ball to everyone in the circle. He would look each person in the eye and give the ball to whomever we asked him to pass it. At last, at last, he was hearing us and responding. We video–taped the whole out–coming; it is still a treasure to watch. Just imagine five adults standing in a circle, all of them with tear–filled eyes, watching a child they had so wanted to get to know for so long. He was emerging from his shell, and here he was.

Andrew even wanted to play with his brother. At one point, Elijah got upset and walked away from the group. Andrew went over to him, took his hand, and brought him back to the group. What an accomplishment after such a short time! If we never got anything else from the auditory training, I didn't care, because these few moments of finally seeing who Andrew truly was were worth it. I had gotten my thrill of victory!

We headed back to Washington. Victor had to fly back to Colorado and Andrew and I would go solo on the training and at the hotel (which was really becoming claustrophobic). That morning I was startled awake by the words, "Mother, mother, wake up dude!" It was Andrew recognizing me as his mother. Victor's parents had come to Washington with Elijah, for the day. Everyone went to the auditory training office and sat with Andrew during his listening sessions.

In the hotel, Andrew and I were truly getting to know one another. I cherished our time alone together. He would bring me books and want me to read them. He would let me sing him to sleep. Before the training, if anyone tried to sing, he would just scream as loud as he could. He even wanted me to get in the tub with him and play shark. We visited the aquarium, so he could see the real fish. He loved it! I enjoyed rediscovering the child I once knew, as facets of him slowly began emerging. Still, I didn't know whether the changes were due to the auditory training, or just the circumstances that put Andrew and me on a one–on–one basis.

One evening, as Andrew and I were eating dinner at his favorite place for about the twentieth time that week, an elderly woman in the booth next to us began talking to Andrew. He, as usual, failed to acknowledge her. I then explained to her why we were in D.C., and a bit about Andrew. She listened contentedly, and didn't "look" at him with the awkwardness that most people showed. As we were leaving, she looked at me directly and said, "Good luck, hon! Keep up the great work and God Bless You for all that you are doing." A total stranger knew exactly what to say to me at the right time. I so needed that encouragement and will always remember the impact this woman had on me. She restored my faith in mankind.

We were now into our seventh day of the auditory training. Andrew was getting comfortable with the routine and thought he was "Joe Cool," sprawled out on the bean bag with those headphones on. Victor's sister, Brenda, and her fiancé, Jay, visited us at the hotel. We watched *Batman* on pay–per–view television. Andrew watched the movie in his fashion of watching TV—he doesn't seem to be looking, but he is. During the scene where the penguin steals a baby, Andrew was moved to tears. He cried so much I had to walk with him, up and down the hall, to calm him down. This was another first–time experience since the training.

We were getting closer to the last day. Brenda and Jay went back to Pennsylvania, leaving Andrew and me alone again. The people at the hotel were getting to know us, and were wondering exactly how long we were staying. Our hotel stay was never uneventful: A fire alarm which proved to be false had us running outside, I set off our smoke detector when my bagel got caught in the toaster, and Andrew went to the bathroom all over the booth at his favorite restaurant. When the last day of the auditory training arrived, I was ecstatic.

In spite of all the changes we had seen in his behavior, I decided not to waste any time or money on another hearing test, certain that Andrew wouldn't cooperate.

After loading all our belongings into the car, I drove out of that garage in D.C. and have not looked back since. I left with a different child than when I arrived.

After our eleven stressful days, we headed to the beach for a vacation. It was fun to watch Andrew enjoy the sand, even though the sound of the ocean still seemed to bother him. As an eventful ending to our vacation, Elijah managed to fall off the playground equipment and break his arm. I was about to lose it! I had just been through a nightmare experience and now I had to deal with a broken arm. At least the plane ride home went smoothly. Andrew played nicely and had no fits, and Elijah was exhausted because of his broken arm and slept most of the way.

When I arrived home, it was great to watch Andrew emerge slowly. He would walk with me to take Elijah to school and I did not have to drag him by the arm while he screamed. He began to sit for a snack at preschool. Even his teacher noticed differences. He did not bite others as often. He was using more words to ask for things. He began talking to people on the phone. He would go to the playground and play on the equipment and not just sit and watch the sand run through his fingers. After a while, we went to the beach again and at last he was at peace with the ocean and even swam in the water. He became completely toilet trained, both day and night, an accomplishment I once thought I'd never see. Every once in a while he forgets to pull his pants back on and will walk out naked, but I am sure that will all come together for him in time. It is great to watch him walk out of a building and be able to find the car, whereas before, I'd hang on to him for dear life because he would just run in any direction, not understanding where he was going. He always seemed to be lost and unaware of things around him. He even recognizes familiar places now, especially a toy store. He chooses the toys he likes and plays with them in the manner they were meant to be played with.

One of my personal disappointments came from friends and family. I guess since Andrew wasn't instantly cured, they didn't seem to relish my little victories with me. Only one of my friends called to see how the training went and was sincere about it. The others just did not seem to recognize the magnitude of the ordeal I had just gone through. I have gotten over all the resentment and realize most people don't understand things unless they have experienced them. My friends and family supported me as much as they knew how, and although it may not have seemed like enough to me at the time, it truly was, and I thank them for not turning their backs on Andrew.

It has now been almost two years since the auditory training, and we have all grown and learned from Andrew's new found independence. The list of changes goes on and on. He goes to a great facility for speech, occupational and physical therapy, and they use a brushing technique with pressure which has helped tremendously. His ability to communicate and concentrate is so much better.

We have great hopes for Andrew, and the auditory training has given us the chance to expand those hopes. Still to this day we praise it to everyone we can. The training helps most children on just one try, but I am sure we will repeat it right before first grade. Maybe when he is older we'll be able to get an accurate hearing test.

So many things which seem uneventful to parents with "normal" children have occurred for us. I am just thankful we were given the opportunity to have the training done. He understands everything we say, comes when he is called, and his appetite is near–normal. He can sit at the table with us during dinner for much longer periods of time without being bothered by the sound of chewing. He still has occasional temper tantrums, and we hoped Vitamin B6 would help, but it seemed to make him more hyper and jittery so we had to discontinue it. His screaming occurs much less frequently though, and when he does scream, there will be a word in there, like, "STOP!" He is five years old, and still receives speech, occupational, and physical therapy. He will be starting a regular kindergarten class in the fall, with an aide just for the beginning. We have learned that it is important for him to do as much as possible without the aide, and she will give him as much space and independence as he can possibly handle. We don't think he will need her for long.

I continue to read and pray for all the miracles God has to offer. When my patience level is low, and I feel defeated again, I always turn to the books about autism written by the parents and children who have overcome so much, and I find my strength once again. May we all continue to use our ability to communicate by helping all who need comforting with words. And so to all of you who have written your stories, THANK YOU THANK YOU from the bottom of my heart for the hope, the miracles, and the insight you have offered. You have helped me cope. You have all had your share of the thrill of victory and the agony of defeat, and you are all truly heros. ■

Afterword

by Jackie McBurnie Rockwell

As a speech–language pathologist and audiologist, I have worked for over twenty years with children and adults who exhibit problems in the areas of learning and communication. During this time, I have attended hundreds of workshops and conferences in an attempt to continually improve my diagnostic and therapy skills. I have worked with thousands of individuals who exhibited a broad range of disorders, including mild to severe articulation problems, apraxia, central auditory processing problems, delays in language development, and problems of fluency.

These individuals have carried diagnostic labels such as developmentally delayed, developmentally disabled, communicatively impaired, mentally retarded, learning disabled, dyslexic, autistic, attention deficit disorder, pervasive developmental disorder, and most recently, multisensory developmental disorder. Some individuals exhibited problems at birth or as toddlers. In others, problems weren't identified until school age, and parents often had to battle the medical and educational communities to get the diagnosis made. In still others, difficulties in communication were a result of stroke or head injury. Whatever the cause, time of onset or diagnosis, the one thing so many of my clients had in common was a sensory one—problems dealing with auditory information.

Auditory problems can take many forms and can result in a variety of symptoms. Problems in perception of sounds can result in simple articulation problems or in speech which is unintelligible. Darren White stated in the article, *Autism from the Inside* (*Medical Hypothesis Journal*, Scotland, 1987, 24, p. 223–229),

> I was rarely able to hear sentences because my hearing distorted them. I was sometimes able to hear

a word or two at the start and understand it and
then the next lot of words sort of merged into one
another and I could not make head or tail of it.

Others with auditory problems are highly distractible and
can't filter out unimportant sounds in order to focus on the
important message. Individuals labeled ADD (attention deficit
disorder) or CAPD (central auditory processing disorder) most
obviously suffer as a result of auditory problems, but they are
present in other disabilities as well.

It wasn't until reading Annabel's book, *The Sound of a Miracle*,
that I suddenly realized I'd been treating the symptoms of an
auditory disorder rather than the underlying cause. After
thousands of hours of professional training, it took the words of a
parent to make me look at these symptoms in a new light!

As an audiologist, my training emphasis had been on
identifying hearing loss. Consequently, in testing hearing, neither
I nor the otolaryngologists with whom I worked were concerned
when an individual's hearing fell within the broad range of normal
which is from zero to twenty decibels on an audiogram. Assessing
hearing was always one of the first steps taken when evaluating
children and adults who exhibited communication or learning
problems. I now realize that hearing within the normal range
doesn't necessarily equal normal hearing.

After reading *The Sound of a Miracle*, and learning of the
establishment of the Georgiana Organization for training
professionals in Dr. Bérard's method of auditory integration
training, I trained with Dr. Bérard in April, 1992, in the first course
presented by the Georgiana Organization. As a result of Annabel's
book and Dr. Bérard's teaching, I became a much better speech–
language pathologist and audiologist, having acquired a
background which has greatly aided me as an auditory integration
training practitioner.

Dr. Bérard firmly believes that "hearing equals behavior."
I've come also to believe this. Normal hearing acuity doesn't
always mean normal hearing perception. In fact, hearing better
than the norm (in the negative five to negative ten decibel range)
may frequently result in auditory overload and subsequent
behavioral problems. Hearing which is not equal in both ears is

also likely to result in problems. Unfortunately, in most instances, the person with these problems believes that everyone hears the way he does and consequently doesn't communicate how he's hearing.

Auditory integration therapy is a treatment approach which appears to correct the underlying problem rather than just treating the symptoms. Following AIT, improvements are frequently seen in articulation and language development, in auditory processing areas such as discrimination, comprehension of speech in the presence of background noise, auditory memory skills, and focus of attention. The list of positive benefits can go on and on. As you've read in so many of the parents' articles presented in this book, signs of obvious tension are often significantly reduced following AIT, and a sense of humor often appears to have developed overnight!

How have three years as an auditory integration training specialist changed my perspective regarding the treatment of those with learning, communication, and auditory problems? I now know that, in many cases, AIT should be the first therapy approach used. Auditory integration therapy appears to "set the stage" for so much of the progress which can be made. Following AIT, teachers and speech–language pathologists may see greater progress in all areas than would have been possible without AIT. Though auditory integration training is not a cure, it is an important part of the key for many people exhibiting communication problems, learning difficulties, dyslexia, ADD, and CAPD. In fact, in any problem in which auditory issues may play a role, auditory integration training should be strongly considered.

Through the Georgiana Organization, Annabel and Peter Stehli have made it possible for families and professionals to learn about auditory integration training. As we teach AIT courses in the United Stated and abroad, it has become apparent that AIT, this parent–driven phenomenon, is changing lives. ■

Jackie McBurnie Rockwell, M.S., CCC–A, CCC–SLP

Index